The Rule of Law and the Rule of God

The Rule of Law and the Rule of God

Edited by

Simeon O. Ilesanmi, Win-Chiat Lee, and J. Wilson Parker

palgrave
macmillan

THE RULE OF LAW AND THE RULE OF GOD

First published in 2014 by PALGRAVE MACMILLAN® in the United States—a division of St. Martin's Press LLC, 175 Fifth Avenue, New York, NY 10010.

Where this book is distributed in the UK, Europe and the rest of the world, this is by Palgrave Macmillan, a division of Macmillan Publishers Limited, registered in England, company number 785998, of Houndmills, Basingstoke, Hampshire RG21 6XS.

Palgrave Macmillan is the global academic imprint of the above companies and has companies and representatives throughout the world.

ISBN: 978-1-137-44775-3

Library of Congress Cataloging-in-Publication Data

The rule of law and the rule of God / [edited by] Simeon O. Ilesanmi, Win-Chiat Lee, J. Wilson Parker.

pages cm

Includes bibliographical references and index.

ISBN 978-1-137-44775-3 (alk. paper)

1. Religion and law. I. Ilesanmi, Simeon O., 1963- editor.

BL65.L33R85 2014

201'.7—dc23

2014012990

A catalogue record of the book is available from the British Library.

Design by Amnet.

First edition: October 2014

10 9 8 7 6 5 4 3 2 1

Contents

Acknowledgment

This book is a collaborative effort and has benefited from the sage advice, research, and criticisms of a host of scholars. However, it was the vision, encouragement, and support of the office of the provost at Wake Forest University that provided the impetus for an interdisciplinary conference whose focus became the subject of this book. The editors wish to express their deep gratitude to the former provost Jill Tiffenthaler and former vice provost Mark Welker for their financial assistance. Conference organization requires the help of many individuals on numerous levels. Preparation for the conference would have been impossible without the precise guidance and tireless logistical support of Debra Alty, formerly of the office of the provost, and Sheila Lockhart of the Department of Religion. Special thanks go to Burke Gerstenschlager and Caroline Kracunas of Palgrave Macmillan for their expertise and editorial assistance in preparing this manuscript for publication. Two graduate students, Robert Martin and Kayla Wolfe, provided clerical assistance at critical stages. We thank our families for their understanding and support during the many hours of effort devoted to completing this work. Finally, we would like to thank the contributors of this volume for the great care with which they prepared their essays for this publication.

The Rule of Law and the Rule of God: An Introduction

Simeon O. Ilesanmi, Win-Chiat Lee, and J. Wilson Parker

I

Aristotle's observation that we are by nature political animals has been widely recognized as a truism since antiquity. Equipped with a social instinct implanted by nature, human beings have sought a community of some kind with a view to some good. One may add to this that religion and law have both played significant roles in the organization of these communities, as well as providing norms governing the activities of their members. They have coexisted both in harmony and in conflict with each other through the ages and under a great variety of cultural contexts. The historical and normative issues stemming from the relations between the two are complex and have been studied by scholars of many disciplines. The purpose of this book is to renew our exploration of some of the normative issues involved from a multidisciplinary perspective in the light of our more recent experiences of the interaction between religion and the rule of law.

The primary sense in which the word "rule" is used in the title concerns governance. In this sense, the particular vision of social and political life or the system of governance informed and legitimated by the undergirding worldview can be understood as that worldview's rule. Ordinarily, this refers to the normative structure that governs how power is distributed in society, how members of society are supposed to act, and how various sectors of society are supposed to relate to each other. While some societies permit a wide dispersal of power among their citizens, for example, through a scheme of constitutionally protected rights that they enjoy, other societies concentrate political power in the hands of one or a few individuals who presumably exercise it on behalf of and for the benefit of the rest of the population.

In this sense, the rule of law and the rule of God denote two competing regimes or conceptions about how we ought to live, including the shape and purposes of the various institutional structures that govern our lives. Of course, this ideological battle about how and whether to draw a boundary between the sacred and the secular is not new, but it has assumed heightened urgency and global significance in the last two decades, thanks to a series of events involving many state and non-state actors. Scholars were often blindsided by this development because of the post-Enlightenment predictions that increased exposure to modernizing influences would precipitate the gradual, if not rapid, extinction of religion. Max Weber was representative of this tradition when he characterized the modern society as a successor to the old order, whose authority was legitimized by tradition and charisma, for its acceptance of "the belief in the validity of legal statute and functional 'competence' based on rationally created rules."[1] Religion straddles the realms of both tradition and charisma in Weber's theory, since it is a conduit for the transmission of what he calls "the authority of the 'eternal yesterday', i.e., of the mores sanctified through the unimaginably ancient recognition and habitual orientation to conform," as well as a signification of "the absolutely personal devotion and personal confidence in revelation, heroism, or other qualities of individual leadership."[2] From this viewpoint, then, the birth of the modern state is the outcome of a process by which the realm of politics and law is gradually emancipated from the encumbrances of religion and constituted into increasingly autonomous political institutions.

Differently put, the Weberian point is that the modern society is committed to the rule of law while the traditional society governs itself by the rule of religion. The differences between the two are not inconsequential, for the basic features typically attributed to one are denied to the other. For instance, the rule of law is defended for the ends it is intended to serve within society and the institutional attributes believed necessary to achieve these ends. It seeks to "protect against anarchy and the Hobbesian war of all against all," to "allow people to plan their affairs with reasonable confidence that they can know in advance the legal consequences of various actions," and to "guarantee against at least some types of official arbitrariness."[3] Achieving these ends requires the existence of commensurate institutional devices, such as "comprehensive laws, well-functioning courts, and trained law enforcement agencies."[4] But do societies whose pillars of political and legal life are built on the authority of religious ideas necessarily lack these teleological and institutional attributes? The verdict on this question may not be as conclusive as Weber believed it to be.

What is certain, according to one of the contributors to this volume, is that "religion will not go away but is in fact shaping global and local social life so the idea of a purely secular future is not really a viable one."[5] Religion is too much embedded in the modern psyche and structures to be dismissed as ephemeral. From the push for political liberalization in the Islamic world to the debate about citizenship and dress code in French schools and the reemergence of "family values" politics in the United States, religion is a major player in the cultural project of shaping the social and political landscape of contemporary societies.

But the terms of its engagement with the institutions of modern life must be reexamined and possibly redefined. This is necessary, in part, because of the controversies arising from the very meaning of religion. While some understand religion as "primarily a set of beliefs—beliefs that are capable of being adopted, rejected, modified or refined at the will of the believer," others see it as "a way of structuring and living a communal existence in fidelity to religious teachings and cultural practice."[6] Similarly, law is no less resistant to a clear and rigid definition because of its conceptual variability as a result of context and association with a diversity of subject matters. This conceptual ambiguity further compounds questions about how the two systems should interact with each other, and how their comparative desirability as normative frameworks for creating a just and effective polity is to be evaluated.

There is a second sense of the word "rule" that is also important to this book. As the later Wittgenstein and his followers have impressed upon us, we are also rule-conscious and rule-governed creatures. This view has implications for our understanding of political and social life, broadly construed. Since human affairs involve institutions and social practices constituted and governed by rules, we may reasonably assume that attending to the rules people are following in the course of their activities would give us insight into the meaning of those activities or the motive and reason behind them. In this way, the rule of law and the rule of religion, understood as political institutions and social practices, can be fully appreciated only in the light of the rules constituting and governing their activities.

However, not only are the rule of law and the rule of religion themselves constituted and governed by rules, but as institutions and practices they also generate norms, arguably also in the form of rules, to govern the behavior of the members of their communities. In the case of the rule of law, for example, laws (i.e., rules governing individual acts) are made or identified by following certain other laws (i.e., institutional rules). (This is the classic Hartian way of understanding the rule of law.) In this way, both the rule of law and the rule of religion can be understood to be a rather complex web of the rule of rules.

The centrality of rules to human governance—be it the rule of law or the rule of religion—only serves to hit home the ontological and epistemological uncertainties concerning rules. Regardless, it highlights two basic anthropological truths, namely, that humans (as both agents and observers) are confronted with uncertainties and choices even as their options are supposedly dictated by rules; and reflection and interpretation, in the light of other background values, are necessary to determine what the rules are (and indeed, whether the relevant norms are rules). If clarity and predictability are important functions that the concept of rules is supposed to provide in the attempt to impose some hermeneutical order on human affairs, then our actual experience has often diverged from this expectation.

But we need not despair in the face of this lack of certainty and definition. Indeed, for our purposes in this book, this only opens up the opportunity for a more productive and meaningful dialogue to help shape our understanding of the rule of law and the rule of religion and how the two should relate to one another, not only in a general way, but also as a matter of interpreting the law of a particular country or even the divine commands of a particular religion.

II

Whether the cultural complexes of law and religion should be seen as alternative or complementary systems is a question addressed by each of the two authors in Part I. Mark Lilla examines the languages of political theology and political philosophy as two alternative systems of legitimacy, one on the basis of divine revelation and the other on "the consent of the governed, whatever their religious conviction."[7] The challenge of our age, as Lilla understands it, is whether these two intellectual traditions, or modes of political discourse, are willing to engage, let alone, understand each other. There seems to be little or no evidence of that possibility, at least now. What we can infer, on the basis of historical experiences, is that any attempt by either side to impose its vision of ideal political life on the other would likely worsen the contemporary global situation characterized by mutual ideological suspicion. This is because neither position is of a transient historical significance or an exclusive preserve of any particular society or geographical part of the world.

While there may be good reasons to be skeptical of a project of political legitimacy anchored in the assumption of "a divinely revealed nexus between God, man, and world," none of the paradigmatic historical responses to this project has been satisfactory. Hobbes's proposal to separate the sphere of God and the sphere of man and Rousseau's liberal theology that seeks to make religion intellectually attractive to the modern mind both engendered reactionary and messianic religious and political outlooks. Yet, Lilla does not foreclose the possibility of a credible alternative to political theology. He finds this in "the renewal of traditional political theology from within,"[8] which is a posture of standing firmly within the faith and reinterpreting political theology "so believers can adapt without feeling themselves to be apostates." If properly done, such internal renewal of religious discourse can make it "easier, not harder, [for believers] to enjoy the fruits of modern existence" without insisting on the preservation of "the habits and mores of a supposedly purer time."[9]

One way this critique of religion might proceed, as William Schweiker's chapter shows, is by "shift[ing] the discussion from one centered on sources of political authority and its relation to religious revelation to the question of how religious sources can and ought to be interpreted."[10] Religions, according to Schweiker, are not self-contained entities whose demands believers seek to discover and then passively apply to their lives; rather, they are fruits of "the labor and disputes of interpretation."[11] The core and scope of human identity and existence are not exhausted by religion; it is just one of the diverse ways of being human. Historical religions are nothing more than particular expressions of the "teeming welter of symbols, stories, ideas about God and God's relation to the world."[12] In fact, Schweiker sees conscience, not religion, as denoting "the totality of a human life involved in its moral and spiritual struggle."[13] It is in exercise of conscience, especially when not coerced by the state and its instruments of power, including law, that one is able to engage and participate in the interpretive endeavor to make sense of life and give shape to it.

But not all interpretations or traditions of interpretations are credible. Those that attempt "to make a local God—or a local way of thinking about God in terms of just one or two ideas—into the universal God" are, Schweiker argues, hypertheistic and symptomatic of theological and ethical distortions.[14] Hypertheism is a bad interpretation because it results in "a tyranny of the soul"[15] and violates human dignity. In contrast, interpretations that see the social order as "a complex interaction among various domains—politics, education, media, economy, religious associations—which limit each other's power and also cannot justly violate human dignity and thus the freedom of conscience" are borne out of monotheistic faith and cosmopolitan orientation to life. The challenge for every historical religion is how to restrain the tendency toward hypertheism while nurturing "a cosmopolitan outlook dedicated to responsibility for the integrity of human life"[16] in all its diverse expressions.

III

In Part II we turn to more specific questions about the relation of religion to the rule of law. Free exercise of religion is a fundamental right in the

American constitution and also a central value in liberal political philosophy. To this way of thinking, no doubt one of the functions of the law is to protect the liberty to practice the religion of one's own choice and to prevent it from being infringed upon by either the government or other citizens.

One way to protect religious liberty is to require the state not to establish a particular religion or religious view. This can be translated into a requirement of state neutrality among differing religions and religious views in setting its policies and making and applying its laws. Frank Ravitch examines how the US Supreme Court attempts to apply this approach as a matter of constitutional law. While neutrality might seem to be a viable legal concept that a court could evenhandedly apply across a range of cases, Ravitch contends that the Supreme Court's use of neutrality in religion cases has not provided an analytical basis for the Court's results but has merely been a post hoc justification for decisions that were derived from other analyses. Ravitch argues that "the Court's formal neutrality approach is especially dangerous, because the formalistic approach leaves little room for introspection, and its very nature makes it less likely to account for nuances or context."[17] The essence of his critique is his contention that "there is no neutral foundation or baseline that can be used to prove that something is 'truly' neutral, neutrality is nothing more than a buzzword and a dangerous one at that, because it implies that the supposedly neutral approach should be taken more seriously because it is actually neutral."[18]

Ravitch also finds analyses that rely upon notions of religious liberty to be problematic. While recognizing that articulating the contours of liberty as a concept may be more easily done than identifying the contours of neutrality, Ravitch finds the Court's analyses no more satisfying: "There is no single concept of religious liberty that can claim historical preeminence. So any claim to liberty must operate from a context or baseline that is only self-justifying."[19]

Limits will need to be set on the individual's free practice of religion in the public sphere so as not to either infringe others' right to do the same or impair the state's ability to perform certain legitimate functions that, among other concerns, might also prove to be essential in the protection and promotion of religious practices. Where the line ought to be drawn around the free practice of religion is a difficult issue. Much of the debate on this question in American law and politics centers on the question of religious accommodation or religious exemption.

Michael Curtis's chapter tips the delicate balance against religious accommodation in the case of gay marriages. The central concern, for Curtis, is the respect for what is essential to an individual's identity. He argues that in the case of gay marriage, exemptions from antidiscrimination laws advocated by some (including some scholars) that would allow religious objectors to refuse to facilitate such marriages are misguided. This is because, in Curtis's analysis, what is at stake from the impact of such religious exemptions is much more than just inconveniencing married gay couples. Sending away a gay couple, married or not, for example, by a commercial establishment to seek overnight accommodation elsewhere because of the religious objection of the operator of the establishment is an attack on the dignity of the gay couple, regardless of whether the objector's refusal to serve the gay couple is preannounced or not.

Curtis's case against religious exemptions from laws prohibiting discrimination against married gay couples is made by using the analogy of civil rights legislation that prohibited discrimination on the basis of race or, more poignantly, discrimination against interracial couples. It is unacceptable that one uses religious grounds to seek exemptions from laws that prohibit racial discrimination. True, the relevant religious beliefs may no long be popular. That, in Curtis's view, may very well be the result of the civil rights legislation and its enforcement. More importantly, whether the relevant religious belief is acceptable or widely accepted is not the business of the government to determine and beside the point in any case for the purposes of religious accommodation.

In a different national setting, concern for equal legal recognition and protection against arbitrary discrimination is also at the heart of Ilesanmi's chapter. One sociological similarity that Nigeria shares with the United States is cultural pluralism. Ilesanmi argues that the tendency by scholars to focus exclusively on the non-adoption and free exercise clauses in the Nigerian Constitution as adequate mechanisms for protecting the country's religious pluralism and the secular character of the state is mistaken. According to him, existing interpretations of both clauses have encouraged rigid ideological positions among religious and nonreligious partisans and have failed to grasp the real nature of the moral hazards that are inherent in a religiously pluralistic society. He contends that a more adequate test for determining the extent to which the Nigerian Constitution takes cognizance of the country's religious pluralism is its articulation of the norms for opposing inequality and discrimination among the citizens. By examining the involvement of the Nigerian government, at both the federal and state levels, in religious pilgrimages, he shows the precarious status of these norms and the imperative to defend their lexical priority over the other constitutional provisions on religion.

IV

Part 3 returns to some of the issues concerning the relation of law to religion, but with a special focus on Islam. Given the geopolitical, economic, and religious importance of Islam in the contemporary world, there may be no better illustration of the complexity of those issues than what this religion has brought to both the Western and non-Western worlds in recent decades. Partly due to immigration, there has been a steady increase in the presence of a Muslim minority in Western Europe and North America whose religious practices pose new and difficult challenges to the West's commitment to religious pluralism. Unfortunately, much of the debate has to take place in the post-9/11 atmosphere of fear and intolerance, resulting from acts of terrorism and the radicalization of some factions of Islam. However, commitment to religious pluralism is not only an issue for the non-Muslim majority in the West, but also one for its Muslim minority, and indeed countries with a Muslim majority as well.

As do some of the previous chapters, Andrew March's contribution also deals with the question of religious accommodation and the tension between liberalism and religion, but from an opposite direction. Instead of asking whether a liberal society can accommodate certain religious practices, March's chapter deals with the question of whether religion—more specifically, a theocratic religion requiring those who are faithful to it to live under its divinely revealed law—can find a way to accommodate a liberal, secular regime and accept such a regime as politically legitimate. The case in point for March is Islam. According to the classical Islamic theocratic principle of legitimacy, a state is legitimate only to the extent in which its legal order approximates and expresses the divinely revealed law of sharia. The question of what attitude toward a liberal secular regime an Islamic theocratic view would endorse is particularly pressing given the political condition under which many Muslims in the West are now living—as a minority in a mainly liberal, secular state.

March's concern about accommodation or acceptance from the Islamic theocratic perspective is more than just toleration of or minimum interaction with a liberal secular regime. Rather, he seeks a meaningful way for such a theocratic view, without abandoning its core theocratic commitments, to participate in what John Rawls calls, "the overlapping consensus," which is the basis of the social contract of a liberal society. The key to forging the way ahead in this direction, March suggests, lies in the Islamic legal theory of "purposes of sharia," (*maqasid al-shari'a*). This theory of purposivism takes what is important about a norm to be not so much that it is compatible with the text, but more that it is compatible with the goods and interests that God seeks to protect through the law. In this way, a non-Islamic (including a secular) society can be considered from the Islamic theocratic perspective to be *sufficiently* just if its law seeks to protect the same kind of goods and human interests that are the purposes of sharia, without providing the punishments for moral crimes that are called for in the revelatory texts. But in March's account, while purposivism might offer Islamic theocrats the best prospect of a meaningful dialogue with liberalism, there is no assurance as to how such a dialogue will turn out.

The purpose of sharia (i.e., the set of human interests God seeks to protect through sharia) includes, most importantly, the preservation of religion, life, property, lineage, and reason. March focuses on the preservation of religion in his discussion in part because this is the point where the difference between the Islamic theocratic view and liberalism might turn out to be the greatest and most significant. Liberalism protects mostly individual "negative" liberty rights in relation to the practice of religion. This may not be sufficient for and may even be in conflict with the more "positive" preservation of religion called for in the Islamic theocratic view. March argues that purposivism provides one of the most flexible and complex frameworks for understanding religious freedom in a diverse society but in a way that is more appealing for the more conservative and traditional Muslims. The theory of purposivism also illustrates the kind of internal renewal of political theology that Lilla believes is necessary for a healthy interaction of religion and law.

Even a monotheistic faith of the sort described by Schweiker in chapter 2 sometimes needs to be defended, but not all methods of defense are compatible with a cosmopolitan conscience or a liberally construed purposivism. John Kelsay's chapter focuses on this issue in his examination of the debate among Muslims about the propriety of taking up arms to resolve a perceived conflict between existing systems of law and the authority of God. Although the various groups involved in this debate are similarly committed to the juridical method of "articulating a 'fit' between historic precedents and current circumstances,"[20] a method Kelsay designates as sharia reasoning, they differ in their interpretations of religious laws and in their understanding of the kinds of conduct permitted to rectify any ostensible injustices attributable to the secular systems.

Anita Allen's chapter discusses a number of legal cases in the United States involving restrictions placed on the modesty garb worn by Muslim women in public, especially the *niqab*, which covers the whole face of the woman except her eyes. This piece of modesty headgear brings into sharp focus the conflict between the free exercise of religion and other legitimate interests of society. While laws banning or restricting the wearing of such modesty headgear are controversial all over the world, in the United States they also run up against the constitutionally protected right of the free exercise of religion. Among the legitimate public interests that are in conflict with wearing the *niqab* in public is, for example, the need to establish the identity of the person or to observe a person's demeanor when providing court testimony.

In reviewing a number of cases involving the *niqab* in the United States, Allen argues that accommodation can be made in most cases to address the legitimate interests of the state without infringing upon the woman's right to practice the modesty requirement she believes to be required by her religion. In any case, in Allen's view, wearing the *niqab* is an essential part of some of these women's religious identity and therefore we should try to accommodate this practice as much as we can.

The modesty headgear worn by Muslim women is also the focus of Sahar Aziz's contribution. Freedom of religion and equality are again at issue. In Aziz's view, Muslim women suffer discrimination, in an intertwined way, on three fronts: religion, gender, and race. Hence their predicament cannot be fully comprehended without appreciating the intersectionality of the three dimensions of discrimination.

The headscarf worn by many Muslim women in public is symbolic of the complexity of the predicament of Muslim women in America. Nevertheless, it is essential, in Aziz's view, that Muslim women be left alone to make the choice to wear such headscarves in public as an assertion of their individual identity. After the 9/11 terrorist attacks, however, the headscarf has acquired yet another symbolic meaning in the non-Muslim world. To many, it is now also associated with a vilified religion and terrorism—an association that has led to documented cases of discrimination against Muslim women in employment, as well as harassment and physical assaults against them (and their children) because the headscarves they openly wear identify them as "enemies." Again, these acts of discrimination against Muslim women, Aziz argues, cannot be overcome without addressing all of its three dimensions and how they intersect.

V

We close the book with a chapter by Richard Miller and a postscript by Wilson Parker. Miller's concluding chapter is a "bookend" to Mark Lilla's opening chapter. Where Lilla questions the inevitability of the Western approach to the rule of law and the rule of God, speculating that Hobbes' "Great Separation" between religion and secular government was neither inevitable nor necessary, Miller marshals arguments as to why post-Hobbes liberal democracies in fact have the balance between law and the right to religion. In his view, such a balance is attributable to the requirement in liberalism that the state remain neutral among comprehensive doctrines of the good, including religions. Such state neutrality provides the broadest framework for fair and stable social cooperation and coexistence among adherents of different religions and other worldviews and accounts for two of liberalism's most basic principles, namely, the respect for conscience and equal liberty. In making his defense of the liberal democratic approach to religion, Miller offers critiques of the contributions of Kelsay, Ravitch, Allen, March, Curtis, and Ilesanmi to this volume.

Much has happened in the world since 2010 when the idea for this book was first conceived. In a postscript that drives home the significance of some of these issues to the world we live in, Wilson Parker offers his account and observations of two separate events that took place in 2011—the "Arab Spring" and the European Court of Human Rights' decision on the Italian practice of displaying crucifixes in public school classrooms.

Notes

1. Max Weber, "Legitimacy, Politics and the State," in *Legitimacy and the State*, ed. William Connolly (New York: New York University Press, 1984), 34.
2. Ibid.
3. Richard H. Fallon, Jr., "'The Rule of Law' as a Concept in Constitutional Discourse," *Columbia Law Review* 97, 1 (1997): 7–8.
4. Rachel Kleinfeld Belton, *Competing Definitions of The Rule of Law: Implications for Practitioners* (Washington, DC: Carnegie Endowment for International Peace, 2005), 3.
5. William Schweiker, "Monotheistic Faith and the Cosmopolitan Conscience," in this volume.
6. Carolyn Evans, "Introduction," in *Law and Religion in Theoretical and Historical Context*, ed. Peter Cane, Carolyn Evans, and Zoe Robinson (Cambridge, UK: Cambridge University Press, 2008), 8.
7. Mark Lilla, "The Return of Political Theology," in this volume.
8. Ibid.
9. Ibid.
10. Schweiker, "Monotheistic Faith."
11. Ibid.
12. Ibid.
13. Ibid.
14. Ibid.
15. Ibid.
16. Ibid.
17. Frank Ravitch, "Grappling With Neutrality," in this volume.
18. Ibid.
19. Ibid.
20. John Kelsay, "The Just War Argument in Islam," in this volume.

PART I

FUNDAMENTAL CONCERNS

CHAPTER 1

THE RETURN OF POLITICAL THEOLOGY

MARK LILLA

For over two centuries, from the American and French revolutions to the collapse of Soviet communism, world politics revolved around eminently political problems: war and revolution, class and social justice, race and national identity; these were the questions that divided us. Today we have progressed to the point where our problems again resemble those of the sixteenth century. As we find ourselves entangled in conflicts over competing revelations, dogmatic purity, and divine duty, we in the West are disturbed and confused. We find it incomprehensible that theological ideas still inflame the soul, stirring up messianic passions that leave societies in ruin. We had assumed this was no longer possible, that human beings had learned to separate religious questions from political ones, and that fanaticism was dead. We were wrong.

Let me offer an example. In May 2006, Iranian president Mahmoud Ahmadinejad sent an open letter to President Bush that was translated and published in newspapers around the world.[1] Its theme was contemporary politics and its language that of divine revelation. After rehearsing a litany of grievances against American foreign policies, real and imagined, Ahmadinejad wondered, "if Prophet Abraham, Isaac, Jacob, Ishmael, Joseph, or Jesus Christ (peace be unto him) were with us today, how would they have judged such behavior?" He then offered the following prophecy:

> Liberalism and Western style democracy have not been able to help realize the ideals of humanity. Today these two concepts have failed. Those with insight can already hear the sounds of the shattering and fall of the

> ideology and thoughts of the Liberal democratic systems. . . . Whether we like it or not, the world is gravitating towards faith in the Almighty and justice and the will of God will prevail over all things.

This is an extraordinary statement. Yet although it received serious attention in many parts of the world, in the United States it barely received notice—except by our two leading scholars of religion and politics, comedians Jon Stewart of *The Daily Show* and Stephen Colbert of *The Colbert Report*. This puzzled me. For all our concern about terrorism and radical Islamism, we apparently still find it hard to believe that *theological ideas* can put fire in the minds of men. We have become extremely adept at finding other explanations of political behavior. We claim we no longer believe that history is a one-way railroad leading all societies inevitably toward modern secular life, but I think deep down we do. We still maintain an implicit faith in a modernizing process, which is why we always blame delays or regressions on extenuating circumstances like poverty or colonialism. This implicit faith still shapes the way we see political theology today, as an atavism requiring psychological or sociological analysis but not serious intellectual engagement. Proponents of political theology, even if they are learned professionals preaching hate or doctors building bombs, appear to us primarily as frustrated, irrational representatives of frustrated, irrational societies, nothing more.

But let us assume that is not right. Let us assume that political theology is still a force to be reckoned with. How do we begin to understand it? The case of contemporary Islam is on everyone's mind, yet some thoughts can be so fraught with anger and ignorance that they are paralyzing. All we hear are alien sounds, motivating unspeakable acts. So let me suggest an alternative approach, which is to take a second look at our *own* (Western) history and experience with political theology.

For, contrary to our prophets of secularization and modernization, the history of political theology in the West did not end with the birth of modern science, or the Enlightenment, or the American and French revolutions, or any other definitive historical moment. Political theology was a presence in Western intellectual life well into the twentieth century, by which time it had shed the mind-set of the Middle Ages and found modern reasons for seeking political inspiration in the Bible—often with disastrous results. This is a forgotten story that I would like to revisit in this essay, and then I will offer some thoughts about what that story might have to teach us about the challenge of political theology today.

Let me begin with a definition, which I hope will help avoid misunderstanding. By political theology, I mean the following: a doctrine that legitimates public authority, and the institutions that exercise it, on the basis of a divine revelation. As construed here, my subject is not the practice of religion in the wide sense, for some religions have never had political theologies, and many societies without a prominent political theology—like our own—still practice religion. Theology is an intellectual discipline; it is a way of thinking. It begins by assuming a divinely revealed nexus between God, man, and world, which it investigates rationally. Political theology, as I wish to define it, derives principles of political legitimacy from that nexus—nothing more, nothing less.

Yet why is there political theology? Attempts to answer this question date back to antiquity, but we don't need history to understand how it is possible. Imagine human beings who first become aware of themselves in a world not of their own making. Their world has unknown origins and behaves in a regular fashion, so they wonder why that is. They know that the things they themselves fashion behave in a predictable manner because they conceive and construct them with some end in mind. They stretch the bow, and the arrow flies; that is why they were made. So, by analogy, it is not difficult for humans to assume that the cosmic order was constructed for a purpose, reflecting its maker's will. By following this analogy, they begin to have ideas about that maker, about the maker's intentions, and therefore about the maker's personality.

In taking these few short steps, the human mind finds itself confronted with a picture, a theological image of the divine nexus. Believers have reasons for thinking that they live in this nexus, just as they have reasons for assuming that it offers guidance for political life. But how that guidance is to be understood, and whether believers think it is authoritative, will depend on how they imagine God to be. If God is thought to be passive, a silent force like the sky, nothing in particular may follow; he is a hypothesis we can do without. But if we take seriously the thought that God is a being with intentions and that the cosmic order is a result of those intentions, then a great deal can follow. The intentions of such a God reveal something humans cannot fully know on their own. This revelation then becomes the source of God's authority, over nature and over us, and we have no choice but to obey him and see that his plans are carried out on earth. That is where political theology comes in.

Historically, most civilizations known to us, from ancient times to the present, have legitimated public authority and institutions through some sort of political theology. The law had a divine sanction, and political discourse was about how to interpret that sanction. The great attractiveness of political theology was, and is, its comprehensiveness. It offers a way of thinking about the conduct of human affairs and connects those thoughts to loftier ones about the existence of God, the structure of the cosmos, the nature of the soul, the origin of all things, and the end of time.

As we know, for more than a millennium, the West took inspiration from the Christian image of a triune God ruling over a created cosmos and guiding men by means of revelation, inner conviction, and the natural order. But this Trinitarian theological picture was always difficult to translate into political form. After the Hebrew Yahweh revealed his law, he remained transcendent, leaving it up to human beings to bring their lives into accord with his will. But by sending his Son to man, the Christian God condescended to enter our world, compromising his transcendence. The Messiah became flesh, much like an immanent God of the pagans. But he did not remain with us on earth; he departed, much like the absent God of the ancient gnostics, with the promise to return at the end of time. From that point on, our relationship with God is to be governed by love and grace, not by law, and it is infused with the constant presence of the Holy Spirit. Stranger still, this epoch is not the final one in human history; it contains within itself the promise of still another, an infinite stretch of time in which "all things will be made new" by the Messiah's return and God's Last Judgment.[2]

All told, this was a magnificent picture of divine and human relations. But it was not at all clear what political lessons were to be taken from it. Were Christians supposed to withdraw from a corrupted world that had been abandoned by the Redeemer? Were they called upon to rule the earthly city with both church and state, inspired by the Holy Spirit? Or were they expected to build a New Jerusalem that would hasten the Messiah's return?

Throughout the Middle Ages, Christians were involved in endless disputes over these questions. The City of Man was set against the City of God, public citizenship against private piety, the divine right of kings against the right of resistance, church authority against radical antinomianism, canon law against mystical insight, inquisitor against martyr, secular sword against ecclesiastical miter, prince against emperor, emperor against pope, pope against church councils. We've all heard this story.

I wonder, though, whether we fully grasp its implications. The profound political problems of Western Christendom were not accidental; they had roots deep in, and solely in, the ambiguities of Christian revelation and theology, which never quite managed to develop a coherent and authoritative political doctrine, given its commitment to the Trinitarian idea. Judaism had its *halakha*, and Islam had its *sharia*; those laws covered every aspect of human life for believers. But no such law existed in Christianity, only endless dispute about the believer's relation to the world and thus to political authority. It was this void that eventually opened a path for new thinking about political life. In other words, it was not the strength of Christian political theology that eventually provoked the rise of modern political philosophy; it was its unique theological weakness that translated into weak and self-contradictory institutions, opening all political theology to a new intellectual challenge. And the thinker who formulated that challenge in its most radical and enduring form was Thomas Hobbes.

With Hobbes, too, we feel ourselves on familiar ground: the war of all against all; life as nasty, brutish, and short; and, of course, that troublesome absolute sovereign. But Hobbes's novelty and importance for us do not rest on these commonplaces or on his political theory, narrowly defined. Rather, they rest on his novel approach to political theology—which was, quite simply, that he showed the Christian West how to let God be when thinking about politics. Traditionally, political theology interprets a set of revealed divine commands and applies them to social life. In his "Leviathan," published in 1651, Hobbes simply ignored the substance of those commands and talked instead about how and why human beings believed God had revealed them. This was a very old question that Hobbes managed to make the decisive question. He did the most revolutionary thing a thinker can ever do—he changed the subject, from God and his commands to man and his beliefs. If we do that, he suggested, we can begin to understand why religious convictions so often lead to political conflicts—at least in the Western Christendom. And once we do, we can find ways to contain those conflicts.

The political crisis of Hobbes's time created an audience for his ideas. In the midst of religious war, his view that the human mind was too weak and beset by passions to have any reliable knowledge of the divine seemed commonsensical. It also made sense to assume that when man speaks about God he is merely expressing his own ignorance and fears. Fresh from the Wars of Religion, Hobbes's readers knew all about fear. But what about revelation? Hobbes knew it is impossible to refute belief in divine revelation; he wagered, though, that he could disempower prophets simply by casting philosophical suspicion on them, which he did with great malice and skill. He laid down a fiat: the new political thinking would simply no longer begin with God's politics. Instead, it would concentrate on men as believers in God, slyly replacing political theology with political anthropology. In doing so, it would replace God's legitimate authority over man with man's legitimate authority over himself.

That was the decisive break in the history of political thinking in the West, which I have called the Great Separation.[3] I hasten to add, though, that this separation is not identical with what we usually think of as the separation of church and state. The problem of church and state is a traditional Christian problem, and throughout its history, Western Christendom found different ways to parcel out responsibilities between the two. The Great Separation effected by Hobbes was of a different order altogether: it offered a new way of separating political discourse from theological discourse. Once that was achieved, the problem of church and state returned and is still with us today, though we speak and think about it differently in different countries. It turns out you can wear a headscarf to school in Holland but not in France; Germany pays its ministers with public funds, while Spain does not; Canada and Britain give public funds to religious schools, yet this is unconstitutional in the United States. What unites Western nations today is not how they separate church and state, but the principle by which they do it. What we share is the principle that the legitimate exercise of public authority depends entirely on the consent of the governed, whatever their religious conviction. And for that we have Hobbes to thank.

The story I have told thus far is familiar and concludes with what sounds dangerously close to a happy ending, in which all God's children arrive safely in a secular society with liberal-democratic government. This is far from being an accurate rendition of the historical experience of the West, although filling in the gaps to this account cannot be stated in form of a chronicle. Instead, I would like simply to suggest that the Great Separation did not end the debate over political theology; new intellectual moves opened up and were pursued by modern political philosophers and theologians long after Hobbes. I would like to explore the logic of those moves, using the history that followed as background.

Let us begin by recognizing that the Great Separation was neither destined to happen, nor a fait accompli, even in Western Europe, where it was first conceived. Our history with political theology is an extremely parochial one: the political ambiguities of one religion (Christianity) in one region of the world (Western Europe) happened to set off a political crisis that might have been avoided but was not, triggering the Wars of Religion. The resulting carnage made European thinkers more receptive to Hobbes's heretical ideas about religious psychology, which he had stolen from Epicurus, though not to all his political ideas. It was only over time that more liberal political principles could be grafted onto Hobbes's rickety structure, which for some time stood lamely next to the magnificent edifice of Christian political theology. That theology had an extremely long afterlife in the West, and only after the Second World War did it cease to be a political force in continental Europe.

While all this was happening, a radically new intellectual challenge to the Great Separation arose unexpectedly from another quarter. It came from a wholly new kind of political theology that was heavily indebted to philosophy and styling itself both modern and liberal: the "liberal theology" movement that arose in Germany not long after the French

Revolution, first among Protestant theologians, then among Jewish reformers. These thinkers, who abhorred theocracy, also rebelled against Hobbes's vision, favoring instead a political future in which religion—properly chastened and intellectually reformed—would play an absolutely central role.

And the questions these new political theologians posed were good ones. While granting that ignorance and fear had bred pointless wars among Christian sects and nations, they asked the following questions: Were ignorance and fear the only reasons that, for a millennium and a half, an entire civilization had looked to Jesus Christ as its savior? Or that suffering Jews of the Diaspora remained loyal to the Torah? Could ignorance and fear explain the beauty of Christian liturgical music or the sublimity of the Gothic cathedrals? Could they explain why other civilizations, past and present, founded their political institutions in accordance with the divine nexus of God, man, and world? Surely, there was more to religious man than was dreamed of in Hobbes's philosophy.

That certainly was the view of Rousseau, who did more than anyone to develop a modern intellectual alternative to Hobbes's religious psychology. While Hobbes beat the drums of ignorance and fear, Rousseau sang the praises of conscience, of charity, of fellow feeling, of virtue, of pious wonder in the face of God's creation. Human beings, he thought, have a natural goodness they express in their religion. That's what religion at bottom is all about.

This is the theme of his short text, the "Profession of Faith of a Savoyard Vicar," which is found in his 1762 masterpiece, *Emile*. This work tells the parable of a young vicar who loses his faith and then his moral compass, when confronted with the hypocrisy of his coreligionists. He is able to restore his equilibrium only when he finds a new kind of faith in God by looking within, to what Rousseau called his "inner light." There is much we cannot know about God, and for centuries the pretense of having understood him caused much damage to Christendom. But, for Rousseau, we need to believe *something* about him if we are to orient ourselves in the world.

Among modern thinkers, Rousseau was the first to declare that there is no shame in saying that faith in God is humanly necessary. Religion has its roots in needs that are rational and moral, even noble; once we see that, we can start satisfying them rationally, morally, and nobly. In the abstract, this thought did not contradict the principles of the Great Separation, but it did raise doubts about whether the new political thinking could really do without reference to the nexus of God, man, and world. If Rousseau was right about our moral needs, a rigid separation between political and theological principles, while intellectually defensible, might not be psychologically sustainable. When a question is important, we want an answer to it: as the Savoyard vicar says, "The mind decides in one way or another, despite itself, and prefers being mistaken to believing in nothing."[4] Rousseau had grave doubts about whether human beings could be happy or good if they did not understand how their actions related to something higher. Religion is simply too entwined with our moral experience ever to be disentangled from it, and morality is inseparable from politics.

By the early nineteenth century, two schools of thought about religion and politics had grown up in the West. Let us call them the children of Hobbes and the children of Rousseau. For the children of Hobbes, a decent political life could not be realized by Christian political theology, which bred violence and stifled human development. The old habit of looking to God for political guidance would have to be broken, and new habits would have to be developed. For Hobbes, the first step toward achieving that end was to get people thinking about—and suspicious about—the psychological sources of faith.

The children of Rousseau followed a different line of argument. They recognized that medieval political theology was not salvageable, but neither could human beings ignore questions of eternity and transcendence when thinking about the good life. When we speculate about God, man, and world in the correct way, we express our noblest moral sentiments; without such reflection, we despair and eventually harm ourselves and others. That is the lesson of the Savoyard vicar.

In the aftermath of the French Revolution, Rousseau's children found a receptive audience in continental Europe, particularly in Germany. This was the century of "liberal theology," a term that requires explanation. In nineteenth-century Britain and the United States, it was generally assumed that the intellectual, and then institutional, separation of Christianity and modern politics had been mutually beneficial—that the modern state had benefited by being absolved from pronouncing on doctrinal matters, and that Christianity had benefited by being freed from state interference. No such consensus existed in Germany, where the assumption was that religion needed to be publicly encouraged, not reined in, if it was to contribute to society. It would have to be rationally reformed, of course: the Bible would have to be interpreted in light of recent historical findings, belief in miracles abandoned, the clergy educated along modern lines, and doctrine adapted to a softer age. The modern state could then give Protestantism its due in public life, and Protestant theology would reciprocate, by recognizing its political responsibilities, and become the moral foundation of the state. Once these reforms were in place, enlightened politics and enlightened religion would join hands.

This fantasy was not limited to Protestant theologians. In fact, it was shared by many German Jewish thinkers until the First World War. After the French Revolution, German Jews were more quickly integrated into modern cultural life than in any other European country—a fateful development. For it was precisely at this moment that German Protestants were becoming convinced that reformed Christianity represented their national spirit. While the liberal Jewish thinkers were attracted to modern enlightened faith, they were also driven by the apologetic need to justify Judaism's contribution to German society. In Germany they could not appeal to the principles of the Great Separation and simply demand to be left alone. They had to argue that Judaism and Protestantism were two forms of the same rational moral faith, and that they could share a political theology.

For much of the nineteenth century, this consensus held in Germany, making it appear that Rousseau had been right and Hobbes wrong. But by the turn of the twentieth century, the liberal theological house was tottering, and after the First World War it collapsed. It was not just the barbarity of trench warfare, the senseless slaughter, the sight of burned-out towns, and the maimed soldiers that made contemptible a theology extolling "modern civilization." It was that so many liberal theologians—Protestant and Jewish—had hastened the insane rush to war, eager to prove their patriotism and confident that God's hand was guiding German history.

It was also that liberal religion offered no spiritual sustenance to young men and women who had just witnessed the collapse of a civilization. To young Protestants it prescribed a catechism of moral commonplaces and historical optimism about bourgeois life, spiced with deep pessimism about the possibility of altering their lives. To young Jews it preached the ethical message at the core of all biblical faith and passed over in genteel silence the fearsome God of the prophets, his covenant with the Jewish people, and the demanding laws he gave them. To the decisive questions—"Why be a Christian?" and "Why be a Jew?"—liberal theology offered no answer at all.

After the First World War, young German Protestants and Jews began to look elsewhere. But they did not turn to Hobbes or to Rousseau. They craved a more robust faith, based on a new revelation that would shake the foundations of the whole modern order. It was a thirst for redemption. Ever since the liberal theologians had revived the idea of biblical politics, the stage had been set for just this sort of development. When faith in redemption through bourgeois propriety and cultural accommodation withered after the Great War, the most daring thinkers of the day transformed it into hope for a messianic apocalypse—one that would again place the Jewish people, or the individual Christian believer, or the German nation, or the world proletariat in direct relation with the divine.

Young Weimar Jews were particularly drawn to these messianic currents through the writings of Martin Buber, who as a young Zionist promoted a crude chauvinistic nationalism. In an early essay, he called for a "Masada of the spirit" and proclaimed: "If I had to choose for my people between a comfortable, unproductive happiness . . . and a beautiful death in a final effort at life, I would have to choose the latter. For this final effort would create something divine, if only for a moment, but the other something all too human."[5] Language like this drew deeply from the well of biblical messianism, and phrases like "a beautiful death" have discomforting echoes for us today. Yet Buber was an amateur compared with the Marxist philosopher Ernst Bloch, an atheist Jew, who in the Weimar years proclaimed a connection between messianic hope and revolutionary violence, which he celebrated. Bloch was particularly fond of brutal Soviet leaders, famously declaring "ubi Lenin, ibi Jerusalem"—wherever Lenin is, there is Jerusalem.[6]

But it was among young Weimar Protestants that the new messianic spirit proved most consequential. They were led by the greatest theologian of the day, Karl Barth, who wanted to restore the drama of religious decision to Christianity and rejected any accommodation of the Gospel to modern sensibilities. When Hitler came to power, Barth bravely opposed him, but others who borrowed from Barth's messianic rhetoric chose the Nazis instead. A notorious example was Friedrich Gogarten, one of Barth's closest collaborators, who briefly sided with the Nazis in 1933. After Hitler completed his takeover, Gogarten wrote the following: "because we are today once again under the total claim of the state, it is again possible, humanly speaking, to proclaim the Christ of the Bible and his reign over us."[7]

All of this seemed to confirm Hobbes's iron law: Messianic theology eventually breeds messianic politics. The idea of redemption is an astonishingly powerful force. It has inspired people to endure suffering, overcome suffering and inflict suffering on others. It has offered hope and inspiration in times of darkness; it has also added to the darkness by arousing unrealistic expectations and justifying those who spill blood to satisfy them. All the Abrahamic faiths cultivate the idea of redemption, and all try to contain its power to inflame minds and deafen them to the voice of reason. In the writings of these Weimar figures, we encounter what those orthodox traditions always dreaded: the translation of religious notions of apocalypse and redemption into a justification of political messianism, though now under frightening modern conditions. It was as if nothing had changed since the seventeenth century, when Thomas Hobbes first sat down to write his *Leviathan*.

The revival of political theology in the modern West is a humbling story—or ought to be. It reminds us that this way of thinking about God and politics is neither the preserve of any one culture or religion nor does it belong solely to the past. It is an age-old habit of mind that can be reacquired by anyone who begins looking to the divine nexus of God, man, and world to reveal the legitimate political order. This story also reminds us how political theology can be adapted to historical circumstances and reassert itself, even in the face of seemingly irresistible forces like modernization, secularization, and democratization. Hobbes had left the impression that the challenge of political theology would vanish once the cycle of fear was broken and human beings established authority over their own affairs. We still make this assumption when speaking of the "social causes" of fundamentalism and political messianism, as if the amelioration of material conditions or the shifting of borders would automatically trigger a Great Separation. Nothing in our history or contemporary experience confirms this belief, yet somehow we seem unable to let it go.

Rousseau may have been on to something: we seem to be theotropic creatures, yearning to connect our mundane lives, in some way, to the beyond. That urge can be suppressed, new habits learned, but the challenge of political theology will never fully disappear so long as the urge survives. We have learned Hobbes's lesson too well, perhaps, and failed to heed Rousseau's. And so we find ourselves in an intellectual bind when we encounter genuine political theology today: either we assume that modernization and secularization will eventually extinguish it, or we treat it as an incomprehensible existential threat, using familiar terms like fascism to describe it as best we can. Neither response takes us a step closer to understanding the world we now live in.

It is a world in which millions of people, particularly in the Muslim orbit, believe that God has revealed a law governing the whole of human affairs. This belief shapes the politics of important Muslim nations, and it also shapes the attitudes of vast numbers of believers who find themselves living in Western countries—and non-Western democracies like Turkey and Indonesia—that are founded on the modern principles of the Great Separation. There is a political chasm here that we cannot begin to address unless we first recognize the intellectual chasm between us. Although it is possible to translate President Ahmadinejad's letter to President Bush from Farsi into English, its intellectual assumptions cannot be translated into those of the Great Separation. We can try to learn his language in order to create sensible policies for dealing with him, but agreement on basic principles will not be possible. And we must learn to live with that.

Similarly, we must somehow find a way to accept the fact that, given the immigration policies West European nations have pursued over the last half-century, they now are hosts to roughly 20 million Muslims, some of whom have great difficulty fitting into societies that do not recognize any political claims based on their divine revelation. Like Orthodox Jewish law, the Muslim sharia is meant to cover the whole of life, not some arbitrarily demarcated private sphere, and its legal system has few theological resources for establishing the independence of politics. Like all strong traditions of political theology, it cannot countenance the idea that human beings may legitimately exercise authority over themselves without consulting God's revelation. It is an unfortunate situation, but we have made our bed, Muslims and non-Muslims alike. Accommodation and mutual respect can help, as can clear rules governing areas of tension, like the status of women, parents' rights over their children, speech offensive to religious sensibilities, speech inciting violence, standards of dress in public institutions, and the like. But we need to recognize that coping is the order of the day, not defending high principle, and that our expectations should remain low. If a sizable population believes in the truth of a comprehensive political theology, its full reconciliation with modern liberal democracy cannot be expected.

This is not welcome news. For more than two centuries, promoters of modernization have taken it for granted that science, technology, urbanization, and education would eventually disenchant the charmed world of believers, and that with time, people would either abandon their traditional faiths or transform them in politically anodyne ways. They point to continental Europe, where belief in God has been in steady decline over the last 50 years, and suggest that Muslims everywhere will eventually undergo a similar transformation. Those predictions, however narcissistic, may eventually prove right. But we must remember that Europe's own secularization, especially regarding politics, is of relatively recent date. As for the American experience, it is utterly exceptional: there is no other fully developed industrial society with a population so committed to its faiths (and such exotic ones), while being equally committed to the Great Separation. Our political rhetoric, which owes much to the Protestant sectarians of the seventeenth century, vibrates with messianic energy, and it is only thanks to a strong constitutional structure and various lucky breaks that political theology has never seriously challenged the basic legitimacy of our institutions. Americans have potentially explosive religious differences over abortion, prayer in schools, censorship, euthanasia, biological research, and countless other issues, yet they generally settle these differences within the bounds of the Constitution. It is a miracle, and miracles cannot be willed.

We also need to recognize that political theology is highly adaptive and can present, to even educated minds, a more compelling vision of the future than the prospect of secular modernity. It takes as little for a highly trained medical doctor to fashion a car bomb today as it took for advanced thinkers to fashion biblically inspired justifications of fascism and communism in Weimar Germany. When the urge to connect is strong, passions are high, and fantasies are vivid, the trinkets of our modern lives are impotent amulets against political intoxication. This has nothing to do with Islam as a religion, let alone with Arab culture. It has to do with the perennial power of political theology.

Realizing this, a number of Muslim thinkers around the world have taken to promoting a "liberal" Islam. What they mean is an Islam more adapted to the demands of modern social and economic life, kinder in its treatment of women and children, more tolerant of other faiths, more open to dissent. These are brave people who have often suffered for their efforts, in prison or exile, as did their predecessors in the nineteenth century, of which there were many.[8]

But now as then, their efforts have been swept away by deeper theological currents. The history of Protestant and Jewish liberal theology reveals the problem: the more an Abrahamic faith is trimmed to fit the demands of the moment, the fewer reasons it gives believers for holding on to that faith in troubled times, when self-appointed guardians of theological purity offer more radical hope. Worse still, when such a liberal faith is used to bestow theological sanctification on a single form of political life—even an attractive one like liberal democracy—the more it will be seen as collaborating with injustice when that political system fails. The dynamics of political theology seem to dictate that when liberalizing reformers try to conform to the present, they inspire a countervailing and far more passionate longing for redemption in the messianic future. That is what happened in Weimar Germany and is happening again in contemporary Islam.

But that is not the only alternative. There is another kind of transformation possible in these faiths, and that is the renewal of traditional political theology from within. If liberalizers are apologists for religion at the court of modern life, renovators stand firmly within their faith and reinterpret political theology so believers can adapt without feeling themselves to be apostates. Luther and Calvin were renovators in this sense, not liberalizers. They called Christians back to the fundamentals of their faith, but in a way that made it easier, not harder, to enjoy the fruits of modern existence. And they did this, not by speaking the apologetic language of toleration and progress, but by rewriting the language of Christian political theology and demanding that Christians be faithful to it. Renewal, though, is a high-risk venture. One can renew a political theology in a way that renders it more open to modern individualism and the institutions of the modern state, or one can renew it in a way that preserves the habits and mores of a supposedly purer time. Those seem to be the two great options before Muslim political theology today.[9]

In the end, though, what happens there will have very little to do with us or our desires. We have little reason to expect that societies in the grip of any powerful political theology will follow our unusual path. This does not mean that those societies necessarily lack the wherewithal to create a decent and workable political order; it does not even mean that they have nothing to teach us about our own failings. But it does mean that they will have to find the theological resources within their own traditions to make renewal happen. All we can do is observe, without any illusions about the deep political differences between us, or how history is drawing us together.

Fantasies of historical inevitability die hard. Like notions of divine providence, they reassure us of the legibility of the world. It satisfies no deeper yearning to learn that our most basic political principles arose in response to the unique theological challenges of Christendom, that they faced serious intellectual challenge from within the modern West, and that the temptation to challenge them with a potent political theology has always been present. There is something grand in viewing modern political thought and practice as the result of larger, impersonal forces—and something comforting, too, since it relieves us of responsibility for understanding the alternatives before us and choosing between them. It helps us to forget that societies are heirs to the Great Separation only if they wish to be.

Notes

1. See, for example, Steven Weisman, "Iranian Writes to Bush; No R.S.V.P. Is Likely," *The New York Times*, May 9, 2006, A14. Full text of letter available at https://web.archive.org/web/20070707160708/http://www.president.ir/eng/ahmadinejad/cronicnews/1385/02/19/letter.pdf.
2. Rev. 21:5.
3. Mark Lilla, *The Stillborn God: Religion, Politics, and the Modern West* (Alfred A. Knoph N.Y. 2007), 55.
4. Quoted in Mark Lilla, "The Politics of God," *Current* 497 (2007), 18
5. Gilga A. Schmidt, ed., *The First Buber: Youthful Zionist Writings of Martin Buber* (Syracuse, N.Y., 1999), 107, 185.
6. Ernst Bloch, *The Principle of Hope*, trans. Neville Plaice, Stephen Plaice, and Paul Knight (London, 1986), 610.
7. Friedrich Gogarten, Einheit von Evangelium und Volkstum? (Jena, Germany, 1933), 5, 11, 24.

8. See, for example, Ursula Gunther, "Mohammed Arkoun," in *Dictionary of Literary Biography: Twentieth-Century Arab Writers*, Vol. 346, edited by Matthew Gruccoli (Gale, 2009), 15–23.
   See also, discussions of Shaker al-Nabulsi, http://www.almuslih.org/index.php?option=com_content&view=article&id=271:the-passing-of-shaker-al-nabulsi&catid=38:obstacles-to-reform&Itemid=207 and http://www.memri.org/report/en/0/0/0/0/0/0/1221.htm
9. See, for example, discussion of Khaled Abou El Fadl and Tariq Ramadan in Mark Lilla, "The Politics of God," *Current* 497 (2007), 23.

CHAPTER 2

Monotheistic Faith and the Cosmopolitan Conscience

William Schweiker

The central focus of this book draws us into a question sweeping the globe, namely, what is the relation between, on the one hand, religious convictions—say, beliefs in God and ideas about revelation and sacred scriptures—and, on the other hand, political loyalties, including ideas about the rule of law. Three things about this topic seem obvious, at least to me: first, religion will not go away but is in fact shaping global and local social life, so the idea of a purely secular future is not really a viable one; second, the rule of just law is at risk in part because of disputes raging in many countries about the pressure that religious and cultural diversity puts on legal systems; and third, global dynamics—economic, cultural, technological, environmental, and so on—arising out of modern social conditions are going to spread and to accelerate, thereby forging deep connectivity among the peoples of the world that can be the cause of conflict as well as cooperation.[1]

In this essay, I will focus on the first aspect of the topic, that is, the interaction of the religions with other social, political, and global forces. Of special interest to me is the need to change the terms of the current debate about religion and politics. In this regard, a preliminary clarification of procedure is in order.

1. Argument and Approach

To start with, I want to explore, through a couple of steps of reflection, the symbolic and conceptual richness of monotheistic faith, not only to understand the dangers it poses for social and political life, but also to find resources for living the religious life in humane, free, and cosmopolitan ways. My central aim is to shift the discussion, from one centered on sources of political authority and its relation to religious revelation, to the question of how religious sources can and ought to be interpreted (see Lilla's contribution to this volume). The root issue, as far as I can tell, is how the religions are *interpreted*; what we actually see on the world stage are different strategies of interpretation. As Terry Eagleton has put it:

> A good many of the influences we undergo have to be interpreted in order to affect our behavior; an interpretation is a creative affair. It is not so much that the past shapes us as the past as we (consciously or unconsciously) interpret it. And we can always come to decipher it differently.[2]

The question of interpretation is more complex and contentious than appeals to authority precisely because every supposed authority for ordering and directing social and political life must itself be interpreted.

The focus on the interpretation of sources of authority means that I adopt a hermeneutical approach to social life. I agree with various theorists, ranging from Augustine and Cicero in the ancient world to moderns like Alexis de Tocqueville, Max Weber, and more recently, Anthony Giddens, Charles Taylor, and others, that we cannot understand social systems—politics, economics, media, for instance—without understanding the beliefs and values that motivate human action.[3] Those beliefs and values, especially religious ones, are not self-interpreting. The religions do not each have just one meaning or way of living, but, rather, each are rich and complex constellations of symbols, ideas, narratives, and practices that can be understood and lived in different ways. It is this fact that explains the diversity of ways of being Christian (Orthodox, Catholic, Protestant—of various kinds) or Buddhist (Zen, Theravada, Mahayana) or Jewish (Orthodox, Reformed, Hassidic).[4] The global reality in which we now live is provoking specific interpretations in each of the religions. One strategy I am going to call "hypertheism" and will explore it in a few moments; another strategy, and the one I will press, focuses on the "cosmopolitan conscience." So, I intend to complicate the picture of how the religions are understood, especially the picture of monotheism, and then I will try to respond to our situation in light of that revision, by introducing the idea of the cosmopolitan conscience, which will require reclaiming some ancient ideas in our global context.

Shifting the discussion in this way will be difficult, I admit, because of entrenched ideas that are shaping current debate. The terms of the debate have in fact set up battle lines that are appealing to many people, since they cast options into an easy either/or. We are told that there are people who believe in democracy, the rule of civil law, and the use of reason to orient human affairs and thus affirm, in some way, the "secular realm"; although, conversely, there are religious believers, often conceived as intolerant fundamentalists, who, again we are told, oppose all of these ideas in the name of religion. That picture is hardly adequate to what we mean by the "secular," as many thinkers have argued. More important for my reflections is the fact that the either/or picture is a faulty understanding of religion and its relation to social and political reality.

The root idea animating the current debate is that reason is on the side of those who seek democracy and the rule of law; revelation, conversely, is on the side of religion. What is more, revelation and reason represent—and must represent—two absolutely different sources of authority for the conduct of human life. Sometimes called the "theologico-political problem," after the work of the philosopher Benedict de Spinoza, at issue is how to justify the organization of political life and so the use and distribution of power and authority. Further back in history, the problem is seen in the clash between Creon and the title character in Sophocles' play *Antigone*. Creon insists on loyalty to the polis, whereas Antigone claims to be commanded by the gods to bury her brother who lies dead and unburied in the street under order of Creon for attacking the polis in a flagrant act of treason. The clash between familial piety, political loyalty, and the command of the gods comes to frightening and tragic end in the play. The question seems obvious. Is our political life justified by appeal to some supernatural revelation so that political organization must conform to the will of God? Conversely, is it possible to base politics on rational deliberation and the will of the people?

Under these terms of debate, our reflections could—if we are not careful—exclude understanding the complexity of the religions and thus the diversity of ways they can be lived. When we allow ourselves to be led into either appeals to reason or revelation alone, we are blinded to other possibilities found in the religious traditions. In fact, there is the possibility of living the religious life humanely and reasonably in a way that is also open to religious meanings in the social order, meanings that are often concealed in other cultural and social events. I will be presenting this kind of position through the idea of the cosmopolitan conscience.[5] This will also entail a shift from thinking about social life in the context of a "religious cosmology" or trying radically to separate religious beliefs and practice from social existence—say, in thinking religion is purely a private, individual matter—to careful reflection on the interactions among domains of social life, including religious and political existence. I am mindful that some advocates of religion and some critics of religion will think that this position is not religious enough or, conversely, not secular and rational enough. But that judgment merely signals that they are committed to the either/or dyad, either revelation or reason. I am trying to change the terms of the debate.

Now before further exploring monotheistic faith, the current lines of debate, and also the cosmopolitan conscience, something more needs to be noted about the perspective and method of these reflections. About perspective, I engage our topic as a scholar of and a participant in the Christian tradition. Thus, in discussing the monotheistic traditions, I claim real expertise in only one of them. The justification for broad language is the fact that the perspective I adopt seeks to account for the distinctive struggle and agency of human beings and our existence as part of the natural world. The monotheistic religions make claims about "humanity before God" and thus assert something about our shared humanity.[6] The idea of conscience, as I will show later, captures something about our shared humanity; that is why appeals to the freedom of conscience are a danger to every form of political and religious tyranny, local or global, because that freedom is about human dignity.

With respect to my own tradition and perspective, my argument unfolds, methodologically, a "theological" horizon of reflection within "ethics." What does that mean? Ethics is careful and critical thinking about how we should live, as persons and communities, in ways that are good, just, and responsible. Every ethics also entails some account of reality within which human beings must orient their lives. That account of reality might be partly a theological one in the sense that it presents ways to conduct human life before God. But this can be done in different ways, say, envisioning a religious cosmology wherein everything finds its source and place in relation to God, or conversely, a more differentiated account of the interaction of domains of life, what I am calling a cosmopolitan one. There is no need to be believer or theologian to ponder these things, but merely have an interest, a nagging worry, or a curiosity about the relation between ideas about God and what is morally good and right. Theological and ethical reflection might, in fact, result in the denial of God or at least some ideas of God, and for moral reasons as well as theological ones. That too will be part of my argument. In order to understand that possibility, which might be a surprise, coming as it does from a theologian, we need to be clear about the meaning of "theology," since there are many ways the term is used.

In a general way, theology is thinking and talking (*logos*) about God (*theos*). In this sense, any talk about God—from the quiet prayers of the faithful to popular arts forms, from the study of Torah among Jews to musing on the "god-gene" by biologists—are forms of "theology."

However, a general definition does not help much. Theology in a strict sense is not confession or catechism or Bible study or prayer or authoritarian pronouncements or the band R.E.M. singing about "Losing My Religion." Theology, properly speaking, is a form of critical thinking and rational reflection asking about the meaning and truth of religious convictions and practices. In this precise sense, theology aims to identify and criticize confused, stupid, vicious, and silly ideas of God—of which there are many—in order to speak rightly of the divine. If ethics is about a way of life worthy of human beings, then theology, we can say, is about beliefs and practices worthy of what is sacred, holy. Here too there is a difference important for my argument. We can practice theology in the strict sense inside of a religious cosmology and so never ask how it might accord or not accord with other ways of knowing the world and ordering social life. Conversely, we can see theology as a mediating form of thinking that critically differentiates and inter-relates realms or domains of social life. In this way, theology is not locked into a specific religious cosmology, but it is thinking at the junctures of forms of thought and social realities. In what follows, then, I want to isolate a problem within certain expressions of monotheistic faith and to outline the "cosmopolitan conscience" as an ethical and theological response to it. As my reflections proceed, keep in mind the account of ethics and theology just noted: ethics is human reasoning about the conduct of life; theology considers the beliefs and practices about the sacred and divine, and it tests a religious outlook, even a cosmology, for its truth and meaning.

Turning now to the popular criticism of monotheistic traditions in our global age and so the usual terms of debate, I will then nuance and revise that debate by isolating the distortion that we can call "hypertheism." This religious distortion is actually a betrayal of monotheistic faith—theologically and ethically—even though its roots are in monotheism. That idea in hand, I will then conclude with the cosmopolitan conscience.

2. Monotheistic Faith and Its Problems

In order to understand what I mean by "hypertheism," we need to be clear about the meaning of "monotheistic faith," since it is a complex phenomenon. Theism is, first, a specific type of religion, one that entails belief in a "God," a distinction necessary because not all religions, as some versions of Buddhism shows, are defined in relations to gods. Monotheism, then, is a form of religion with only one God, not many. That is to say, monotheism is a theistic form of religion—a belief in and relation to divine reality—but it is not polytheistic; there are not many gods, as in some versions of Hinduism or the pantheon of gods in Greco-Roman

Hellenistic religion, but only one God. The God of monotheistic faith is believed to be ultimately real, but the sum total of reality does not equal God. Thus, monotheism rejects pantheism since God in some ways "transcends" reality. A key question, then, is how the one God relates to the rest of reality—to physical nature, to history, to social and political systems, and to the anxieties and joys of personal life.

The monotheistic religions (Judaism, Christianity, and Islam) are teeming with ideas, symbols, and narratives to speak about how God relates to the rest of reality: Political images are used, so God as sovereign; familial ones, too, and thus God as "parent"; and physical, as well as animate images, are also used, like God as a rock or God as a mother hen tending her brood. Metaphysical ideas have been put to work to explain God's relation to the world, so God as first cause and last end. Mystical thinkers speak of God as the dark night of the soul or the abyss of mystery. God is love, to use an image from the Gospel of John, and so on and so on. This is important: there is no single idea of God somehow dictated by "revelation" because the "revelation" is a welter of ideas, images, and metaphors that have to be interpreted. Even the idea that God is a supernatural person is, in fact, only one idea of the divine in the monotheistic traditions. And what is more, "God," the divine reality, is not the same as ideas about God. The word "God" is actually a term for a reality that we cannot adequately or exhaustively know because our terms for "God" are derived from non-divine reality, like hens or rocks or persons. In classical Christian thought, the various ways of speaking about God have been divided into metaphysical and moral attributes of God. But the point is that the ideas used to express God's relation to human and nonhuman reality are almost endless. This means—crucially—that monotheistic faith requires and provokes interpretation.

We need to note, second, that monotheism is not only belief about the nature of divine reality distinct from nontheistic, polytheistic, and pantheistic forms of religion. Monotheism is also about how human beings can and should relate to the one and true God. This is why we speak of "monotheistic faith." But what does faith mean? That too, as we all know, is a complicated question, and it is one that has filled the pages of theological treatises throughout the centuries. It is not possible to explore all of the meanings of faith in this essay. Drawing on and amending the work of H. Richard Niebuhr, we can say that faith is trust in God as the source of life and the value of existence, devotion to what furthers God's purposes for human and nonhuman life, and active obedience to the divine will.[7] So defined, faith is given expression in basic human sensibilities—like trust—but also specific beliefs, say, about God's will, and also religious practices, such as worship or ascetic spiritual disciplines, from prayer to fasting. How faith is interpreted will determine the way in which a believer is to relate to

God. If we say that "obedience" to God's will is basic, that can, at least in principle, orient life very differently than trusting in or devotion to God's love for all reality. Again, this too will be important in a moment for understanding what I mean by hypertheism, as only one way—and a dangerous one at that—of interpreting the complexity of monotheistic faith.

If this is a rough and ready understanding of monotheistic faith—that is, trust, devotion, and obedience to the one God of reality whose relation to reality is spoken about in many different ways, none of which exhaust what we mean by the divine reality—then the problems of monotheism start to become clear. The root of these problems, I am suggesting, is when the rich diversity of ways of speaking about God and faith are reduced to just a few ideas, and the diversity of religious ideas and practices is enfolded within a self-contained and seamless cosmology. It is the complexity of monotheistic faith—not its simplicity—that is the real problem but also the real possibility. What then are the problems? Let us return to the current terms of debate and so the either/or between reason and revelation that characterizes the theologico-political problem.

The discussion of religion on the global scene indicates what is perceived to be a major problem facing the great monotheistic religions in an age of global diversity and interaction. In brief, the claim is that monotheism—the belief in one God of all reality—is somehow inimical to human diversity. The criticism is that these religions are inherently dangerous and tyrannous because the very idea of there being one and only one God, and that this God is to be the center of complete devotion by persons and communities, means that the diversity of human beliefs and practices cannot be tolerated. In other words, belief in a universal God, a global God, is supposedly destructive of local identities and differences. Monotheism, so the criticism goes, is inherently intolerant and by its own logic demands that the whole of life be placed under the sovereignty of the one God.

Further, there are three great monotheistic religions—Judaism, Christianity, and Islam—and it is not surprising, the critic notes, that these communities have been in conflict throughout the centuries about which is the one, true religion, and also, especially with Christianity and Islam, missionary, conquering, and colonial powers. From crusades to forced conversions, genocide to terrorist attacks, benign despotism to full-blown theocracy, these traditions, the criticism concludes, are the historical and social expressions of the dangers inherent to monotheism itself. As soon as the rule of God is made the supreme authority and focus in life, then the rule of law must bow to divine sovereignty and to the manipulation of those who serve as the ministers of God's sovereignty: religious leaders, political authorities, and, more often than not, men within a patriarchal social structure. Everything is then submitted to and ought to conform to "revelation." Now, please notice: this criticism contends that the only proper image for God in monotheistic faiths is a political one—a sovereign tyrant—and that the only meaning of faith is obedience and, further, these are to be parts of a comprehensive revealed religious vision of reality.

3. Clarifying the Criticism

Let me probe this criticism of the monotheistic faith, in the hope of providing a more nuanced account of the challenge that monotheism poses, and then outline a response to that challenge. I am trying to change the terms of the debate—from the either/or of reason versus revelation—to explore the complexity of religion and strategies of interpretation. In other words, rather than casting the topic of our discussion in terms of competing forms of "authority," say, rational deliberation or appeals to revelation, I am focusing my inquiry on strategies of interpreting the religions. These points will help me isolate a danger in monotheistic faith usually missed by the standard criticism but also, and importantly, identify resources for a different way of living religiously.

In terms of the popular criticism of monotheism, the world is divided into two options, a kind of "clash of civilization" as the late Samuel Huntington called it.[8] On the one side are some believers, as well as those who want, for political or moral reasons, to show deference to religion, and so they insist that evil expressions of religion, monotheistic or otherwise, are not really religion. We hear that Islam has been hijacked by extremists, for instance. Or we somehow imagine that "fundamentalism" in the various religions—Judaism, Christianity, or Hinduism, for example—is really the result of nonreligious forces, say, poverty or political struggles. The strategy is to demarcate religion—which is supposedly always good—from aberrant nonreligious forms that infect and destroy religion. The task then is to get the true religion because it will be good and just and loving. On the other side, are those—like some of the so-called New Atheists—for whom religion, root and branch, is the problem. Religion preys on human fear and ignorance and drives human beings to do the most heinous actions in the name of their "god." The only escape is to "break the spell" of the god-delusion, as Daniel Dennett puts it.[9] Once clearheaded thinking is in place, we can form societies freer from the tyrannies of religion and the evil they do.

These lines of argument, based on the contrast of "reason or revelation," face massive historical and comparative problems. It is hard to sustain the idea that the horror worked on human existence or the natural world by the religions is somehow greater than those worked by modern rationalized societies. Human history is a sad chronicle of conflicts among Buddhists no less than among Hindu, wars among members of indigenous tribes in the Americas, and the horror over the last century of state-run and executed tyranny by atheistic political regimes. The body counts are high on all sides. More pointedly, religious fundamentalism and extremism seems to be the late-born twin of modern social structures; they are different expressions of modernity. We might even say that the pressure to see the world in an either/or—either reason or revelation—itself is a modern enterprise, but that is a topic I cannot explore here. The main and essential point is that we cannot easily separate "religion" from how it is hijacked. The religions—every religion—as lived human realities are as ambiguous as human beings. That is just another way of saying, seeing it from the inverse side as it were, that monotheistic religions are exceedingly rich in how to speak of God and of faith. This richness is also the possibility for distortion because the religions can be interpreted in endless ways. The question is what to do about this ambiguity.

Another feature of the popular criticism of monotheism has a long history, reaching from the ancient world to modern thinkers like Thomas Hobbes, David Hume, and others, but it too has problems. Monotheism, psychologically, is supposedly rooted in human fear or a slavish desire for eternal reward (i.e., for "heaven"). Human beings face the terrors and uncertainties of life that drive them to superstitious beliefs. As Hume puts this in his treatise *The Natural History of Religion*:

> The primary religion of mankind arises chiefly from an anxious fear of future events; and what ideas will naturally be entertained of invisible, unknown power, while men lie under dismal apprehensions of any kind, may easily be conceived.[10]

We could, quite easily, race through Freud, Nietzsche, and other critics of religion to make much the same point. Popular today is the attempt to explain religion in terms of utility function and so to use economic rationality to explain the appeal of religion rooted in the quest for rewards. Further, the attempt to isolate "the" cause of religion is even found among the defenders of religion. There are those who contend that the origins of religious sensibilities are what is most honorable and noble in human life, the depths of love and the purity of justice and compassion. The twentieth century Christian theologian, Paul Tillich, argued that Christian faith is a matter of ultimate concern, and it provides the "courage to be" in the face of the threat of nonbeing and death. It finds expression—he goes on to argue—in love and justice.

There are problems with accounts of the origin of religion in terms of fear, or desire for reward, or simply ultimate concern. It is difficult, I would say impossible, to isolate a single source of religion, psychologically or historically, or, for that matter, any other human phenomenon. Human beings and human societies are more complex than these accounts, and any attempt to reduce the complexity of experience and the motivations for action are wide of the mark. We have already seen this complexity in the idea of faith itself—which includes sensibilities, like trust, but also beliefs and practices. But that means that religion, like everything human, has multiple sources.

It might seem that I have in fact deflected or even dispelled the popular criticism of monotheism and the usual terms of debate, and in some respect, that is the case. Does that mean that I do not think the theologico-political problem is a genuine problem? Not in the least. My concern is not to dispel the criticism or the problem so much as to nuance and to focus thinking on the right point. I agree with those thinkers, ranging from the Hebrew prophets to modern thinkers, who insist that one task of critical thinking—maybe a basic one—is the critique of religion. The task is to focus that critique on the right point, so that on the other side of critique we can advance constructive thinking, including a constructive interpretation of religious life. I have intimated that deeper than the problem of the conflict of "authorities"—reason or revelation—are conflicts of interpretation, that is, how to read and understand the teeming welter of symbols, stories, and ideas of about God and God's relation to the world. Behind questions of authority are to be found the labor and disputes over interpretation. And that is because disputes about power and authority never escape the more basic question of meaning. So far in these reflections I have explored the popular criticism of monotheism as a version of the theologico-political problem rooted in the either/or structure of reason versus revelation. Our inquiry has allowed us to see what is too often concealed in the current debate, namely, a certain instability in how monotheistic faith can be lived that arises from the complex and ambiguous symbolic richness of religion. Having changed the terms of the debate from a focus on authority to a focus on interpretation, let me now center the analysis where it needs to be directed—that is, the symbolic richness—and introduce the idea of "hypertheism" on the way to what I want to say about the "cosmopolitan conscience."

4. Hypertheism and Conscience

What do I mean by "hypertheism?" By this idea is meant the attempt to enfold all of life within a specific interpretation of "God" when "God" is only rightly known, and can be completely known, and loved within the confines of one special community. In terms used before, it is to insist on a distinctive kind of religious cosmology. We might say that it is the attempt to make a local God—or a local way of thinking about God in terms of just one or two ideas—into the universal God. This can be found in any form of theism, that is, any religious form that focuses on devotion to a god. So, we could have polytheistic hypertheism in which beliefs about many gods, say, a pantheon, provide a framework within which some one community, and it alone, rightly knows and loves what is truly divine. It is possible something like this was at work in Imperial Rome with the cult of the emperor. It might also be found in ancient Egyptian religion, which reacted with vicious force against the attempt by the Pharaoh Akhenaten to introduce monotheistic religion.[11] Or there could be pantheistic forms of hypertheism. On this outlook the nature system, as interpreted by some community or thinker, is the one and only true belief; however, some strident forms of ecological holism may be hypertheistic, among some proponents of "Gaia," for example. My concern is with monotheistic hypertheism. Here the distortion is twofold.

We have seen that for the great monotheistic religions, thinking about God—even based on some supposed revelation—cannot be the same as God. God is not our thinking about God and further there is a rich treasure trove of images, stories, and symbols to think about God. In truth, God is not a Christian God or a Muslim God or a Jewish God or a Hindu God. As Rabbi Jonathan Sacks has rightly noted, "God is the God of all humanity, but between Babel and the end of days no single faith is the faith of all humanity."[12] The diversity of human faiths does not imply a diversity of gods. Yet insofar as members of any religion claim ultimate truth for their all-too-human interpretation of the divine, it is not clear what status other communities can and ought to have in orienting society. Hypertheism is the term for the conviction of a community or tradition that its faith and interpretation of God are one and the same with the divine, obviously true and ultimately real. Hypertheism claims that a community's vision of God and it alone is sufficient to speak of the mystery, power, and truth of the divine. Accordingly, human life must become enfolded within that community's vision and faith and every aspect of existence made to conform to its convictions about God. It is to institutionalize a religious cosmology. Hypertheism is a term for the flaw of monotheistic religion that endangers the meaning and purpose of diverse forms of human life. It is the attempt to simplify and unify beliefs about God into one form that is then used to structure the rest of social, political, and personal life.

In this light, it would be less of a problem if hypertheism were only a matter of "political theology," as Mark Lilla uses the term in his contribution to this volume.[13] In that way it would be a reduction of monotheistic faith to focus just on divine sovereignty and human obedience.

Of course, hypertheism can take political form, but something more is at stake that also cuts against the very insights of monotheistic religions, theologically and ethically. How is that the case?

Believing that there is but one, living God means—by implication—that every human being, indeed all reality, has some relation to this God; there is, as it were, no utterly godless condition. We can call this the universal or global impulse of monotheistic faith. Granting the wild diversity of specific societies and persons, the obvious diversity does not deny some relation to the one God. But then a question I raised before returns in a new light: How is God related to the wild diversity of human societies and peoples? Hypertheism is the outlook that God relates to the human world only in terms of the specific interpretation of God claimed by a particular, local tradition, say, evangelical Christianity. The diversity of human existence is enfolded into one outlook, one worldview. Yet in making this claim, a hypertheistic outlook actually denies a basic theological insight, that is, that all people must, in some way, have a relation to God in and through the particularities of their local forms of life. A hypertheistic outlook must equate God with its interpretation of God and thus violate monotheistic faith. Further, hypertheism also denies a basic moral insight of monotheistic faith. Getting these two problems clear—a theological and an ethical one—is important for what I want to say about the cosmopolitan conscience. We need to probe deeper into monotheistic faith.

Consider first the ethical problem. Although it is not often noted, the Abrahamic monotheistic religions have generated within themselves an account of the human self, or in classical terms, an idea of the soul, which asserts—and asserts strongly—that religious conviction cannot be coerced. These religions insist there is a fundamental freedom in human existence that ought not, and in fact cannot, be violated: the free human act of holding convictions. Just like the experience of love or joy, genuine faith—trust, devotion, obedience—cannot be manufactured, forced, or coerced. There is something about the phenomenon of faith—the very way in which our most deeply held identity-conferring convictions arises in human existence—that resists tyrannous imposition. Can someone be forced to trust someone? Can devotion be purchased against someone's will? Although someone may be forced into compliance through coercion or fear, is that true obedience? In a word, there is something about the very dynamics of faith that resists coercion, and the same would be true of love or hope or joy.

The monotheistic religions insist that each person's relationship to the living God must be a matter of faith, that is, trust, devotion, and obedience. This means, surprisingly, that these religions acknowledge at their core a domain of human freedom that cannot be violated in the name of God. This is not to say that these religions have not in fact and historically tried to coerce faith. Obviously they have; those are expressions of hypertheism often in the shape of gas chambers, crusades, and persecutions. So, when law as a mechanism of political power and order and a hypertheistic outlook about how to interpret ideas, symbols, and stories about God collude, danger threatens a society, not only its politics but also its religious forms. There is the assumption that somehow citizens can be legitimately coerced to accept real or authentic religion. Yet the attempt to coerce faith through the collusion of religion and law is, I am claiming, itself a religious and moral distortion. The tyranny of the soul called hypertheism is a distortion within monotheism that finds its roots in monotheistic conceptions of the divine.

The term for the way in which basic convictions, like faith, cannot be coerced is, at least within Christianity, connected to the idea of "conscience." The idea of conscience (syneidesis), as S. Fischer-Fabian notes, is the "moral judging of self-consciousness" and it implies a judgment and a "knowing-with" of self and moral claims not reducible to religious or political authority.[14] The idea is found in Greek, Stoic, and biblical sources. In fact, the witnesses of conscience span the ages: Socrates, Thomas More, Martin Luther, Gandhi, and Mandela, to name just a few. Now, my concern in this essay is not to probe the concept of conscience and its forms, social origin, or even its psychological, cultural, or biological roots. We cannot explore further cases of conscience or those who acted on conscience. Rather, I am interested in how this discourse, this idea, arises within religious contexts precisely to challenge unbridled religious authority claimed through the reduction of the richness of monotheistic faith, that is, hypertheism.

The key insight in the development of the notion of conscience is that human beings are creatures who must decide how to live with respect to some idea of what is good and some standard about what is right. The sense of the good and the right, the idea of conscience implies, is not some specific faculty of the human brain or the soul or simply the result of social forces adopted through education or socialization, although each of these has been offered as a theory of conscience. More precisely, "conscience" is a concept for the totality of a human life involved in its moral and spiritual struggle. Conscience is a way to speak about the meaning and purpose of being human with respect to the demand to orient life responsibly amid its goods, vulnerabilities, threats, and distortions. When conscience is distorted or mistaken, then human life is distorted or mistaken. People should never act against conscience, as moralists throughout the centuries have argued. Yet that does not mean that people might not be mistaken, even distorted. It does mean that people cannot be compelled to violate the primary mode of being, their humanness. Various metaphors have been used in Christian thought to explore the senses linked to conscience: it can sting; the conscience can be terrified or despairing; it can be a goad to action; it can testify to the integrity of a life, a person can have a free conscience. There is a certain awakening to life when the voice of conscience arises through the dimensions of our mortal being within the wider compass of life.

The idea of conscience brings us back to the theological problem. Interestingly, some Christian theologians see conscience as an inchoate and vague sense of God. Although God is not equivalent to our words about God, there is a testimony to divine reality in our sense of what is good and right. And this means, as various forms of natural law and other types of ethics argue, that religious convictions cannot violate moral standards. In this respect, both Creon and Antigone are wrong but for different reasons: because Creon deifies the state, he asks Antigone to violate her conscience in relation to her duties to her brother and the gods; Antigone apparently cannot resolve the claims of conscience consistent with political loyalty to her community with loyalty to her family. The theological error of confusing our ideas about God with God too easily leads to a violation of conscience, the attempt, that is, to coerce convictions. The monotheistic traditions believe the oneness of God is what backs the claim that human beings—every person—has a depth and freedom that should not be violated. In other words, conscience mediates between the global God and the specific and located nature of every human life. When conscience is violated, say in hypertheistic modes, we isolate a theological distortion, that is, we confuse ideas about God with God, and also make a moral distortion and violate human dignity.

My point is that hypertheism can obviously take political forms, but more profoundly and more insidiously, it is a denial of the freedom of moral conscience through a reduction in how to understand religious meanings. Hypertheism is a tyranny of the soul. And this is the case on the two levels I have mentioned. First, recall that a hypertheistic outlook is a distortion of monotheistic faith because it confuses how we think about God—the images, symbols, ideas, stories of God and God's relation to the world—with the divine reality itself. But God is not equal to how we speak about God. Indeed, the whole point of theology, in its strict sense, rests on this insight. We need to think critically about the meaning and truth of religious claims because those claims are not identical with the reality about which they speak. It is not surprising, then, that hypertheistic outlooks exchange theology for indoctrination. And, second, hypertheism is an ethical distortion. In the name of faith, it violates the freedom of conscience that is a condition of faith as well human moral and political actions.

Taken together the theological and the ethical distortions demarcate the distinct challenge that hypertheism found among monotheistic religions seems to take, at least in our time. Our response must answer the question: Can we imagine a way of inhabiting these traditions that avoids this threat that is lodged in the very heart of monotheism or must we reject religious convictions altogether in the name of the rule of law in our troubled global times? Answering this question brings me to the possibility of the cosmopolitan conscience.

5. The Cosmopolitan Conscience

Thus far in these reflections I have been engaging the criticism usually associated with the theologico-political problem, not in order to deflect or defeat the criticism of religion, but rather to focus it properly and note the genuine richness and ambiguity of religion. The complicated question—and one that is on the horizon of my reflections—is to decode the social and historical conditions that provoke hypertheistic interpretations of monotheistic faith. I have intimated, but have not tried to establish, that one historical and social situation that provokes hypertheism is a period in which there is intense concern for political authority marked by a desire to reduce social complexity. The available symbols, ideas, and stories about God and faith are then too easily reduced just to the dyad: sovereign God and obedient faith. In this light, it is not surprising that our global age is provoking forms of hypertheism in and through the increasing connectivity among peoples. But there are no doubt other situations that could provoke other forms of hypertheism less focused on political authority but no less dangerous to human life. I have tried, then, to isolate what I take to be an instability or ambiguity in the monotheistic faith that opens the possibility for hypertheism. But please notice: the problem of hypertheism does not arise from revelation, whatever that might mean. It is, importantly, an intellectual and rational problem about how to interpret religious sources, which means that any answer to this distortion will also need to be a correction in thinking rather than simply abandoning revelation.

If that correction is at least a plausible suggestion, then we confront not a critical but a constructive question: namely, how can and ought we to conceive the religious life in ways that escape the dangers of hypertheism? Further, each person can ask that question, whether a believer or not, since what we are seeking is sane, just, and stable ways of social life. Furthermore, something like the problem of hypertheism can appear within any complex social reality that requires interpretation and that in fact includes human social life as such. For instance, when the richness and ambiguity of our political ideas get reduced to a simple set of ideas that are supposedly self-evident—my country is right or wrong; freedom is only conceivable in Western democratic forms; all social life is driven by a struggle for power—then problems beset the social order. Although I am concerned here with the challenges to social life found in monotheistic faith, it does not miss the implication of my argument for other social forms. And, further, I have tried to isolate within monotheistic faith resources for countering hypertheism, resources that focus on the relation of God to reality and the noncoercive nature of the human conscience. I can now weave those insights together and propose the idea of the cosmopolitan conscience. My remarks are limited; an entire exposition would take a book.

I have already indicated the meaning of conscience, that is, the moral labor of human existence through which identities are formed with respect to convictions about what is good and right but that also entail a realm of freedom that ought not and cannot be violated by religious or political authority. I have also shown that this idea arises within monotheistic faith in terms of the very dynamics of faith itself. This is why, I judge, the Christian tradition, especially in its prophetic and Protestant forms, has developed a vision of society that insists on the separation of powers, including the separation of religious conviction and political authority and the rule of law. Stated differently, once we grasp the meaning of the freedom of conscience, then any vision of an undifferentiated religious cosmology where everything is placed in an immediate relation to God and under religious authority is no longer possible. Rather, the social order is a complex interaction among various domains—politics, education, media, economy, religious associations—that limit each other's power and also cannot justly violate human dignity and thus the freedom of conscience. From that vision, I would also suggest, follow basic ideas about the origin, legitimacy, and rule of law. But the basic point, which is too often missed in the current discussion, is that monotheistic faith is one deep source of our ideas about freedom of conscience. I have been interpreting that faith from the perspective of this kind of freedom.

One consequence of my argument is to show that the diversity of images, ideas, stories, and practices within the monotheistic tradition can lead to grave theological and ethical distortions, but this diversity also opens the possibility for freer and more humane ways of religious life. And the main move, I can now say, is to shift from what I have called a "religious cosmology" to a cosmopolitan outlook. What does that mean?

Arising in the ancient world among Hellenistic Christian and non-Christian thinkers, the idea of cosmopolitanism was that each person was a citizen of the world rather than just some local community. The idea was that the bonds of human association reach far beyond our local communities. Admittedly, that is an implausible idea. People are not citizens of the whole world precisely because, thankfully, there is no one single global political order. Given this, the idea of cosmopolitanism in current thought, what some have called "rooted cosmopolitanism," is the idea that affirms shared human bonds, insists on human dignity, and demands for justice, in and through the particularities of communities and traditions. This possibility arises, as Joshua Yates has noted, once we are able to conceive of the world as a single place and also that there is shared humanity where the ideas of world and humanity are not descriptive claims but necessary moral categories for our global age.[15]

Because of the dynamics of our age, we must insist on the particularity and locality of human communities, traditions, and persons. Yates quotes Ulf Hannerz this way:

> As the world becomes increasingly a single place, I believe there is a growing need to cultivate a cosmopolitan imagination, a sense of informed citizenship of the world which combines a sense of human compassion and responsibility for the welfare of humanity with respect for, even appreciation of, cultural diversity.[16]

Although there is much more that could be said about the relation between imagination and conscience, my point is that the cosmopolitan conscience is precisely the sense of responsibility and also freedom of our moral being lived within the complexity of global realities. It is, more pointedly, a way of inhabiting local traditions—including religious traditions—in a way that combats their hypertheistic interpretations because it is at the core of how we live with the complexity of religious and cultural resources the demand to respect and enhance the integrity of forms of life, personal, and social. To cultivate the cosmopolitan conscience, then, is to cultivate a way of understanding and living with particular religious and cultural resources and identities in a way that uses them for responsible and compassionate action rather than seeking to enfold human life within those resources. It is, to put it pointedly, to live mindful of the ambiguities of traditions and human life and to decide to confront that ambiguity freely and responsibly for the sake of the global future. It is to decide that appeals to authority—reason or revelation—must first be interpreted in ways that promote free and responsible existence if they are to claim the right to order social existence.

What I am suggesting is that we can release the power of an idea at the roots of monotheistic faith—the freedom of conscience—as a guide for the creative and reconstructive work of living religiously in a global age, an age in which the religions are not going to go away, and therefore an age in which we need humane ways of being religious. This approach to religious life insists that a faith is not genuine that tyrannizes the soul and that a religious cosmology is unwarranted. What is needed is a cosmopolitan outlook dedicated to responsibility for the integrity of human life with its cultural, social, racial, sexual, and religious diversity. In this respect, my argument has not been developed from within monotheistic cosmology, but, ethically and theologically, has sought to ponder how we can and ought to live in our global times with respect to critical reflection on the meaning and truth of religious sources. I am proposing, in a word, that one way to combat false and dangerous interpretations of religion is actually to live the religious life more deeply, more freely, within the richness and complexity of a religion's forms of thought and life. It is to use resources to block the distortion of resources.

6. Conclusion

I realize, of course, that this will sound like a tall order, and maybe too tall and demanding an order for most people, including myself, to undertake. And I realize, of course, that much more needs to be said about what is meant by responsibility, its norms and values, the relation between imagination and conscience, and whether or not it is realistic to think that religious people can in fact adopt this outlook. But those are merely some of the challenges put to theological and ethical reflection in our global age. The root question is whether or not we will ourselves rise to this challenge and decipher the religions differently.

Notes

1. The literature on globalization is of course massive. See, for example, John Tomlison, *Globalization and Culture* (Chicago, IL: The University of Chicago Press, 1999) and William Schweiker, *Theological Ethics and Global Dynamics: In the Time of Many Worlds* (Oxford: Blackwell, 2004).
2. Terry Eagleton, *On Evil* (New Haven: Yale University Press, 2010), 11.
3. See, for instance, Charles Taylor, *A Secular Age* (Cambridge, MA: Harvard, 2007) and Anthony Giddens, *Modernity and Self-Identity: Self and Society in the Late Modern Age* (Stanford, CA: Stanford University Press, 1991).
4. For a discussion of differentiations within the religions, see W. Schweiker, ed., *The Blackwell Companion to Religious Ethics* (Oxford: Blackwell, 2005).
5. Throughout this essay I am drawing on and expanding arguments made in David E. Klemm and William Schweiker, *Religion and the Human Future: An Essay in Theological Humanism* (Oxford: Wiley-Blackwell, 2008).

6. See W. Schweiker, M. Johnson, and K. Jung, ed., *Humanity before God: Contemporary Faces of Jewish, Christian and Islamic Ethics* (Minneapolis, MN: Fortress Press, 2006).
7. See H. Richard Niebuhr, *Radical Monotheism and Western Culture* (Louisville, KY: Westminster/John Knox Press, 1993).
8. See, for example, Samuel Huntington, *The Clash of Civilizations and the Remaking of the World Order* (New York, NY: Simon & Schuster, 1998) and also Martin E. Marty, *When Faiths Collide* (Oxford: Blackwell, 2005).
9. Daniel Dennett, *Breaking the Spell: Religion as a Natural Phenomenon* (New York, NY: Penguin, 2007).
10. David Hume, *The Natural History of Religion*, ed. J. Fieser (New York, NY: Macmillan/Library of Liberal Arts, 1992), 62.
11. See Jan Assman, *Moses the Egyptian: The Memory of Egypt in Western Monotheism* (Cambridge, MA: Harvard, 1998).
12. Jonathan Sacks, *The Dignity of Difference: How to Avoid the Clash of Civilizations* (London: Continuum, 2003), 55.
13. See also Mark Lilla, *The Stillborn God: Religion, Politics, and the Modern West* (New York, NY: Vintage, 2007).
14. S. Fischer-Fabian, *Die Macht des Gewissen: Von Sokrates bis Sophie Scholl* (München: Th. Knaur, 1987).
15. See Joshua J. Yates, "Mapping the Good World: The New Cosmopolitans and Our Changing World Picture," *The Hedgehog Review* 11, no. 3 (2010): 7–29.
16. Ulf Hannerz, "Journalists, Anthropologists and the Cosmopolitan Imagination" cited in Joshua J. Yates, "Mapping the Good World," 10.

PART 2

Limits in the Construction and Application of Free Exercise and Establishment Doctrine

CHAPTER 3

GRAPPLING WITH NEUTRALITY AND LIBERTY UNDER THE RELIGION CLAUSES

FRANK S. RAVITCH

INTRODUCTION

The US Supreme Court's decisions relating to law and religion have often been criticized. The source of the criticism frequently depends on the issues involved and the decision in a given case. There is no doubt, however, that some of these cases have occupied a central role in the evolving culture wars played out every day in the United States.

Cases involving law and religion have often resulted in inconsistent outcomes, and even more important, in inconsistent use and application of legal tests. When one evaluates these cases, however, one sees the same principles being used by different courts and different justices in entirely inconsistent ways. While this is especially true of the principle of neutrality, it is also sometimes true of the principle of religious liberty. This essay evaluates both of these principles and how they have been applied in a variety of cases. Interestingly, this analysis leads to the conclusion that neutrality is not possible and certainly has not been achieved by any of the conflicting decisions that attempt to apply this principle in the Religion Clause context. Religious liberty may be a more robust principle in some contexts, but it has proven equally empty in others.

NEUTRALITY

Neutrality, whether formal or substantive, does not exist in the Religion Clause context. Others have recognized this.[1] Still others have come part way to this conclusion by suggesting that neutrality is inherently dependent upon the baseline we choose to use in describing it, and thus it doesn't exist apart from these baselines.[2] Claims of neutrality cannot be proven. There is no independent neutral truth or baseline to which they can be tethered.[3] This fact is important because it means that any baseline to which we attach neutrality is not neutral, and claims of neutrality built on these baselines are by their nature not neutral. This might seem circular (i.e., since there is no independent state of neutrality from which to derive neutral rules or applications of rules, there can be no neutral results and no means by which we can prove a given baseline is neutral), yet examples of the Supreme Court attempting to use neutrality as a guiding principle are readily available.[4] The Court has used varying concepts or baselines of neutrality,[5] and in several cases justices in the majority and dissenting opinions claimed to be relying on the same or similar principles of neutrality, yet they reached opposite conclusions.[6]

This critique of neutrality applies to both the recent Court's use of "formal neutrality" (a concept explained further below) and to earlier Courts' "substantive neutrality" or "separation as neutrality" approaches (also explained further below). Much attention will be paid in this paper to the concept of formal neutrality, which seems most pervasive today, at least in cases involving aid to religious entities or individuals, equal access, and Free Exercise Clause exemptions. As will be seen, the critique of neutrality provided herein applies to any claim that a given approach is "neutral" in regard to the many highly contested questions arising when government and religion interact in our complex regulatory state. In the end, as with interpretive claims based on hard originalism, neutrality requires value choices that are often masked under the cloak of evenhandedness or other mostly rhetorical devices.

Steven Smith has explained:

> [T]he quest for neutrality, despite its understandable appeal and the tenacity with which it has been pursued, is an attempt to grasp at an illusion. Upon reflection, this failure should not be surprising. The impossibility of a truly "neutral" theory of religious freedom is analogous to the impossibility, recognized by modern philosophers, of finding some outside Archimedean point . . . from which to look down on and describe reality. Descriptions of reality are always undertaken from a point within reality. In the same way, theories of religious freedom are always offered from the viewpoint of one of the competing positions that generate the

> need for such a theory; there is no neutral vantage point that can permit the theorist or judge to transcend these competing positions. Hence, insofar as a genuine and satisfactory theory of religious freedom would need to be "neutral" in this sense, rather than one that privileges one of the competing positions from the outset, a theory of religious freedom is as illusory as the ideal of neutrality it seeks to embody.[7]

Others have also acknowledged the illusive and malleable nature of neutrality.[8] The Court's use of the term until recently was often symbolic—not in the sense that William Marshall's fascinating work has used that term,[9] but rather in the sense that the Court was trying to send a message that it was being balanced in its resolution of the issues that it decided.[10] Of course, despite protestations otherwise, this was not always so. Still, the Court did not use neutrality as the be all or end all concept in actually deciding cases. Rather it had to also rely on other principles because neutrality is so malleable—Steven Smith has even argued parasitic.[11] If there is no such thing as neutrality—or at least neutrality as more than a buzzword—this seems a logical state of affairs. The Court suggests that it is acting neutrally, but it can only define this neutrality by reference to other principles (which are not neutral).

The current Court, however, has begun to rely on neutrality more directly.[12] Neutrality is no longer a background principle that the Court sees no need to consistently define. Rather it is an actuating principle that the Court apparently believes must be given a formalistic definition that can be rigidly applied.[13] As will be seen, the Court connects its formal neutrality with what appear to be arguments for formal equality between religion and non-religion.[14] Yet, the current Court's neutrality is no more neutral than past Courts' neutrality. In fact, because of its formalistic nature, it is potentially "less neutral"—if it is possible to be less than something that doesn't exist—because, at least potentially, if a government action or inaction meets the Court's definition of neutrality (and the element of individual choice discussed below), pesky things such as the effects of the program need not be considered.[15] This is particularly problematic because the Court does not explain why its formal neutrality is neutral given the competing views of neutrality, and the Court uses terms such as "entirely neutral,"[16] and "neutral in all respects."[17] By relying on the term in this direct, yet unsubstantiated, manner the Court gives it extra power.

Not to be outdone, the justices who reject the Court's formal neutrality have begun strenuously arguing for a return to substantive neutrality,[18] or sometimes to separation as neutrality, as the guiding principle.[19] The battle thus joined, the justices argue over the meaning of neutrality, which, as I have suggested is like arguing over the real location of Oz. Neither side is forced to confront in any serious way the interpretive presumptions that inform its chosen neutrality position, although the substantive neutrality wing often openly acknowledge their reliance on separation (without, of course, explaining how separation is in fact neutral). As will be seen, substantive neutrality—at least as envisioned by Douglas Laycock—has something important to lend to this debate, but not because it is neutral.

The current Court's formal neutrality approach requires a law or government policy to be facially neutral in regard to religion.[20] In the aid context, there is an additional element to the formal neutrality approach.[21] Any benefit or funding that flows to religious entities must do so as the result of the choices of private individuals.[22] As will be seen below, this approach has not been applied in all aid cases, but to the extent it has been applied, the private choice element may have lost its substantive bite.[23]

The current version of neutrality, which has become dominant in the aid, equal access, and Free Exercise contexts, is intensely formalistic, and it appears to minimize the effects of government programs and actions.[24] Establishment Clause jurisprudence has traditionally been fact sensitive, but the Court's formal neutrality approach lacks the tools to enable it to deal with the many situations to which it will invariably be applied. The more flexible *Lemon* test[25] was much maligned because of the questionable distinctions drawn by the Court.[26] Thirty years from now the Court's apparent move toward a formal neutrality test might be viewed in the same way. Formalism does not necessarily beget clarity, and in the end when the issues that arise are complex and fact specific, the more formalistic the test the less clarity it will likely bring in the long run—either because it must be contorted to fit the diversity of situations to which it will be applied or because it will ignore context and function, somewhat like a bull in a china shop.

The Court's formal neutrality approach reminds me of a quotation from Professor Philip Kurland's classic 1961 article, "Of Church and State and the Supreme Court,"[27] which has influenced the Court's formal neutrality approach. In describing a "neutral principle" that would "give the most appropriate scope to the Religion Clauses," Kurland explained:[28]

> This "neutral principle" has been framed in reliance on the Aristotelian axiom that "it is the mark of an educated man to seek precision in each class of things just so far as the nature of the subject admits," rather than the Platonic precept that "a perfectly simple principle can never be applied to a state of things which is the reverse of simple."[29]

Although it may at first seem an odd thing for a legal academic to state, I am inclined to favor the Platonic precept over the Aristotelian axiom upon which Professor Kurland relied, at least when it comes to formal neutrality. The vast web of factual scenarios involved in funding cases and equal access cases—situations where the Court has already clearly applied formal neutrality—is indeed the reverse of simple, and formal neutrality is an intensely simple concept (although in no way perfect). Although Professor Kurland may have advocated a version of formal neutrality, it is unlikely he was advocating the kind of acontextual neutrality toward which the Court has been headed.

Lurking underneath the Court's formal neutrality is the notion that religion has no special status, and thus there is no need to differentiate between religion and non-religion if the government is acting "neutrally."[30] A corollary to this notion is the argument that by treating religion differently, one is being hostile to religion. Thus, it is discrimination and hostility to religion if religious organizations are not given access to the same benefits as secular organizations,[31] and at the same time there is nothing wrong with failing to provide religious exemptions to "generally applicable" laws, even if those laws interfere with core religious practices.[32] There would be significant problems with the Court's implicit presumptions even if neutrality were a real and attainable concept, but if neutrality is nothing more than an empty construction,[33] the Court's other presumptions are even more problematic.

To understand the current Court's notion of neutrality, it is useful to explore several of the cases where the Court has used neutrality analysis in varying contexts. Thus, in this paper we will look at two cases to see the formal neutrality doctrine in action. The cases are *Zelman v. Simmons-Harris*[34] and *Employment Division v. Smith*.[35] These cases each represent a major area where the Court has used a version of the formal neutrality concept:[36] *Zelman* in the government aid to religious schools context[37] and *Smith* in the context of exemptions to "generally applicable" laws under the Free Exercise Clause.[38] Before analyzing these cases, however, it is useful to further answer the question, "What is neutrality?" or, at least, what does it pretend to be?

The answer to the question—"What is neutrality?"—is central to the discussion of neutrality's place in Religion Clause jurisprudence. Thus, my answer that neutrality, at least in the Religion Clause context, is a myth, may seem wholly unsatisfying. Yet can there be some use for a concept that is impossible to achieve? Neutrality is nothing more than a variable social construction, and formal neutrality is nothing more than a rigid judicial construction.[39] Each relies on a baseline that is not provably neutral, but each has a value because people take solace in the notion of neutrality.[40] Even if objectivity does not exist in contested spaces, there may be value in the perception of objectivity.

This sounds a bit odd at first, but it actually tracks much of what the pre-Rehnquist Court did with the concept of neutrality. Neutrality was mentioned quite a bit in numerous contexts; sometimes the Court used a vague adjective to describe it, such as "benevolent neutrality."[41] Yet the Court never relied exclusively on the principle, supplementing it with separationism or accommodationism.[42] For those who did not dig too deeply, there was always the reassuring tone of neutrality. For those who did dig, it was apparent that the Court could not substantiate its claim to neutrality, but the Court had the other principles to fall back on, and one could support or attack those other principles without focusing on whether they were neutral in application or effect.[43] It would not be a reach to read some of these cases and perceive that the Court was essentially saying, "we are following a separationist principle or an accommodationist principle that we think is more neutral than the alternatives in this context, but neutrality is only the lofty goal of the Religion Clauses, not something we can prove with absolute certainty."

I do not defend the earlier Courts' use of the term. It was in a sense false advertising, because there is no way to prove that separationism or accommodationism is inherently more neutral than other principles.[44] Yet the implicit message that was at least potentially infused in these earlier decisions (i.e., we know that neutrality is just a lofty goal, and we are only using it to describe the outcome in this case vis-à-vis the alternatives) is less troubling than claims that both the mode of analysis and the results *are* neutral, and that the alternatives are not. The latter is the message of the formal neutrality approach. The current Court has converted the neutrality principle from a lofty, albeit impossible, goal to both the means and ends of Religion Clause analysis.[45]

Of course, even though neutrality as a lofty principle is less problematic than formal neutrality because it is not used to reach or empower outcomes, it is no more neutral. Moreover, in two contexts it has been used to (or argued to), empower results. These two contexts are substantive neutrality and separation as neutrality. As will be seen, one conception of substantive neutrality has some merit but not because of the neutrality claim. This conception of neutrality is far more nuanced and sophisticated than other neutrality claims. It recognizes there is no agreement about what neutrality is. I am referring to Douglas Laycock's construction of substantive neutrality.[46] Laycock is not alone in arguing for substantive neutrality. Scholars, as well as justices of the Supreme Court,[47] have argued for some form of substantive neutrality. Professor Laycock, however, provides the best and most succinct conception of substantive neutrality. His substantive neutrality has a lot to recommend it. Still, as I hope to show, substantive neutrality may have a lot of substantive value—but no "neutrality." This might seem a bit nitpicky since the approach has a lot to offer; although Professor Laycock may have made a wise choice among potential baselines, his choice and the resulting baseline are no more provably neutral than the Court's formal neutrality.

Professor Laycock's formulation of substantive neutrality is reflected in the following quote:

> My basic formulation of substantive neutrality is this: the religion clauses require government to minimize the extent to which it either encourages or discourages belief or disbelief, practice or nonpractice, observance or nonobservance. If I have to stand or fall on a single formulation of neutrality, I will stand or fall on that one. But I must elaborate on what I mean by minimizing encouragement or discouragement. I mean that religion is to be left as wholly to private choice as anything can be. It should proceed as unaffected by government as possible. Government should not interfere with our beliefs about religion either by coercion or by persuasion. Religion may flourish or whither; it may change or stay the same. What happens to religion is up to the people acting severally and voluntarily; it is not up to the people acting collectively through government.[48]

Professor Laycock suggests that neutrality depends on the baseline one sets in defining it, and that there are varying baselines.[49] The baseline approach, however, is problematic because there is no super-baseline to determine whether a given baseline is neutral.[50] Yet the very term neutrality asserts an epistemic (in the sense that it suggests some theory or way to know something is neutral) and arguably a teleological claim. A given baseline might be a useful paradigm for Establishment Clause jurisprudence, but unless one can demonstrate the neutrality of the baseline itself, the baseline cannot support claims of neutrality.

The *Zelman* case is a good example through which to view this observation. If the Court had held that vouchers are unconstitutional when given for attendance at religious schools, but that districts can maintain vouchers for secular private schools and of course can maintain the secularized public schools without any voucher program, would the result encourage secularism? Would such a limitation advance private choice or would it place burdens only on the private choice of religious individuals because they must choose between a secular education free of charge and their values? Yet, under the Court's holding, which allows vouchers to be used at religious schools, there is a powerful argument that religion, and particularly more dominant and well-funded religions, will benefit from an infusion of government funds,[51] and that private choice will be skewed toward sending one's children to schools with whose faith mission one disagrees simply to keep them on a level playing field with other kids in the area who may face no such conflict.[52]

Which of these options is neutral? Which encourages or discourages religion the most? These are actually two very different questions. The first is unanswerable in any objective way unless one has a magic key to demonstrate that a contested account of neutrality is actually neutral. Yet the second question is answerable, even if it is not precisely so. More importantly, even though the answer may be contestable, the contestability of the answer is more open to debate when it is not appended to the concept of neutrality. The answer must be debated on its merits, without regard to the unprovable claim that it is neutral,[53] and thus neutrality should have no power in the interpretive process. As Steven Smith has implied, calling a result neutral adds nothing of value to an argument.[54] I would add that doing so may obfuscate the nature and value of other principles that undergird an argument or may unnecessarily prop those principles up.

Yet, as will be seen, this does not destroy the force of Laycock's principle.[55] Significantly, the fact that divorcing Laycock's substantive principle of Religion Clause jurisprudence from neutrality does not undermine that principle demonstrates the lack of import the neutrality concept has. As between formal neutrality and substantive neutrality, substantive neutrality is the better option, not because it is more neutral—neither option is neutral—but because it is still useful even when divorced from its neutrality claim. The Court's formal neutrality hinges too much on neutrality as a real concept, or at least on formal equality as neutrality,[56] and although a more sophisticated and consistently applied version of the equality principle could have independent value,[57] the formal equality as formal neutrality version has little to offer, since its claim to neutrality (and its implicit claim of equality) cannot be proven.

Separation as neutrality is another concept of neutrality that has at times been linked to substantive neutrality. The separation as neutrality approach was used in early cases, such as *Everson v. Board of Education*,[58] *McCollum v. Board of Education*,[59] and *School District of Abington Township v. Schempp*,[60] and is currently favored by a minority of justices.[61] Of course, it is no more neutral than formal or substantive neutrality. Consider both arguments in *Everson*.[62] The majority held that funding the transportation of students to parochial schools did not violate the separation principle because it simply demonstrated neutrality between religion and non-religion.[63] The dissenting opinions argued that neutrality mandated a separationist outcome, and thus the funding was unconstitutional.[64]

Assume the funding is constitutional as the majority held. How is it neutral? Putting aside for the moment that, as Justice Jackson pointed out in his dissenting opinion, the funding only went to Catholic school students and not to other parochial or secular private school students,[65] the bulk of the funds going into private hands for transportation will go to those attending religious schools. The Court noted that parochial schools were the primary venues for private school students in that area and even if the program allowed transportation funding to all private schools,[66] the denominations with the largest number of schools would receive the largest benefit.

The reasons the Court gave for upholding the program, save one, made some sense. That one—that the funding regime and its practical outcome are neutral—is simply not true. The funding could provide additional encouragement for families to send their kids to private school, and especially to parochial schools, which were the largest constituency of private schools in Ewing Township. Admittedly, this is not a huge windfall for religion, and in fact, it would be allowed under the facilitation test I have proposed elsewhere; speaking of neutrality simply covers over the real world impact of such a funding regime given religious and private school demographics.

The dissents' position, however, would be no more neutral, because to deny funding under the facts in the case would give added encouragement for people to send their kids to the public schools. For those who chose not to do so because of their religious convictions, the denial of funding would add an additional cost (in addition to property taxes to support the public schools and parochial school tuition) not borne by those who decide to send their kids to the secularized world of the public schools. This *may* be justifiable under the separation principle, but it would end up discouraging religion. Neutrality talk adds nothing to the analysis except perhaps a rhetorical justification (as it did for the majority).

Issues surrounding government interaction with religious entities have become increasingly complex over the last hundred years or so as government, both state and federal, has grown and gotten involved in many areas of life where there was traditionally little or no government participation or regulation. It is hard for government to act neutrally when its actions or failure to act in the same situation can have massive repercussions.[67] This creates problems for any neutrality test that must be applied to this massive web of government action and inaction. At the theoretical level, such a test can make no absolute claim to neutrality because there is no principle of super-neutrality that can be used to demonstrate its neutrality; thus contested perspectives necessarily enter the process of developing such a test.[68] It would solve the problem if one could prove neutrality by looking at the effects of a court's approach, but as the above examples demonstrate, this is impossible to do without presuming that a certain baseline is neutral and using the presumed baseline to justify the neutrality of outcomes.[69]

Although Laycock's theory is highly useful in the Religion Clause context, the Court has unfortunately chosen to pursue the "formal neutrality" approach in regard to a number of issues. We can explore some of these issues through three landmark cases, each applying a version of the formal neutrality approach.

A. ZELMAN V. SIMMONS-HARRIS

Zelman is a significant case for several reasons. It is the first US Supreme Court case to uphold a government funded educational voucher program; thus it is quite significant from the education policy perspective, as well as the law and religion perspective. Additionally, a majority of the Court affirmed the use of formal neutrality, holding if a program is neutral on its face and functions through "true private choice," the program is constitutional.[70] Finally, although the majority opinion purports to consider whether private individuals who channel the government money to religious schools had real choices, the opinion expands the pool of "choices" to include public magnet and charter schools, leaving open the possibility that the comparison group could be further expanded to include all public schools, at least in districts that have open enrollment or public school choice programs.[71]

The *Zelman* Court ostensibly followed the *Lemon* test as modified in *Agostini v. Felton*.[72,73] The Court first held that *Zelman* did not present a secular purpose issue because the goal of providing a better education to students in the Cleveland School District was an adequate secular purpose[74]—indeed at least in government aid and equal access cases, it is hard to imagine a situation where there would not be an adequate secular purpose. Thus, the case centered on the effects of the program,[75] as have several other funding cases.[76]

Yet there is a significant catch. The two factors that determine whether an indirect aid program meets the *Zelman* test are (1) the program must be neutral on its face, and (2) the money must flow through individuals who have "true individual choice" regarding where to direct the aid.[77] If a program is neutral on its face between religious and nonreligious entities, it is highly unlikely it would ever fail the secular purpose test. Nor is there a significant distinction between direct and indirect aid. So long as the government entity drafting the program relates the aid that flows to religious institutions to the number of individuals who choose to use the private service, it does not matter whether the check is written from the government directly to the religious institution.[78] It is not a stretch to say that, at least in cases of government aid to religious institutions, the test is one of facial neutrality plus a private "circuit breaker" (i.e. the money ostensibly flows to the religious institution because of the choices of private individuals).[79] Significantly, the "circuit breaker" element is connected to the Court's broader neutrality analysis. It is the private individual choice that makes a facially neutral program entirely neutral.[80]

This raises the question, however, about what constitutes "true private choice" under the Court's analysis. The Court's answer to this question is significant because it involved a statistical sleight of hand that could potentially make all public schools the relevant comparison group to religious schools for purposes of government aid programs. This would be so even in areas with no secular private schools or where such private schools cannot afford to take voucher students, so long as secular private schools would be included in the program *if* they existed.[81] This makes the Court's new test an exercise in almost pure formalism.[82] If a program is neutral on its face—it does not specify religious entities as beneficiaries—and there is some government or nonreligious private entity that the recipients could conceivably choose to attend, the test is met because the program is neutral on its face and provides "true private choice,"[83] even if virtually all funding going to private organizations goes to religious organizations.[84]

If this program really were neutral, and neutrality is an appropriate actuating principle under the Establishment Clause,[85] the Court's approach would be perfectly acceptable. Conversely, if the Court's approach is not neutral, calling it neutral should give it no further power, and it should be adequately supported by some other principle. In fact, if it is not neutral, having the Court pronounce its neutrality is especially dangerous; the Court would simply be placing the label of neutrality on analysis that is neither neutral nor likely to lead to neutral results and using the label to validate its approach. The Court could call its undergirding principle "Ralph," and it would have the same descriptive accuracy. In fact, Ralph might be more descriptively accurate because people would still have to determine what the essence of Ralphness is, and the nature of the term does not suggest that it has any extra power or reality until it is defined.

This might seem a bit tongue-in-cheek, and it is to a point, but it demonstrates the serious problems with claims to neutrality. Since there is no neutral foundation or baseline that can be used to prove that something is truly neutral, neutrality is nothing more than a buzzword, and a dangerous one at that, because it implies that the supposedly neutral approach should be taken more seriously because it is actually neutral.[86] Legal tests and definitions of neutrality do not make an approach neutral, they are simply tests or definitions, and neutrality is nothing but extra baggage.[87] As was explained above, this doesn't mean that conceptions of neutrality—such as Douglas Laycock's substantive neutrality[88]—aren't useful tools, but it does mean that they aren't neutral and should gain no additional validity from the use of that term.[89]

This suggests that the Court's formal neutrality approach is especially dangerous because the formalistic approach leaves little room for introspection, and its very nature makes it less likely to account for nuances or context. Supporting such a rigid regime with a concept that can't be proven is particularly dangerous, since once the formalistic test controls outcomes there will be little opportunity to adapt to varied circumstances without sacrificing the clarity such formalistic tests are intended to create. Thus, courts applying the test must either rigidly apply a test that has never adequately justified itself because it is based on a nonexistent principle, attempt to modify the test in its application to varied circumstances without the help of a useful guiding principle, or in the case of the Supreme Court, abandon *stare decisis* and either overturn the decisions giving rise to the approach or apply the approach in a manner that goes against its underlying purpose.[90]

B. Employment Division v. Smith

Smith demonstrates the application of the formal neutrality principle in the Free Exercise Clause context. Two members of the Native American Church were denied unemployment benefits after being fired from their jobs at a substance abuse rehabilitation center.[91] They were fired because they had used peyote, an illegal substance under Oregon law, during religious rituals.[92] Oregon law stated that being fired for misconduct—which is how the firing was characterized—precludes the receipt of unemployment benefits.[93] Neither had abused peyote, and there was no evidence that they used it anywhere other than in religious ceremonies.[94] In fact, it would violate the tenets of the Native American Church to use peyote outside of appropriate religious rituals because the substance has significant religious import for members of the faith.[95] Oregon, unlike many states and the federal government, did not have a religious exemption for Native American peyote use under its general drug laws.[96] Thus, the Court had to decide whether the two men denied unemployment benefits had a constitutional right to an exemption to the drug laws given the religious nature of their peyote use.[97] An exemption would preclude the denial of unemployment benefits based on misconduct.[98]

The backdrop of legal precedent seemed to favor the men, but that precedent—contrary to popular belief—was anything but clear or terribly helpful to religious minorities. The precedent many thought would be the key to the decision was *Sherbert v. Verner*,[99] which held that a state must have a compelling governmental interest for denying unemployment benefits to a person who was fired for refusing to work on her Sabbath.[100] Relevant, but not decisive to my reading of the *Sherbert* opinion, was the fact that the state unemployment laws contained a number of exemptions for nonreligious reasons.[101]

Another decision, *Wisconsin v. Yoder*,[102] was also potentially relevant. In *Yoder* the Court held that Amish families with high school age children were entitled to exemptions from the state's compulsory education laws in the absence of a compelling state interest.[103] The court looked at the Amish community's track record of good citizenship, hard work, and the success of its young people within the community to demonstrate that the state had no compelling interest for denying the exemption.[104] There have been some serious criticisms of the Court's approach in *Yoder*,[105] but for present purposes this basic overview of the Court's holding is adequate.

Given this precedent most people believed that the battle lines in *Smith* would be drawn over whether the state had an adequate compelling governmental interest.[106] In fact, Oregon's attorney general at that time later pointed out that the state never argued for disposing of the compelling interest test,[107] but rather argued that compliance with the state's drug laws satisfied the burden under that test, especially in light of post *Sherbert* and *Yoder* case law.[108] As will be seen, that subsequent case law suggested that *Sherbert* and *Yoder* were primarily paper tigers, at least in the US Supreme Court.

Between *Yoder* and *Smith* the Court decided a string of Free Exercise exemption cases. With the exception of a few unemployment cases, the person seeking the exemption never won.[109] In some cases the nature of the government institution (i.e., the military or prisons) served as a basis for not applying the compelling interest test.[110] In others, the relief requested was decisive in not applying the compelling interest test. For example, cases where the government entity involved would have had to change its policies to grant an exemption.[111]

Finally, there were cases where the court ostensibly applied the compelling interest test, but in a manner that made it anything but strict scrutiny.[112] It should be noted, however, that *Sherbert* and *Yoder* did influence the outcomes of some lower court cases.[113] The *Smith* Court relied on the post-*Yoder* decisions, as well as some pre-*Sherbert* decisions, to hold that *Sherbert* is limited to the unemployment context where there are generally a variety of exemptions built into the unemployment laws.[114] Furthermore, the claim in *Smith* was different from earlier Free Exercise cases granting exemptions to unemployment laws because the claimants in

Smith sought an exemption based on illegal conduct; however, the claimants in the earlier cases sought an exemption based on religious conduct that was otherwise legal.[115] *Yoder* was harder to distinguish, but the Court created the concept of hybrid rights; cases in which the Free Exercise Clause right is connected to some other important right (in *Yoder*, parental rights).[116] This theory works well to distinguish several earlier cases that involved freedom of expression, as well as Free Exercise concerns,[117] but to characterize *Yoder* as a hybrid rights case was a stretch.

This stretch would be more troubling if the traditional story of Free Exercise Clause jurisprudence were accurate, but the reality is that *Sherbert* and *Yoder* were never the panacea they have been made out to be.[118] The idea of a compelling interest test held a lot of promise, but in the hands of shifting majorities on the Court that promise was never realized; although, it was sometimes realized in the lower courts.[119] The relevance of the Court's failure to live up to the promise of *Sherbert* and *Yoder* for future attempts to interpret the Free Exercise Clause is discussed elsewhere.[120] For now, I will focus on the implicit neutrality claim made by the *Smith* Court, and why that claim suffered the same flaws as other neutrality claims in the Religion Clause context.

Divorcing *Smith* from all the important—but for present purposes irrelevant—baggage regarding *stare decises*, and so on, we are left with the basic notion that the Free Exercise Clause does not require exemptions to generally applicable (today the Court might say facially neutral) laws. The argument seems to be that because these laws are religion neutral the Free Exercise Clause has no impact on them except through the political process.[121] This is, of course, a claim of formal neutrality. But how is facial neutrality neutral in this context? We might ask this in the language of *Smith*: how can a law be generally applicable in this context? The concurring and dissenting opinions essentially ask this question and answer that the laws are neither neutral nor generally applicable for Free Exercise purposes.[122]

Here there may be a dichotomy between claims of neutrality and general applicability. The law without religious exemptions is not neutral, whether viewed from the perspective of Free Exercise or from that of the legal regime as a whole. The Court admits as much in suggesting that no one is entitled to a religious exemption and religious minorities might be at a disadvantage when attempting to get exemptions through the political process.[123] Whatever baseline we set for neutrality in this context, neither the result nor the baseline can be proven neutral. Yet, we might set two different baselines for general applicability in this case: one that views general applicability without regard to the nature of the claim, and one that views general applicability specifically in the Free Exercise context.

From the latter perspective, the law is not generally applicable because it places a significant burden on those whose religious practices require a violation of the law. From the former perspective, the law is generally applicable because it applies to all citizens, even if it may have a differing impact on some. This, of course, simply raises the question: how do we choose between these baselines? Certainly we could not choose on the basis of the tortured use of precedent by both the majority and dissenting opinions. So what really allowed the justices to choose? We will, of course, never know for sure, but it seems the majority presumed that it is religion neutral to analyze the general applicability of the law without regard to the nature of the claim.[124] Otherwise, the Court's reasoning makes no sense. If the law was not religion neutral in the Free Exercise context, then it is not generally applicable because it would apply differently to different religious groups. The Court's approach is one of formal neutrality because it is concerned only with the facial neutrality of the law and not with its practical effects. The concurring and dissenting opinions seem to assume that the law is not generally applicable or religion neutral in the context of a Free Exercise claim.[125] Thus, for purposes of the present discussion we will focus on the majority opinion.

Whether the decision in *Smith* is a valid interpretation of the Free Exercise Clause (I will suggest elsewhere that it is not) cannot be determined based on the implicit neutrality claim or on the presumption regarding the general applicability of the law. Rather, we must look elsewhere. The governing precedent was mixed; although it does seem the majority opinion took some liberties with precedent. In the end the Court had to answer the question, as the *Sherbert* Court tried to do, "What does the Free Exercise Clause mean and how should it be applied to exemptions from laws that are not directly aimed at religion?" By relying on general applicability and facial neutrality the Court never seriously engages this question. The answer is presumed—general applicability and neutrality are determinative because that is what the Free Exercise Clause requires. Why? Because generally applicable laws cannot burden Free Exercise in a constitutionally significant way. Why? Because we said so. The Court might be able to justify this approach with an appropriate mode of Religion Clause interpretation, but neutrality is not such a mode and general applicability is used as a stand in for neutrality. Even if we were to argue that general applicability has meaning separate from its implicit neutrality claim, we are left trying to determine if the laws of general applicability approach used by the Court is adequately supported by an appropriate mode of Religion Clause interpretation. Neutrality is used here to avoid carefully answering the tough question of what the Free Exercise Clause requires and why.

Liberty

If neutrality does not work as the underlying principle for interpreting the Religion Clauses, what about other principles such as liberty and equality? These principles have sometimes been connected to neutrality, but they are capable of definition without being tethered to neutrality claims. This section will explore the concept of liberty under the Religion Clauses. The religious liberty principle has obvious relevance to Free Exercise Clause jurisprudence, but it can also be relevant in the Establishment Clause context.

The problem with religious liberty is defining it. As with neutrality there are varying concepts of religious liberty, and the choice between these conceptions can affect outcomes under the Religion Clauses.[126] Neutrality asserts a claim of balance that is impossible to achieve regardless of the baseline asserted. No conception of neutrality can be neutral in the Religion Clause area. Liberty suffers a similar, but somewhat different, problem. No one conception of religious liberty can claim to be the correct conception of liberty, unless as some contend there is a clear historical understanding of religious liberty.[127] As will be seen, despite some excellent arguments to the contrary, there is no single concept of religious liberty that can claim historical preeminence. So any claim to liberty must operate from a context or baseline that is only self-justifying.

Yet, unlike neutrality claims—which even when limited to a given approach or baseline suggest that some state of affairs is actually neutral, liberty claims don't inherently suggest any sort of absolute state of liberty.[128] Rather they only suggest that a given approach may protect religious liberty in a given context or that a given conception of liberty is consistent with the intent of the framers. When our suggested liberty approach infringes on the liberties of others, however, the concept of liberty loses much of its force because, as with neutrality, we end up with an explicit or implicit balancing of interests usually accompanied by the claim that one side of the balance fosters religious liberty more than the other.[129] This suggests that the liberty concept, to the extent it is useful, is likely to be more useful in the Free Exercise context than the Establishment context because religious liberty claims are less likely to conflict in the former context.

Scholars and judges seem to understand, or at the very least intuit this, because most of the "liberty talk" in the Religion Clause context occurs in discussion of the Free Exercise Clause.[130] This does not mean that liberty has not been discussed in the Establishment Clause context,[131] only that discussion of the concept is less common in that context than it is in the Free Exercise context. When it is used in connection with the Establishment Clause, it is rarely used in a helpful way; although, there are exceptions.[132] When a judge or scholar claims that separationism promotes religious liberty, we might question whose religious liberty and how. Conversely, when a judge or scholar claims that some form of governmental recognition of religion promotes religious liberty, we might ask the same questions. Each approach *may* promote the religious liberty of some but only at the expense of others.[133] How are we to weigh whose religious liberty is more important and why without relying on some concept other than liberty?

In the Free Exercise context the liberty concept poses fewer problems, assuming there is a sound basis for using it. When one seeks an exemption to a "generally applicable" law, the liberties of others will rarely be directly interfered with; although when the liberties of others are affected, such as when a seniority system is involved, the questions get harder. Thus, one can say that requiring exemptions to generally applicable laws, at least when such exemptions do not interfere with the rights of others, promotes religious liberty.[134] It may not be the only way to promote religious liberty, and more importantly, saying that it promotes religious liberty does not mean that it is necessary to the existence of religious liberty generally or required under the Free Exercise Clause. Of course, if it creates more religious liberty for more people than the alternatives, without interfering with the rights of others or conflicting with other valid Religion Clause principles, and especially if one can find support in other modes of Religion Clause interpretation, the use of religious liberty to justify exemptions to generally applicable laws under the Free Exercise Clause makes sense.[135] As will be seen, the only valid Religion Clause principle with which exemptions might be said to interfere is separation. In the Free Exercise context, the ebb and flow of Religion Clause jurisprudence would favor what I will argue is a strong Free Exercise argument supported by liberty and several other principles over a weak separation argument.

So we are left with a concept that is quite malleable, but for which—at least in some contexts—a useful baseline may be found. This leaves the problem of determining what baseline(s) of liberty may be useful, why the arguments against neutrality baselines don't apply to these views of religious liberty, and in what contexts and to what extent liberty should be used in deciding questions under the Religion Clauses.

A. Framing Religious Liberty

Given my argument there is no way to establish a neutral baseline for neutrality claims in the Religion Clause context, how can a baseline or baselines for a similarly malleable concept such as liberty be found? The difference lies in the concepts themselves. Neutrality suggests a state of balance between various interests that is simply impossible to achieve in the Religion Clause context, given the religious diversity and massive role of government in the United States. Liberty is malleable like neutrality, but it doesn't suggest any universal epistemic claim. The problem with liberty is that there is no way to choose between conceptions of liberty from within the liberty principle itself. This it shares with neutrality. But unlike neutrality, government can act in a manner that promotes liberty.

To say X is neutral to a degree means that X is also not neutral to a degree, and in a complex area, such as the Religion Clauses, we must be able to explain how X is then neutral. To say that X promotes religious liberty to a degree can be taken at face value and debated. If someone says that Y also promotes religious liberty that too is possible. If X and Y conflict, we have no basis within the liberty principle to choose between them barring a clear historical argument (which as will be seen is lacking). Yet, unlike neutrality, which falls under its own weight and cannot be demonstrated by using any other principle, a given conception of liberty may be supported when other principles interact with it in the Religion Clause context. Thus, there may be more than one valid concept of religious liberty, and when and how these concepts can be used, and how they can be justified, will depend on other principles.

The difference between neutrality and liberty is that one is impossible to achieve in the Religion Clause context and the other may be achievable to a degree. Yet we might argue that we can achieve neutrality to a degree through concepts like formal neutrality or separation as neutrality, so how is that any different? The answer is that the presumption is simply wrong. Formal neutrality doesn't create neutrality in any sense. It is only useful to those who already believe that formal neutrality is neutral. There are strong factual and theoretical arguments demonstrating that formal neutrality does not lead to neutral results. The same is true for separation as neutrality. If the "private choice" or separation arguments are to be supported, they must be supported by something more than the unprovable claim that they are neutral. Neutrality adds nothing of value to the discussion other than the illusion of an objective underlying principle (i.e., a legal justification). To say that giving an exemption to a generally applicable law promotes religious liberty (at least for those getting the exemption) is a verifiable statement, even if it does not by itself answer the question of whether such exemptions are mandated under the Free Exercise Clause or how we would choose between that argument and one that suggests religious liberty may be promoted in the absence of such exemptions; everyone is still guaranteed the liberty of conscience to believe what they will and the ability to practice their faiths to the extent that general laws are not infringed.

Given the malleability of the liberty concept, how can we pick any single conception of religious liberty for use in Religion Clause analysis? The answer is that we don't have to. What we need to do is understand how the liberty principle might interact with other modes of Religion Clause interpretation on given issues, and this engagement will help us understand when liberty is a helpful concept in addressing Religion Clause issues and, if so, what conception of liberty. The good news is that, despite all the debate over the proper role of liberty in Religion Clause jurisprudence vis-à-vis other principles, most conceptions of liberty share a great deal in common in the Free Exercise context—the major exceptions being the approach espoused by the *Smith* Court and the strict separationist argument that Free Exercise exemptions violate the Establishment Clause.[136]

In the Establishment Clause context both the role and meaning of religious liberty are more hotly contested. For now, the short answer is that the liberty concept should have little or no role in Establishment Clause cases, unless those cases involve questions of equal access or similar speech concerns as Professor Brownstein suggests.[137] Under the Free Exercise Clause the liberty principle has a more important role to play, and the arguments for robust Free Exercise protection supported by numerous scholars and judges—albeit through somewhat different approaches—are favored by the ebb and flow of Religion Clause principles over either the *Smith* Court's approach or the strict separationist approach.

B. To Whom Does Religious Liberty Apply?

A significant question remains regarding religious liberty. Assuming we can support the liberty principle in some contexts, to whom does it apply? Does it apply only to individuals or does it also apply to groups of people or religious entities? If it does apply to groups or religious entities, how might it do so? The implications of these questions are important because religious liberty of individuals is less likely to substantially conflict with other principles in the Establishment Clause context. Recognizing liberty in the contexts of groups or entities might lead to arguments that the majority has the right "to use the machinery of the state to practice its beliefs,"[138] because a dominant group could rightly assert that denying public recognition of their faith artificially separates their religious beliefs from the panoply of rights they can petition for in the public sphere and thus interferes with their religious liberty. I use the term "rightly" in the preceding sentence to point out that without some other principle to counterbalance it, the recognition of group-based religious liberty would potentially point out the inherent problems with the traditional separationist idea that religion is relegated to the private sphere.[139] For many people of faith, religion doesn't function that way. The ability to seek public recognition of religion is part of religious liberty for many people. This does not mean the private sphere/public sphere dualism suggested by many separationists isn't a useful pragmatic cutoff for such claims of religious liberty. It simply means that it isn't an obvious or self-justifying cutoff if we recognize religious liberty for groups.

Religious liberty for religious entities poses a slightly different concern. Certainly, it would violate most baselines of religious liberty for the government to intentionally discriminate against a religious entity,[140] but would it violate religious liberty if a religious entity claimed that the government denied it access to a funding program to which nonreligious entities have access?

Religious liberty would seem to obviously apply to individuals to the extent it applies at all, but from this simple statement one might assume that the reason for this is some notion from classical liberalism that religion and rights are individualistic.[141] Classic liberal theory, however, is not what drives this assertion. Rather, the assertion is driven by the pragmatic reality that Free Exercise rights are often asserted by individuals, and state action that interferes with religious practices generally affects individuals at least. Additionally, as has been well stated, there is a textual basis for finding an individualized right under the Free Exercise Clause, even without resort to originalist arguments. This doesn't answer the question of whether there may also be group or institutional rights. The question of whether there is any sort of individual religious liberty right under the Establishment Clause will be severely limited by analysis elsewhere in this book, suggesting that the liberty principle plays a minimal role in Establishment Clause analysis.

What about group and institutional liberty interests? It would be easy to write these off by stating that the Free Exercise concerns of groups or institutions are better analyzed under other modes of Religion Clause interpretation, such as equality, but in some cases the burden on a group or institution may in fact be a relatively direct burden on the individuals involved in the group or institution. Yet allowing group or institutional rights in the Establishment Clause context might support factions "using the machinery of the state to practice their beliefs."[142] In fact, Justice Scalia suggested such a right in the school prayer context in his dissenting opinion in *Lee v. Weisman* and Justice Stewart did the same based on group Free Exercise rights in his dissenting opinion in *School District of Abington Township v. Schempp*.[143] This argument suggests that some segment of the population is denied Free Exercise rights when the government is denied the ability to sponsor organized prayer, and so on.

This analysis enmeshes the question in the Court's Establishment Clause jurisprudence because if there is a group Free Exercise right to engage in religious practices using the machinery of the state, there are few governmentally sponsored religious ceremonies or symbols that could be precluded under the Establishment Clause. Of course, some have argued that such a result is precisely what is mandated by the interplay between the Religion Clauses.[144]

The above concerns militate against recognizing group or institutional liberty rights under the Free Exercise Clause, but other contexts may favor such rights. Consider the facts underlying *City of Boerne v. Flores*[145] or *Lyng v. Northwest Indian Cemetery Protective Association.*[146]

In *Boerne* a church was denied the ability to meet the needs of its congregation because of local zoning regulations, and in *Lyng* sacred Native American lands were paved over for a highway project, thus effectively destroying the religious practices of several tribes. Although the *Boerne* was a case about the constitutionality of the Religious Freedom Restoration Act,[147] like *Lyng*, it demonstrates how institutional or group Free Exercise concerns may be quite important and pose no conflict with the Establishment Clause.

The ebb and flow of Religion Clause principles allow the possibility of accounting for both concerns under the liberty principle. After all, if no one principle is consistently dominant in Religion Clause interpretation, but rather a set of valid modes of interpretation ebb and flow based on context, one need not choose between no recognition of group or institutional Free Exercise rights or always recognizing such rights. It is quite possible to argue that religious liberty principles should apply when a religious group or institution seek an exemption to government action that does not violate the Establishment Clause. In other words, the liberty principle need not support groups or institutions using the machinery of state—or combining with the machinery of the state—to facilitate their religions in society at large, in order to allow groups or institutions to seek exemptions to government action that may substantially burden their ability to carry out their religious functions in a nongovernmental context.

A Note about Epistemology

During the conference at Wake Forest that gave rise to this book, I had a fascinating exchange with Professor Richard Miller about what he saw as a potential claim in my paper that neutrality itself is impossible because there is no way to ever know that something is neutral. Miller's insight was important and helpful, and it gave me an opportunity to clarify the limits of my argument and think further about my own views on the role of neutrality outside those limits. Miller had no serious disagreement with my neutrality argument, so long as it was limited to the legal context in which I applied it, that is, that the Supreme Court's use of neutrality in the Religion Clause context has been nothing more than illusion, and neutrality in that legal context is impossible to achieve given the vast number of religions and the vast amount of government activity in the United States.

We began to part ways a bit on my broader assertion that neutrality is impossible in most highly contested areas because there is no Archimedean point from outside of such debates that would allow someone to judge whether there is a neutral answer. Given Miller's prominent role as an ethicist and scholar of religion, this ended in a debate about epistemology that I found both exciting and intellectually stimulating. It caused me to think a great deal about the broader implications of my argument. In the end, however, my conclusion is that there is no way to determine neutrality in highly contested issues, at least not in a manner that would allow someone to do so from outside of the contested positions. With that said, I am approaching neutrality here from a legal realist sort of position, and therefore I am looking at neutrality of results and principles. I do not deny that one might view neutrality as an aspiration, even in contested spaces. I simply deny that there is any way to know whether one has achieved neutrality from within the contest; in many cases it may be impossible to achieve neutrality, even if there were a way to know that one had achieved it.

Neutrality to me does not seem a helpful concept at the metaphysical level because it implies a sort of balance that simply cannot be determined from within disputed positions. That does not mean that one can't come to a decision that is seen as better or more just from within a given framework. It simply means that whatever neutrality claims are made for such a result will only be seen as such by those who share that framework or find some of its claims appealing enough, or more importantly, consistent enough with one's preconceptions, to accept the result as "neutral."

The extent to which Rawlsian Liberalism inherently leads to rejecting conceptions of neutrality such as mine, as Miller suggested it does, is unclear. It seems quite plausible that Rawlsian notions of what might be called neutrality, neutral principles, or neutral treatment are really more about an aspiration to neutrality than an epistemological notion that there is a way to know that something is "truly neutral" in a contested space. To the extent that such aspirations operate in the realm of ethics, I have no serious disagreement with many of Miller's choices, not because they are neutral in any metaphysical sense, but because they seem good aspirations and perhaps may come closer to what many or most people would consider neutral; however, this is a perception—a practically and ethically valuable perception—of neutrality, not any sort of tangible neutrality.

In the end, however, my dialogue with Miller taught me a lot. He and I may have significant disagreement about the ability to know that something is neutral in contested spaces, but we seem to have significant agreement on the possibility of ethical precepts that may guide a lot of people. I don't see these precepts as in any way inevitable or neutral, but that does not make them less valuable. It simply recognizes what I see as an inescapable epistemological reality. No doubt Miller disagrees with this, and I thank him for his thoughtful expression of his disagreement.

Notes

1. See, for example, Steven D. Smith, *Foreordained Failure: The Quest for a Constitutional Principle of Religious Freedom* (New York: Oxford University Press, 1995), 96–97 [hereinafter *Foreordained Failure*]. "The foregoing discussion suggests that the quest for neutrality, despite its understandable appeal and the tenacity with which it has been pursued, is an attempt to grasp at an illusion."
2. See, for example, Douglas Laycock, "Formal, Substantive, and Disaggregated Neutrality toward Religion," *Depaul Law Review* 39 (1990): 1005. "Substantive neutrality requires a baseline from which to measure encouragement and discouragement. What state of affairs is the background norm from which to judge whether religion has been encouraged or discouraged? This question also require judgment; there is no simple test that can be mechanically applied to yield sensible answers."
3. Smith, *Foreordained Failure*, 96–97.
4. See generally, Frank S. Ravitch, "A Funny Thing Happened on the Way to Neutrality: Broad Principles, Formalism, and the Establishment Clause," *Georgia Law Review* 38 (2004): 489.
5. Ibid.
6. See, for example, *Mitchell v. Helms*, 530 U.S. 793, 809–11 (2000) (plurality opinion); ibid., 877–84 (Souter, J., dissenting). Plurality relied on formal neutrality, and Justice Souter's dissent rejected formal neutrality in favor of a form of substantive neutrality that is not necessarily decisive. See also, *Sch. Dist. of Abington Tp. v. Schempp*, 374 U.S. 203, 215, 222–27 (1963); ibid. at 311–13, 317 (Stewart, J., dissenting). Majority equating separation with neutrality and dissent suggesting that accommodation is consistent with neutrality, but coercion is not.
7. Smith, *Foreordained Failure*, 96–97.
8. See generally, Ravitch, "A Funny Thing Happened on the Way to Neutrality," 489.

9. William P. Marshall, "'We Know It When We See It': The Supreme Court Establishment," *Southern California Law Review* 59 (1986): 504. It advocates an approach that is more focused on the symbolic impact of government action than on government involvement with, and support of, religion.
10. Of course, although the Court may have been trying to send the message that it was being balanced in its religion clause decisions, that message presumed that there is a way to be balanced in such cases, and of course many people disagreed that the Court was balanced. See, for example, Frederick Mark Gedicks, *The Rhetoric of Church and State: A Critical Analysis of Religion Clause Jurisprudence* (Durham, NC: Duke University Press, 1995), 26–27.
11. Steven D. Smith, "Symbols, Perceptions, and Doctrinal Illusions: Establishment Neutrality and the 'No Endorsement' Test," *Michigan Law Review* 86 (1987): 268, 325–31 [hereinafter *Symbols, Perceptions, and Doctrinal Illusions*].
12. *Zelman v. Simmons-Harris*, 122 S.Ct. 2460 (2002); *Mitchell*, 530 U.S. 793 (plurality opinion).
13. *Mitchell*, 530 U.S. at 837 (O'Connor, J., concurring in the judgment). In her concurring opinion in *Mitchell*, Justice O'Connor decried the central role of neutrality in the plurality's approach. "The plurality's treatment of neutrality comes close to assigning that factor singular importance in the future adjudication of Establishment Clause challenges to government school aid programs."
14. See generally *Zelman*, 122 S. Ct. 2460.
15. *Zelman*, 122 S. Ct. at 2484–85 (Stevens, J., dissenting); *id.* at 2485–86, 2490–97 (Souter, J., dissenting); *id.* at 2507–08 (Breyer, J., dissenting).
16. Ibid., 2473.
17. Ibid., 2467.
18. Ibid., 2485 (Souter, J., dissenting).
19. Ibid., 2484 (Stevens, J., dissenting).
20. *Zelman*, 122 S. Ct. 2460.
21. Ibid.
22. Ibid., 2460.
23. See Ravitch, "A Funny Thing Happened on the Way to Neutrality," 513–23; Ira C. Lupu and Robert W. Tuttle, "*Zelman's* Future: Vouchers, Sectarian Providers, and the Next Round of Constitutional Battles," *Notre Dame Law Review* 78 (2003): 938.
24. *Zelman*, 122 S. Ct. 2460; Steven K. Green, "The Illusionary Aspect of 'Private Choice' for Constitutional Analysis," *Willamette Law Review* 38 (2002): 549.
25. See *Lemon v. Kurtzman*, 403 U.S. 602, 612–13 (1971). A test, based on earlier cases, which required that government action have a secular purpose, a primary effect that neither advances nor inhibits religion, and that there can be no excessive entanglement between government and religion.

26. Michael W. McConnell, "Religious Freedom at a Crossroads," *University of Chicago Law Review* 59 (1992): 127–34; Michael Stokes Paulsen, "*Lemon* Is Dead," *Case Western Reserve Law Review* 43 (1993): 800–13.
27. Philip B. Kurland, "Of Church and State and the Supreme Court," *University of Chicago Law Review* 29 (1961): 1.
28. Ibid., 2.
29. Ibid.
30. *Zelman*, 122 S. Ct. at 2467–68; *Mitchell*, 530 U.S. at 826–29 (plurality opinion); cf. *Good News Club v. Milford Central School*, 533 U.S. 98, 110–12, 114 (2001). This case addresses viewpoint discrimination.
31. *Good News Club*, 533 U.S. at 118–20; *Mitchell*, 530 U.S. at 826–29 (plurality opinion).
32. *Employment Division v. Smith*, 494 U.S. 872 (1990).
33. See Ravitch, "A Funny Thing Happened on the Way to Neutrality," 498–523, 531–44.
34. 122. S. Ct. 2460 (2002).
35. 494 U.S. 872 (1990).
36. In both cases formal neutrality.
37. *Zelman*, 122 S. Ct. 2460.
38. *Smith*, 494 U.S. 872.
39. Frank S. Ravitch, *Masters of Illusion: The Supreme Court and the Religion Clauses* (New York: NYU Press, 2007).
40. Laycock, "Formal, Substantive, and Disaggregated Neutrality toward Religion," 998; Smith, *Symbols, Perceptions, and Doctrinal Illusions*, 313, 329, 331.
41. *Walz v. Tax Comm.*, 397 U.S. 664, 669 (1970).
42. Douglas Laycock, "The Underlying Unity of Separation and Neutrality," *Emory Law Journal* 46 (1997): 43 (separation); Michael W. McConnell, "Accommodation of Religion," *Supreme Court Review* (1985): 3–6 (accommodation).
43. Smith, *Symbols, Perceptions, and Doctrinal Illusions*, suggests that it would be impossible to prove neutrality, so the other principles couldn't be accurately defined by the neutrality ideal.
44. It is possible that concepts such as separation and accommodation might serve as baselines for neutrality, which requires the setting of baselines. See Laycock, "Formal, Substantive, and Disaggregated Neutrality toward Religion," 996, 998, 1004–5; there is no place from which someone can prove that any such baseline is neutral. Smith, *Foreordained Failure*, 96–97.
45. See *Zelman*, 122 S. Ct. 2460.
46. Laycock, "Formal, Substantive, and Disaggregated Neutrality toward Religion," 1001–6; Laycock, "The Underlying Unity of Separation and Neutrality," 68–73.
47. Perhaps the most eloquent plea for substantive neutrality in recent years has come from Justice Souter. See *Zelman*, 122 S. Ct. at 2490–92; *Mitchell*, 530 U.S. at 877–84 (Souter, J., dissenting); Liza Weiman Hanks, "Note,

Justice Souter: Defining 'Substantive Neutrality' in an Age of Religious Politics," *Stanford Law Review* 48 (1996): 903.

48. Laycock, "Formal, Substantive, and Disaggregated Neutrality toward Religion," 1001–2.
49. Ibid., 994, 996, 1004–5.
50. Cf. Thomas S. Kuhn, *The Structure of Scientific Revolutions*, third ed. (Chicago: University of Chicago Press, 1996). Kuhn discusses paradigms in the sciences and asserts that there is no super-paradigm to decide between conflicting paradigms.
51. See *Zelman*, 122 S. Ct. 2484 (Stevens, J., dissenting); *id.* at 2485 (Souter, J., dissenting); Steven K. Green, "Of (Un)equal Jurisprudential Pedigree, Rectifying the Imbalance between Neutrality and Separationism," *Boston College Law Review* 43 (2002): 1111.
52. *Zelman*, 2494–97.
53. Smith, *Foreordained Failure*, 96–97; Smith, *Symbols, Perceptions, and Doctrinal Illusions*, 314.
54. Smith, *Symbols, Perceptions, and Doctrinal Illusions*, 268, 325–31.
55. See Ravitch, "A Funny Thing Happened on the Way to Neutrality," 544–58.
56. See generally *Zelman*, 2460.
57. See Christopher L. Eisgruber and Lawrence G. Sager, "Equal Regard," in *Law & Religion: A Critical Anthology*, ed. Stephen M. Feldman (New York: NYU Press, 2000), 200–225.
58. 330 U.S. 1 (1947).
59. 333 U.S. 203 (1948).
60. 374 U.S. 203, 215, 222–27 (1963).
61. The most prominent proponent of separation as neutrality is Justice Stevens. *Van Orden v. Perry*, 125 S. Ct. 2854, 2882–88 (Stevens, J., dissenting). Moreover, Justice Souter's substantive neutrality approach seems to reflect the separation as neutrality principle, although not by itself. *Zelman* at 2485 (Souter, J., dissenting).
62. See generally *Everson*, 330 U.S. 1.
63. Ibid.
64. Ibid., 19 (Jackson, J., dissenting); ibid., 29 (Rutledge, J., dissenting).
65. Ibid., 20–21 (Jackson, J., dissenting).
66. *Everson*, 330 U.S. 4–6, 16–18.
67. Smith, *Symbols, Perceptions, and Doctrinal Illusions*, 329–31. This is also reflected in the differences between the majority and dissenting opinions in *Zelman*. See *Zelman*, 2460.
68. Cf. Kuhn, *The Structure of Scientific Revolutions*, which makes a similar argument about the lack of a super-paradigm in the sciences that would allow someone to select between various contested scientific paradigms.
69. Laycock, "Formal, Substantive, and Disaggregated Neutrality toward Religion," 994, 996, 1004–5.
70. *Zelman*, 2466–68, 2473; ibid., 2476–77 (O'Connor, J., concurring).
71. Ibid., 2491 (Souter, J., dissenting).
72. 521 U.S. 203 (1997).

73. Ibid., 2465–66; *id.* at 2476 (O'Connor, J., concurring).
74. Ibid., 2465.
75. Ibid.
76. This is especially true since the Court rolled the entanglement prong of the *Lemon* test into the effects prong. See *Agostini v. Felton*, 521 U.S. 203 (1997).
77. *Zelman*, 2467, 2473.
78. *Mitchell*, 530 U.S. 816 (plurality opinion).
79. Ibid.; *Zelman*, 2467–68.
80. *Zelman*, 2473.
81. Ibid. 2491 (Souter, J., dissenting).
82. Ibid. 2486 ("verbal formalism").
83. Ibid. 2473 (using term "true private choice").
84. Ibid. 2491–93 (Souter, J., dissenting).
85. See Ravitch, "A Funny Thing Happened on the Way to Neutrality," 502–13, which suggested that neutrality is not appropriate as a central actuating principle under the Establishment Clause.
86. Ibid., 502–13.
87. Smith, *Symbols, Perceptions, and Doctrinal Illusions*, 325–31.
88. Laycock, "Formal, Substantive, and Disaggregated Neutrality toward Religion," 1001–06.
89. See Ravitch, "A Funny Thing Happened on the Way to Neutrality," 502–13.
90. Some would argue that is exactly what the Court did in *Mitchell* and *Zelman*. See *Mitchell*, 530 U.S. 837 (O'Connor, J., concurring); ibid., 899–900 (Souter, J., concurring); *Zelman*, 2486 (Souter, J., concurring).
91. *Smith*, 494 U.S. 874.
92. Ibid.
93. Ibid.
94. See Respondents' Brief at 1–5, *Employment Div. v. Smith*, 485 U.S. 660 (1988) (Nos. 86–946, 86–947), 1987 WL 880316.
95. Garrett Epps, "What We Talk about When We Talk about Free Exercise," *Arizona State Law Journal* 30 (1998): 583. "An uncontroverted part of the record was the relentless opposition by the peyote religion to the use of peyote outside the ritual context, and to the use of other drugs and alcohol for any reason whatsoever." See also *Smith*, 913–16 (Blackmun, J., dissenting).
96. See generally *Smith*, 872.
97. Ibid.
98. Ibid.
99. 373 U.S. 398 (1963).
100. Ibid.
101. Ibid., at 406; see also Douglas Laycock, "The Remnants of Free Exercise," *Supreme Court Review* (1990): 50. "The other point in the Court's explanation of its unemployment compensation cases is secular exemptions. If the state grants exemptions from its law for secular reasons, then it must

grant comparable exemptions for religious reasons. . . . In general, the allowance of any exemption is substantial evidence that religious exemptions would not threaten the statutory scheme."

102. 406 U.S. 205 (1972).
103. Ibid.
104. Ibid., at 209–12, 216–18, 222–27, 235–36.
105. *Wisconsin v. Yoder*, 406 U.S. 205, 241–42 (1972) (Douglas, J., dissenting); Stephen M. Feldman, "Religious Minorities and the First Amendment: The History, the Doctrine, and the Future," *University of Pennsylvania Journal of Constitutional Law* 6 (2003). Feldman notes that *Yoder* "illustrates the importance of Christianity for a successful free exercise exemption claim."
106. See Garrett Epps, "To an Unknown God: The Hidden History of *Employment Division v. Smith*," *Arizona State Law Journal* 30 (1998): 1015. "[A] ll the parties were shocked at how the Court had decided [*Smith*]. Most observers, both at the time and later, have concluded that . . . the Court rewrote the entire jurisprudence of the Free Exercise Clause . . . ."; see also ibid., 956–57 nn.11–12, which cites many legal and journalistic commentators criticizing *Smith* soon after it was decided.
107. See Brief for Petitioners, *Employment Div. v. Smith*, 494 U.S. 872 (1990) (No. 88–1213), 1989 WL 1126846.
108. Ibid.
109. In fact, no non-Christian has ever won a Free Exercise Clause exemption case before the US Supreme Court and even most Christians have lost such cases. Mark Tushnet, "Of Church and State and the Supreme Court: Kurland Revisited," *Supreme Court Review* (1989): 381.
110. See, for example, *Goldman v. Weinberger*, 475 U.S. 503 (1986) (military setting); *O'Lone v. Estate of Shabazz*, 482 U.S. 342 (1987) (prison setting).
111. *Bowen v. Roy*, 476 U.S. 693 (1986).
112. *United States v. Lee*, 455 U.S. 252 (1982).
113. Lower court cases went both ways after *Sherbert* and *Yoder*, and although many denied the claimant's exemptions, a number did not. See, for example, *Dayton Christian Schs., Inc. v. Ohio Civil Rights Comm'n*, 766 F.2d 932 (6th Cir. 1985). The school's free exercise rights were violated by application of civil rights laws. See also *McCurry v. Tesch*, 738 F.2d 271 (8th Cir. 1984). The enforcement of state order against the operation of a church school in violation of state law infringed the church's free exercise rights.
114. *Smith*, 883–84.
115. Ibid., 878.
116. Ibid., 881–82.
117. Ibid.
118. Frederick Mark Gedicks, *The Rhetoric of Church and State*, 98–99.
119. Ibid.
120. See Ravitch, *Masters of Illusion*.
121. See generally, *Smith*, 872.

122. Ibid., 891 (O'Connor, J., concurring in the judgment); ibid., 907 (Blackmun, J., dissenting).
123. Ibid., 890.
124. See generally ibid.; ibid., 886 n.3.
125. Ibid., 891 (O'Connor, J., concurring in the judgment); ibid., 907 (Blackmun, J., dissenting).
126. See Perry O. Chrisman, "Confessions of a Baptist Lawyer," *Texas Tech Law Review* 27 (1996): 1041. Chrisman argues that "[i]n no area has the religious right more confused or abused the perception of the law than in the concepts of religious liberty based on the First Amendment protection."
127. See Noah Feldman, "The Intellectual Origins of the Establishment Clause," *New York University Law Review* 77 (2002): 384–85. Feldman asserted that "the history of the idea of liberty of conscience" reveals that early Americans "shared a basic theory of religious liberty and drew on the same sources and Lockean ideas to express their views."
128. See Smith, *Foreordained Failure* ; Ravitch, "A Funny Thing Happened on the Way to Neutrality," 542. It primarily addresses neutrality but also discusses liberty.
129. See, for example, Jonathan C. Lipson, "On Balance: Religious Liberty and Third-Party Harms," *Minnesota Law Review* 84 (2000): 593. Lipson recognizes that "balancing the rights of religious actors and third parties reflects the two competing anxieties that have historically defined the boundaries of our religious liberty jurisprudence."
130. See, for example, Patrick M. Garry, "The Institutional Side of Religious Liberty: A New Model of the Establishment Clause," *Utah Law Review* 2004 (2004): 1163. "The Free Exercise Clause defines a fundamental individual liberty. . . . The Establishment Clause, on the other hand, simply provides a negative check on certain governmental powers and functions."
131. See, for example, Noah Feldman, *Divided by God: America's Church-State Problem—And What We Should Do about It* (New York: Farrar, Straus, and Giroux, 2005).
132. The equal access cases (cases involving access by religious groups to government property on the same terms as other nongovernment related groups) are a good example of the concept of liberty being used helpfully in the Establishment Clause context, but of course, the liberty involved in those cases was both religious liberty and freedom of speech. *Good News Club*, 533 U.S. 98 (2001); *Lamb's Chapel v. Center Moriches Union Free Sch. Dist.*, 508 U.S. 384 (1993); *Widmar v. Vincent*, 454 U.S. 263 (1981).
133. See Smith, *Foreordained Failure*; see also Douglas Laycock, "Religious Liberty as Liberty," *Journal of Contemporary Legal Issues* 7 (1996): 313–14.
134. See generally McConnell, "Religious Freedom at a Crossroads."
135. Cf. Ibid.
136. *Smith*, 872; William P. Marshall, "In Defense of *Smith* and Free Exercise Revisionism," *University of Chicago Law Review* 58 (1991): 319–28. Marshall argues that "[t]he free exercise exemption . . . offends Establishment Clause principles."

137. Alan E. Brownstein, "Interpreting the Religion Clauses in Terms of Liberty, Equality, and Free Speech Values—A Critical Analysis of 'Neutrality Theory' and Charitable Choice," *Notre Dame Journal of Legal Ethics and Public Policy* 13 (1999): 246–56.
138. See *Sch. Dist. of Abington Tp.*, 374 U.S. 203, 226 (1963). The Free Exercise Clause has "never meant that a majority could use the machinery of the State to practice its beliefs."
139. See Philip Hamburger, *Separation of Church and State* (Cambridge: Harvard University Press, 2004), 485.
140. *Church of the Lukumi Babalu Aye v. City of Hialeah*, 508 U.S. 520 (1993). This case was about intentional discrimination and religious gerrymandering by the city aimed at the religious group based on that group's practice of animal sacrifice.
141. See Suzanne Last Stone, "Cultural Pluralism, Nationalism, and Universal Rights," *Cardozo Law Review* 21 (2000), 1215. "[C]lassical liberalism implies that equal citizenship rights reside in the individual rather than in . . . groups."
142. *Sch. Dist. of Abington Tp.*, 374 U.S. 226.
143. Ibid., 312–13 (Stewart, J., dissenting); see also *Lee*, 505 U.S. 645–46 (Scalia, J., dissenting).
144. Ibid.
145. 521 U.S. 507 (1997).
146. 485 U.S. 439 (1988).
147. *Boerne*, 521 U.S. 507.

CHAPTER 4

A Unique Religious Exemption from Antidiscrimination Laws in the Case of Gays? Putting the Call for Exemptions for Those Who Discriminate against Married or Marrying Gays in Context

Michael Kent Curtis

Introduction

1. The Issue

Faced with gay marriage in a few states, the Becket Fund for Religious Liberty and some scholars advocate exemptions from antidiscrimination laws for those with religious or moral objections to "facilitating" gay marriage.[1] Advocates seek exemptions only in connection with gays, and at least initially, they connect the need for exemptions to gay marriage. This essay examines the claim for religious or moral exemptions in a broader social and historical context. It asks why exemptions are sought only in the case of gays and whether the rationale for exemptions can reasonably be confined to "facilitating" gay marriage. Would the claim for exemptions logically support exemptions from antidiscrimination laws in the case of discrimination against single and partnered gays? Why should gays be treated differently from every other group protected by antidiscrimination laws, including Americans of African descent and women? Can a claim for a religious exemption in the case of gay marriage be supported on the theory that a religious and biblical rationale was absent in the case of racial discrimination but is present in the case of gays? Can it be supported on the ground that religious exemptions for discrimination against gays would subject them to only minor inconvenience? Would a similar rationale be persuasive in the case of religious exemptions for racial discrimination?

A. The Merchants: The Restaurateur, the Landlord, the Baker, the Florist, and the Employer

Consider a restaurateur, a landlord, a baker, a florist, and an employer living in an American state in 1950. (I will call them all merchants.) In the absence of a state statute, the restaurateur could refuse to serve black people, the employer could refuse to hire well-qualified black people, the baker and florist could refuse to sell to black people, and the landlord or property owner could refuse to rent or sell real property to black people.

But some states, and finally Congress, passed civil rights laws that banned discrimination. The 1964 Civil Rights Act banned discrimination based on race, religion, or national origin in public accommodations[2] and banned discrimination based on race, religion, national origin, or sex in employment, for most businesses with 15 or more employees.[3]

For our purposes, assume our merchants' state passed an antidiscrimination law that broadly banned race discrimination in public sales and accommodations, in sale and rental of real property, and in employment. Assume the law covered our merchants, bakers, florists, and other groups that generally sell to the public and also covered landlords and employers. The state antidiscrimination law was general, and it provided for injunctions and damages against all these people if they refused to deal with black people (or white people, for that matter).

Our merchants, including the baker and florist, have strong religious views against integration. They object to integration because they believe it will lead to interracial marriage, and they think that "race mixing" violates God's word. The merchants are hardly alone in their opposition to interracial marriage. At the time of the Fourteenth Amendment, a substantial majority of states banned interracial marriage. As late as 1950, 29 states still banned interracial marriage. In 1967, when the Supreme Court struck down the Virginia ban in the aptly named case of *Loving v. Virginia*,[4] 16 states (including Virginia) still prohibited interracial marriage.[5]

Our merchants claim that their religious views should entitle them to an exemption from generally applicable antidiscrimination laws. After *Employment Division v. Smith*, as we will see, their federal constitutional claim to an exemption would be a loser.[6] We assume for purposes of our hypothetical, that it would be a loser in 1950 also. So our merchants turn to their state legislature.

At first, our merchants wanted a general exemption from serving, selling to, employing, or renting apartments to black people. But their state supreme court has recently struck down the state ban on interracial marriage.[7] Now, our merchants are confronted with something more troubling to their consciences: a married or marrying interracial couple. The issue was simple: the merchants wanted an exemption in the commercial sphere for general, and religiously inspired, race discrimination. Is the issue now different because marriage is involved? Must the restaurateur serve an interracial couple, the landlord rent them an apartment on the same terms as whites, and the employer hire a well-qualified spouse of an interracial couple? Must the baker bake a wedding cake or the hotel owner, who regularly rents out space for wedding receptions, rent space for the interracial wedding? Must the florist provide flowers? When one of the employer's white employees marries an American of African descent, may the employer discharge her for that reason?

For our merchants, interracial marriage is a grave sin, a violation of God's word. They do not want to be involved in the sin in any way at all. Still, the law applies. The Constitution does not protect their religiously motivated right to discriminate based on race. On principle these merchants oppose all integration, and they would like a blanket exemption. But as a matter of tactics, they decide to limit their claim initially to interracial marriage—they seek an exemption from facilitating interracial marriage. Interracial marriage strikes them as the most unpopular form of integration, so it seems a good place to start their effort to achieve more general exemptions for race discrimination. So they go to the legislature and seek an exemption for religiously *and morally* motivated discriminators, at least in the case of any connection with interracial marriage. Should they get one?

They seek an exemption only from facilitating racial intermarriage. Facilitating is a slippery term. The baker, the florist, and the hotel owner suggest we start with freeing them from providing goods or locations for the ceremony. The employer wants a broader exemption, one from employing one spouse from an interracial couple; the landlord wants an exemption from renting to them; and the merchant wants an exemption from selling to them. Simply as a matter of public policy, should the legislature grant the exemptions?

No. The important values underlying the need to destroy the racial caste system militate in favor of maintaining the general law and applying it generally. Religious and moral exemptions will undermine the force of the law. They may do more. They may teach merchants that they have a religious right and duty to discriminate. The Civil Rights Act of 1964 (generally without exemptions for religious or moral objectors) helped to solidify public rejection of segregation. A law riddled with exemptions for religiously or morally motivated discriminators would, it is reasonable to suppose, have been far less effective. Indeed, it might have dramatically changed the message sent by the law.

At the other end of the spectrum, as a matter of freedom of religion and freedom of association, a segregationist church need not accept black members, the segregationist minister need not marry them, and the church that has spaces for receptions (limited to its own members) need not accommodate the interracial couple.

As to race today, thanks to civil rights laws and changing public sentiment (probably much influenced by those strong and general laws), the issue of an exemption to allow racial discrimination is remote. But today many states have added sexual orientation to the categories protected by their antidiscrimination laws. Today, as to sexual orientation, religious groups and some scholars are advocating religious exemptions from the law. The advocates for exemptions have chosen to frame the issue around gay marriage.

In what follows, I discuss exemptions from antidiscrimination laws in cases involving for-profit commercial activity—in employment, in housing, in providing commercial services to the public, and in public accommodations. Most of these types of discrimination were prohibited in the 1964 Civil Rights Act[8] and, for housing, more broadly by the 1866 Civil Rights Act, as interpreted by the court.[9] There were limits as to the size of the establishment to which the 1964 Act applied in the case of employment discrimination.[10] The limits were politically necessary to obtain the law, so they made pragmatic sense. Except for a limited exemption for a small owner-occupied boarding house, there were no size limits on public accommodations, and none were explicit under 42 U.S.C. Section 1982 for racial discrimination in the sale or rental of housing,[11] though there were exemptions under the 1968 Fair Housing Act.[12] Certain exemptions, such as for churches hiring ministers, are right as a matter of free speech, free exercise, and association principles and are widely protected by antidiscrimination laws.

Race, gender, and sexual orientation should be treated the same. So if the legislature should not give religious discriminators an exemption in the cases of race and gender, it should not give religious people (or others) who want to discriminate against gays in commercial matters an exemption either. So far the focus has been on policy, and I have only raised the issue and suggested an approach. The argument for this approach will follow. Of course, the legal story is more complicated because of the federal[13] and state Religious Freedom Restoration Acts.[14] But similar policy concerns apply as to the wisdom of exemptions. In any case, it is useful to think about this issue in its historical context.

B. Historical Background

The Declaration of Independence proclaimed "that all men are created equal, that they are endowed by their Creator with certain unalienable Rights" including "Life, Liberty, and the pursuit of Happiness."[15] Most of us now understand the principle to include all people. The preamble of the Constitution announced its purpose to be, among other things, securing "the Blessings of Liberty."[16] Our nation's story has been a story of efforts to expand the promise of American life to more and more people, including blacks, women, people of different religious faiths, of different national origins, and now, haltingly, gays. Expansion has never been easy or linear. Often the efforts have met fierce resistance. Objections to expanding protection for civil rights of blacks and women (as well as arguments in favor of protecting these groups) were often religious and justified by citations from the Bible.[17]

The nation has extended liberty and equality to more and more people by constitutional amendment. The Thirteenth Amendment banned slavery.[18] The Fourteenth sought to provide equal citizenship, to nationalize civil liberty, and to provide equal protection and due process for all persons.[19] The Fifteenth Amendment sought, for black males, to ban race discrimination in voting.[20] The Nineteenth banned discrimination in the right to vote based on sex.[21] The Twenty-Fourth Amendment outlawed the poll tax for federal elections (for Congress and the President).[22] Of course, efforts were made in the states as well. Court decisions sometimes also expanded liberty and equality.

We often think of the Supreme Court as the primary guardian of liberty and equality. Over the long haul, however, the court's record on liberty and equality has been, to put it charitably, mixed. The court even struck down or eviscerated early civil rights and civil liberties legislation.[23]

These amendments to the Constitution sought to expand the promise of American life, and some fine judicial decisions did also. Still, a combination of constitutional amendment and judicial interpretation has been only one route. Congress and the states have passed legislation promoting liberty and equality.[24] Striking gains came from progressive legislation passed in the

1960s, including the Civil Rights Act of 1964[25] (passed pursuant to congressional power over commerce) and the Voting Rights Act of 1965.[26] The 1964 Civil Rights Act barred racial discrimination in public accommodations based on race, religion, and national origin and banned employment discrimination based on race, religion, natural origin, and sex. These laws were designed to prevent, and, when that failed, to punish discrimination in access to places of public accommodation, such as hotels and restaurants, access to employment, and in 1968, access to housing.[27] Another antidiscrimination law was the Equal Pay Act, requiring equal pay for women and men when they do comparable work.[28]

The Civil Rights Acts produced immense changes. They went a long way toward obliterating a racial caste system and toward providing opportunities for women. The 1964 Civil Rights Act had no exceptions for religious (or moral) objectors, beyond protecting the right of churches to hire ministers and other officials of their faith.[29] No general national laws ban discrimination in housing, employment, and public accommodations based on sexual orientation, but many states and localities have passed such laws.[30]

Civil rights laws have enhanced not only equality, but practical liberty as well—the liberty to buy a home or rent an apartment of your choice, to enjoy equal access to hotels, and to take advantage of many more practical liberties. But opponents argued that such laws also contracted liberty, for example the liberty of the employer or the landlord or the merchant.[31] The liberty or values allegedly infringed have included economic liberty and religious liberty.

Almost every step on the road to expanded equality has met determined resistance. That was certainly true for race and gender equality. It is true in the case of sexual orientation, even for very small steps. Over 25 years ago, I tried to get the North Carolina legislature to reduce the "crime against nature" from a felony to a misdemeanor, in the case of consenting adults in private.[32] North Carolina had even prosecuted a married couple for acts in their own bedroom.[33] This small change in a more humane direction was successfully opposed by fundamentalist ministers. Even after *Lawrence v. Texas*, North Carolina still refuses to repeal its crime against nature statute (a felony) as to private, consensual, noncommercial, adult sexual conduct.[34] Of course, after *Lawrence v. Texas* the statute cannot today be generally applied to consenting adults in private.[35]

C. No Constitutionally Required Exemptions Based on Religious Belief

In *Employment Division v. Smith*,[36] the court denied Smith, a member of the Native American Church, a constitutional exemption from generally applicable laws that burdened religious conduct.[37] Smith, a drug counselor, was denied unemployment benefits after he was discharged for violating an Oregon criminal law against illegal drug use.[38] This was so, even though the drug (peyote) was used in a sacred ceremony of his Native American religion.[39]

Court authority on the religious exemption issue has evolved. At first the court denied exemptions for religiously motivated conduct that violated generally applicable laws. A Mormon polygamy case[40] is one of several examples. Next, in unemployment cases and a few others, the court sometimes required exemptions unless the state was pursuing a compelling state interest by narrowly tailored means.[41] In *Smith*, the court departed from that second line of cases. Instead of following the cases requiring exemptions, the court largely returned to its original rule that denied a religious exemption from generally applicable laws that burdened religiously motivated conduct.

After *Smith*, the constitutional case for religious exemptions from generally applicable laws is weak. Congress responded to *Smith* with the Religious Freedom Restoration Act (RFRA).[42] Under the RFRA, the government (state and national) could not substantially burden the exercise of religion unless the government had a compelling interest in doing so and pursued this interest by narrowly tailored means.[43] But, as applied to the states, the court held the RFRA exceeded the power of Congress.[44]

So, religious groups have increasingly sought statutory exemptions from generally applicable laws that others must obey. Their success in obtaining exemptions is remarkable, indeed, stunning. Many states give religious commercial organizations benefits denied to secular ones—to take one example from many, exemptions from health and safety laws for religious day care centers. These exemptions reflect political power. If the rules are unreasonable, no one should have to obey them. If, on the other hand, they offer reasonable protections to children, religious groups should have to obey them just as secular establishments must. The issue here is different.

I. THE ISSUE

Assume a state law bans discrimination based on sexual orientation, as well as race and gender, in housing, employment, and public accommodations. If gays were discriminated against based on sexual orientation in one of these areas, in violation of the state law, should those with religious objections be exempt from civil damages or injunctions for their violation of the law? If so, when? Should the exemption be constitutionally required? Under the rule in *Employment Division v. Smith*, the answer to the constitutional question is no.

Since a federal constitutional exemption from state laws is not available (and the RFRA could not constitutionally be applied to the states), should the legislature engraft a religious or moral exemption onto its antidiscrimination statutes *solely in the case of discrimination based on sexual orientation*? Should it pass state constitutional amendments doing the same thing?

In connection with gay marriage, the Becket Fund for Religious Liberty answers this question, "Yes." The Becket Fund's examples of conflict with sincere religious beliefs include religious objectors who decide not to hire people in same-sex marriages, who refuse to extend spousal benefits to same-sex couples, and who refuse to provide otherwise available housing to same-sex couples. After listing these examples, the Becket Fund advocates legislation to provide "robust" accommodation to religious objectors to same-sex marriage. It also would expand the exemption to other "conscientious" objectors. Since the Becket Fund also lists gay couples, it seems its plan may end up going beyond gay marriage. As a matter of logic, it is hard to see why it should stop at married gays and not include gays living with their partners and single gays.

Assuming the state has a general antidiscrimination law and the legislature passes a religious or moral exemption only in cases of sexual orientation, what should be the dimensions of the claimed religiously or morally justified right to discriminate against gays? Should the right to discriminate be limited only to immediately facilitating the gay marriage itself—baking the wedding cake, providing the flowers, supplying the hotel for the receptions, and so on? Should it, as the Becket Fund apparently advocates, include the right to discriminate against married gays after the marriage? Should it, as the Becket Fund advocates, cover housing, employment, and spousal benefits, such as health insurance? What about gays living with partners and unmarried gays?

If the Becket Fund is correct about exemptions for discrimination against married and marrying gays, and if the right to discriminate expands to cover unmarried as well as married gays (why not, by this logic?), should the state or Congress also, as a matter of sound policy, provide religious or moral exemptions in cases of racial, religious, and gender discrimination? Here we look at legislative policy decisions in commercial transactions, not at what the Constitution requires or provides.

If discrimination based on sexual orientation is closely analogous to discrimination based on race and gender, the policy answer to the questions should be the same: exemptions should be allowed to religious discriminators in race, gender, and sexual orientation cases, or exemptions should be denied to religious discriminators in each case. Should religiously motivated objectors to laws banning race (and gender) discrimination in employment and discrimination in public accommodations, for example, have been exempt from the strictures of the laws? As a matter of public policy, should the 1964 Civil Rights Act—which banned discrimination based on race, religion, or national origin in public accommodations, and added sex to the list in cases of employment—have allowed religiously motivated objectors to discriminate against blacks or women or Buddhists? Should those with religious or moral motivations have been exempt from the ban on discrimination in public accommodations or employment under the 1964 Civil Rights Act?

At the moment, those who advocate exemptions focus on gay marriage. Should religious objectors to interracial marriage now be allowed to (and, after *Loving v. Virginia*, should they in the past have been allowed to) discriminate against interracial couples in employment, housing, spousal benefits, and the rest? If not, why is gay marriage unique? More broadly, why is discrimination against gays unique?

Since I think discrimination based on sexual orientation is closely analogous to racial and gender discrimination, I turn next to that question.

II. The Analogy to Race and Gender

A. *Why Race and Gender Are Analogous*

Both race and gender are genetic. For blacks the slavery experience and its aftermath were particularly awful. For a long time, both black males and women of all races lacked political power. In the South particularly, it was for many years dangerous for blacks to exercise political rights or advocate against the racial caste system. Both blacks and women suffered from denial of the right to vote and from denial of civil rights.

Discrimination based on sexual orientation is closely analogous to racial and gender discrimination. Sexual orientation seems to be significantly affected by biological and genetic factors. At any rate, it is a basic part of who a person is. There has been a long history of persecution and discrimination against gays for their sex lives, including first execution and later long prison sentences. Gays have been subjected to private violence and are more likely to attempt suicide. Because of intense prejudice, they have been victims of employment discrimination—even, until recently, by the US government. Because of pervasive prejudice, gays were afraid to publicly acknowledge their orientation. For many that remains true today. As a result, for many years, gays could not effectively raise their concerns in the political process for fear of retaliation and persecution.

So, as a matter of public policy, legislation protecting people against discrimination based on sexual orientation—for example, in housing, employment, and public accommodations—*generally* should be treated as race and gender discrimination are treated. Whatever one thinks about the role of the courts on constitutional issues, the principle here is directed at legislation and attempted constitutional amendments providing a religious defense for violating antidiscrimination laws that protect gays. Of course, laws banning discrimination based on sexual orientation protect everyone else too, since all people have sexual orientations.

The analogy to race or gender (as with all analogies) is not perfect. Awful and pervasive race discrimination in housing, employment, and public accommodations reached far more black people because they were easily identifiable. Typically, one can tell by visual inspection that a person is an American of African descent or is a woman. That is not generally so for gays. So unless discovered, gays could often escape discrimination and persecution. They could not, however, escape the fear of discovery, discrimination, and persecution, or the chilling effect that fear had. And, except by hiding their identity (for example, by refraining from doing things in public that heterosexuals do, such as holding hands), they could not escape discrimination and persecution.

Fear of discrimination and persecution had a silencing effect for many years. Fear imposed political as well as personal costs. One cost for many years had (and to some extent has) been an inability to advocate for gay rights in the political process. In addition, the personal dilemma of hiding a central part of a person's identity and the fear of confronting prejudice and discrimination impose great emotional costs. As with race and gender, the greatest harm may be to the human spirit, the harm inflicted when gays internalize the message sent by hostility and discrimination. The suicide rate among gay youth is one of many indicators. There were, and are, psychological costs to racial and gender discrimination too.

Of course, once it becomes acceptable, and indeed a religious duty, to discriminate against gay people, the religious discriminators face a serious problem. They have a duty to discriminate, or (as supporters of a right to discriminate frame it) to at least not facilitate the gay lifestyle. But many closeted gays and even out gays might slip through the net due to the lack of an effective detection device. There is no easy solution to this problem, but there is one solution, imperfect though it is. The religious discriminator can post a sign and put a notice on his or her website. "We do not serve gays." "No gays need apply." "We do not rent to gays." There is, of course, historical precedent for this approach: "No Irish Need Apply"; "Whites Only." Once one frames discrimination against gays as the exercise of religion and as a religious duty, of course the religiously motivated discriminator must do what he can.

B. The Attempt to Distinguish Race and Gender from Sexual Orientation Based on a Unique Religious Basis with Reference to Homosexuality

One might seek to distinguish discrimination based on race (or gender) and discrimination based on sexual orientation on the grounds that discrimination based on sexual orientation is sometimes based on sincere religious conviction although presumably that would not be the case for racial discrimination or gender discrimination. Professor Robin Wilson makes this argument in connection with public accommodations and gay marriage: "The religious and moral convictions that motivate objectors to refuse to facilitate same-sex marriage simply cannot be marshaled to justify racial discrimination." An examination of American history shows the proposed distinction is baseless. Slavery, racial discrimination and segregation, and opposition to women's rights were all supported by strong religious arguments bolstered by citations to the Bible. As scholarly work has shown, these religious views were deeply held by many people. That Professor Wilson finds it impossible to marshal religious arguments for segregation is, to a great degree, a tribute to the success of the civil rights movement and civil rights laws, generally without exemptions for religious objectors.

Not only could religious arguments for segregation be marshaled, they *were* marshaled. For example, Senator Robert Byrd of West Virginia cited the Bible in opposition to the Civil Rights Act of 1964. Reverend Jerry Falwell attributed the *Brown v. Board of Education* desegregation decision to Chief Justice Warren's failure to know and follow God's word; Falwell also preached against racial intermarriage.[45] Falwell and Byrd were not alone.

The trial judge who upheld Virginia's antimiscegenation statute in the 1967 case of *Loving v. Virginia* cited the fact that God had put the races on separate continents as proof "that he did not intend for the races to mix."[46] Earlier, in 1867, the Pennsylvania Supreme Court upheld segregation in railway cars.[47] The court explained that "[t]he natural law which forbids [racial intermarriage] and that social amalgamation which leads to a corruption of races, is as clearly divine as that which imparted to [the races] different natures."[48] The Pennsylvania court's appeal to divine authority was used by state supreme courts in Indiana, Alabama, and Virginia to support the validity of statutes banning interracial marriages and by decisions in Alabama and Kentucky to support segregation of transportation and higher education.[49] The latest use of this language came in a 1955 Virginia decision.[50] "[T]he theology of separate races constituted a kind of cultural religion that permeated the hearts and minds of attorneys and judges throughout the courts of the South for a hundred years after the Civil War."[51]

Jane Dailey has explicated the religious and biblical case for segregation.[52] The religious case for racial separation was based on a type of selective biblical literalism. By this reading of the Bible, a reading that cited a number of Bible verses, "God Himself" had drawn boundary lines to keep races and peoples separate, or at least to keep them from intermarriage and having sex across the boundaries. Concern about one type of sexual activity was at the heart of the religious case for segregation. According to segregationists, race mixing would lead to interracial marriage and interracial sex, contravening God's plan. Mississippi Senator Theodore G. Bilbo explained that "miscegenation and amalgamation are sins of man in direct defiance with the will of God. . . ."[53] A professor at Mississippi's leading Baptist institution announced, "[O]ur Southern segregation way is the Christian way. . . . [God] was the original segregationist."[54] A writer in the *Baptist Standard* agreed: "God created and established the color line. . . ."[55]

Although leading clergymen, including Baptist, Methodist, Episcopalian, Jewish, Church of Christ, Unitarian, and other religious leaders, rejected the religious argument for segregation, Professor Dailey shows it was a quite widely held belief.[56] Dailey surveyed a number of sources: resolutions from churches, a resolution from the Daughters of the American Revolution ("racial integrity" was a "fundamental Christian principle"), a decision of the Florida Supreme Court, and letters to Thomas B. Stanley, the Governor of Virginia, in response to the *Brown* decision. Jane Dailey's survey showed that "[m]ost who wrote [Governor Stanley] objected to integration. The most common argument of the dissenters was theological: integration encouraged miscegenation, which contradicted the divine word."[57] The claim that opposition to homosexuality or gay marriage is religious, while opposition to integration and interracial marriage was not, is mistaken.

Of course, humane religious and biblical arguments were made against discrimination based on race, gender, and sexual orientation. Powerful religious arguments were also made against slavery.[58] Although there are problematic Bible passages about homosexuality (and slavery and the subordination of women), there are passages that militate in the other direction.[59]

As in the case of homosexuality, problematic passages were cited to support slavery.[60] As to race, and to some extent as to gender, religious arguments for equality have mostly carried the day. As to sexual orientation, the controversy is continuing, although an increasing number of major denominations are beginning to support gay equality.[61] Still, religious opposition to gay marriage is extensive.

One could dismiss and distinguish segregationist religious views on race and opposition to women's equality as bigotry, but bigotry can be founded on sincerely held religious views. The categories of bigotry and sincere religious belief are not always mutually exclusive. Past advocates of racial and gender discrimination and subordination are entitled to the same presumption of sincerity as current opponents of gay equality. Many believed the religious argument against integration and interracial marriage, just as many people believe the religious arguments against gay equality and liberty.

Opposition to gender equality was also often religious. Although segregationists insisted that God intended the races to remain separate, opponents of gender equality insisted that God had decreed a special (wife and mother) sphere for women who were to be ruled by their husbands.[62] Denial of basic civil rights for married women, denial of the right to enter the professions, to vote, and even to speak in public to men as well as women were all defended as God's plan. The defenders relied on Bible verses.

C. Purported Distinction Based on Hostility to (Presumed) Gay Conduct

One can argue that discrimination against gays is about conduct (gay sex) while segregation was not. But, segregation *was* about conduct: the conduct of race mixing; the conduct of a black person entering a white-only railroad car or a white-only hotel or restaurant; or most dramatically, sexual conduct—blacks having sex with or marrying whites. Fear of interracial sex (sexual conduct) was a leading religious argument for segregation.

Similarly, in the case of discrimination against gays, one can insist on the distinction between discriminating against a person because of who the person is (which is contrary to our most basic commitment to equality) and discriminating based on what the person does (which may seem a matter of prudential judgment and not inherently wrong). But, as the case of racial intermarriage shows, the categories converge. The punishment for interracial sex was based on what the people did. The white person was not punished because of what he or she was, but because of what he or she did. The conduct-based crime supported the racial caste system. The conduct-based crime of sodomy supported another loathsome caste system.

The conduct-versus-identity distinction involves other problems. The facts are complex because of the varieties of sexual orientation. Gay identity cannot be reduced to sex acts any more than the identity of heterosexuals can be so reduced. Gay people are generally attracted to people of the same sex. It is part, and just a part, of who they are, as distinguished from what they do.

Certain types of conduct are closely correlated with identity. Heterosexuals, if sexually active, typically engage in heterosexual sex. Gays, if sexually active, typically engage in gay sex. In this case, and with reference to punishment by the state or denial of equal citizenship by private discrimination in the public commercial sphere, punishment allegedly based on conduct merges with punishment based on identity. In this situation, the distinction between discrimination against the conduct and discrimination against the person is more formal than substantial. And, of course, not all gay or straight people—single or married—are sexually active.

If a conduct distinction is thought to justify discrimination against married gays, just what is the conduct? Marriage is a commitment to love, support, and cherish another person, and it provides certain state privileges, immunities, and duties. If gays are discriminated against because they are married, then the disfavored conduct is shared by straight people, the only difference being that heterosexuals marry persons of a different sex. Is that, as a matter of policy, a substantial basis for putting gays in a uniquely disfavored class—making gays the only covered group denied the general protection of antidiscrimination laws that ban discrimination based on race, gender, religion, national origin, and sexual orientation? If the distinction is based on supposed sexual activity, that is, on the assumption that married gays are having non-procreative sex, then this distinction is flawed too because it is overbroad and under-inclusive. Not all married people are sexually active, and many heterosexuals engage in non-procreative sex.

It is hard to separate, but those who harbor hostility toward gays direct much of that hostility at them because of who gays "are." Hostile feelings make discriminating against gays more attractive. In addition to gay marriage, hostility is also based on presumptions about gays' sexual activity. But a large number of heterosexuals engage in non-procreative sex (including, for example, using birth control and having oral and anal sex), and so far at least, there have not been proposals to allow religiously motivated discrimination in the public commercial sphere against such heterosexuals or against heterosexuals who marry and presumably engage in non-procreative sex. As far as I know, a religious right to discriminate in the public, commercial sphere against straights who engage in non-procreative sex has never been advocated. Indeed, the idea is ludicrous.

III. Refusing to facilitate Gay Marriage or a Broader Right to Discriminate against Gays? Reframing the Issue

Faced with the "threat" of gay marriage, religious conservatives and some scholars[63] advocate (qualified) religious exemptions for individuals who discriminate. Some advocates of exemptions describe them as an exemption from "facilitating" gay marriage. The scope of "facilitating" is vague. After all, employment, housing, or spousal benefits, such as health insurance for a married gay couple, will facilitate gay marriage to some degree—so might renting them a hotel room—and refusal of these benefits and opportunities will to some degree deter it, or at least, help to disrupt it. Groups like the Becket Fund have a robust view of "facilitation," one that apparently includes employment, housing, spousal benefits, and public accommodations.

If there should be a qualified religious right to discriminate in the commercial sphere against married gay couples in employment, housing, businesses serving the public, and public accommodations, should the exemptions also cover single gays, gays with a same-sex roommate or a gay roommate, or gays who live with their partners? If not, what exactly is the basis for discriminating against married but not unmarried gays? Presumably many unmarried gays, like straight people, are often sexually active and many are in monogamous relationships.

For groups like the Becket Fund, is the focus on gay marriage a politically clever way to allow less protection for gays and greater protection for individuals who discriminate against gays in employment, public accommodations, and housing? Again: If exceptions should be included now for those with religious objections to homosexuality, why, as a matter of sound public policy, should they not be included now (and have been included in antidiscrimination law in the past) for those with religious scruples that support gender and race discrimination? If the hotel or restaurant should have a qualified right not to host the married gay couple, what about the married interracial couple? In short, should exemptions have been allowed when religious opposition to integration and gender equality was far more socially acceptable?

The focus on gay marriage by religious conservatives and by academic supporters of religious exemptions is opportune but confusing. We should not limit the discussion to discrimination against marrying or married gays or to gays alone. To do so suggests that gays or married gays should be put in a unique and less robustly protected class, a class distinct from victims of race or gender discrimination. Doing so raises the question I posed at the start of this essay. Should conservative religious believers be allowed a broad religious exemption from bans on, for example, racial discrimination in employment, housing, or public accommodations?

The fundamental issue is far broader than discrimination in connection with same-sex marriage. The exemption issue is broader in at least two ways. First, antidiscrimination laws have prohibited discrimination based on race or gender as well. (They did so when compliance collided with widely and deeply held religious convictions.) For gays, similar legal protection is in its early stages. In contrast to race, gays are not protected by a general national law against discrimination in employment, housing, or public accommodations, though there is protection under many state or local laws.

Second, discrimination against gays has a much broader impact than, for example, merely refusing to bake a wedding cake for a gay marriage. Discrimination need not be in any way connected to gay marriage, though it could be. Narrowing the focus to those unwilling to be seen as assisting gay marriage appears to provide much narrower exemptions than the logic of the Becket Fund approach, for example, seems to advocate. In any case, it fails to fully address the problem of wide-ranging discrimination against married gays or gays in general and the religious basis for that discrimination. It fails to confront the views of many religious objectors to gay equality and liberty, views that would seem to call for more pervasive discrimination than that limited to providing services for the marriage.

Discrimination against gays is not typically tied to gay marriage, though gay marriage may make it easier to identify gays and so practice discrimination against them. A hotel or inn could refuse to serve gay couples because providing the bed would be assisting the "sin." With exemptions from antidiscrimination laws for gay marriage, marriage becomes, in effect, a proxy for being gay.

The obsessive focus on marriage may well obscure the broader protection that proposed exemptions may provide for discrimination based on sexual orientation. At any rate, it is hard to see marriage as a stopping point. Groups seeking exemptions seem to be using the threat of gay marriage to obtain exemptions based on principles that go well beyond services for or in direct connection with gay weddings. If successful, they are likely to weaken antidiscrimination laws that protect gays, even in the great majority of jurisdictions that ban gay marriage. In any case, it is hard to see why discrimination against gays would (or from the religious objector's perspective should) end after the vows are exchanged. This critique does not extend to efforts to provide exemptions for churches and their ministers, for example. These are constitutionally required in any case.

IV. The Laycock Effort at Reconciliation

Professor Douglas Laycock has proposed narrower exemptions than, for example, what the Becket Fund seeks. Laycock and Robin Fretwell Wilson have edited a book dealing with the conflict they see between gay marriage and religious liberty.[64] Professor Laycock suggests the interests of religious minorities (or majorities, depending on the state) and sexual minorities could easily be on the same side.[65] According to Professor Laycock:

> In resisting legal and social pressures to conform to majoritarian norms, they make essentially parallel and mutually reinforcing claims against the larger society. They claim that some aspects of human identity are so

> fundamental that they should be left to each individual, free of all nonessential regulation, even when manifested in conduct. No human being should be penalized because of his beliefs about religion, or because of his sexual orientation. And no human being should be penalized because of her religious practice, or because of her choice of sexual partners, unless her conduct is actually inflicting significant and cognizable harm on some other person.[66]

There is a problem with this worthy and moving effort at reconciliation. The principle that no person should be harmed because of her choice of sexual partners is a worthy one. So is the denial of an exemption for conduct that is "actually inflicting significant and cognizable harm on some other person." The problem is that these principles are inconsistent with the religiously inspired conduct of a person in the private sector (1) who discharges married (or single) gay people from their jobs, (2) who denies spousal or partner health insurance to them, or (3) who refuses to rent an apartment to gay people or to married gay people. The principles are also inconsistent with the conduct of those who discriminate against married or marrying gays in commercial services available to everyone else. Exemptions in all these areas seem to be contemplated by the Becket Fund, at least for the married.[67] An individual who is discharged from a private sector job because of sexual orientation or his or her gay marriage, or who is denied the ability to purchase a house or rent an apartment of his or her choice, is harmed, often very grievously. The problem persists even in the Laycock effort to limit the right to discriminate. Discrimination based on sexual orientation also causes psychological harm.[68] It is a mark of a caste system, which is so regardless of whether the discrimination is motivated by religious belief.

As a constitutional matter, after *Employment Division v. Smith*,[69] a religious objection is not sufficient to bar application of generally applicable laws aimed at conduct (such as discrimination) rather than belief. In contrast, religious beliefs, such as the sinfulness of homosexuality or the sinfulness of interracial marriage, are protected by the First Amendment.

The idea of discriminating against committed, recognized relationships, as opposed to uncommitted, potentially transient ones, is bizarre. As we have seen, the Becket Fund proposes to accommodate religious conduct by individuals who, for example, discriminate against married gays in access to employment, to housing, to public accommodations, and to services of business serving the public.[70]

Professors Laycock and Wilson would accommodate at least some denials of service. They provide more limited exemptions for discrimination based on religious or moral conviction. Professors Laycock and

Wilson focus on discrimination against married or marrying gays, and so does the Becket Fund. Today, in some 20 states, antidiscrimination statutes now protect gays generally, with limited religious exemptions for churches and religious organizations. The religious exemptions that Professors Laycock and Wilson think should be written into these antidiscrimination statutes would often trump the discrimination claim, at least with reference to same-sex couples. For the Becket Fund, the exemptions would seemingly always trump the antidiscrimination claim. In contrast, Professors Laycock and Wilson would recognize some exceptions. Here is Professor Laycock's explanation:

> The scope of any right to refuse service to same-sex couples must depend on comparing the harm to the couple of being refused service and the harm to the merchant or service provider of being coerced to provide service. What is most importantly at stake for each side is the right to live out core attributes of personal identity. In my view, the right to one's own moral integrity should generally trump the inconvenience of having to get the same service from another provider nearby. Requiring a merchant to perform services that violate his deeply held moral commitments is far more serious, different in kind and not just in degree, from mere inconvenience.[71]

To protect against unfair surprise, Professor Laycock suggests a notice on a website or a sign in the door announcing the refusal of service should suffice.[72] (How will it read? "We will not serve gay couples"?) Professor Laycock would perhaps limit the exemption to smaller businesses, but he gives no guidance as to what size limits he would prefer.[73] He also would strike the balance differently if it could be shown that gays were pervasively denied service.[74] Indeed, at times, he seems to narrowly circumscribe the right to discriminate: "[W]hen a particular merchant's refusal to cooperate might actually delay or prevent the conduct he considers sinful, then he loses his rights and has to facilitate the sin."[75] If applied literally, this might swallow many exemptions. On the other hand, allowing discrimination if non-discriminating merchants can be found seems a quite different test.

It is hard to see how this would work in the real world, particularly if applied to housing and employment. An "is there an alternative?" version of a balancing test puts a thumb on the scale in a way that helps the religious discriminator. In the "robust" exemptions sought by the Becket Fund, the problem would be acute. Would the gay person have to prove all or most businesses would discriminate against him or her? The burden, presumably, of proving no acceptable alternatives, is on the plaintiff. By that approach not only must a plaintiff prove discrimination, but what else? That no other (nearby?) swimming park accepts married gays? That another comparable and equally convenient house is not available to married gays, or just that no house is? That a comparable job is not available or that no job is? How many times must the plaintiff be turned down for employment? If the merchant has the burden of showing the exemptions, is he not participating in the sin? By providing information on non-discriminating merchants, he will be facilitating the conduct he refused to be mixed up in.

In support of his effort at a balanced approach, Professor Laycock points to the Equal Access Act, by which both religious and gay clubs have access to school rooms after school hours.[76] (Of course, as Professor Laycock notes, religious conservatives sought to deny equal access to the gay groups.)[77] Free speech and association for both groups is a laudable development. But it is fundamentally different from exemptions from laws banning discrimination based on sexual orientation. Allowing diverse groups to meet to share common values and to express views (whether of acceptance or rejection of homosexuality) does not deny anyone a job or an apartment or access to services the rest of the community enjoys from a merchant.[78] In contrast, religiously inspired discrimination against married gays (or against gays generally) denies them access to public accommodations, employment, services, and housing otherwise generally available to the public.

V. A Principle and Examples of Application

As a matter of principle, discrimination based on sexual orientation should be as disfavored as racial or gender discrimination. Should the Congress have embraced exemptions for race discrimination based on religious beliefs? Consider these cases based on actual experiences, though the facts have been slightly modified.

Case 1. A black former army officer returns to civilian life after service to his country. He takes his daughter to an ice cream parlor in North Carolina to buy an ice cream cone. The proprietor, who is a strong believer in segregation, tells the man that he and his daughter will have to be served at the back, the place for "Negroes." Assume the discrimination violates the public accommodations law unless a religious exemption is included. If the owner bases his refusal on sincere religious belief in segregation, should he be free to treat the former soldier in this way because he is black? Would we be comfortable following, for race discrimination, Professor Laycock's proposed exemption plan for gays (or at least married or marrying gays)? Should we balance the supposedly slight inconvenience of getting ice cream at the back of the store against the supposedly more powerful case of religious conscience?

Case 2. A black child goes with his school class on an outing to Delightful Lake, a small private recreation park. The proprietor refuses to let the black child swim in the lake. Suppose he does so based on a religious conviction against integration. It is a small park. There are other parks. If the parents bring suit on behalf of the child, should they face a religious or moral exemption and have to show no other park would allow him to swim in order to prevail?

Let us suppose that the owner of the lake posts a warning on his website and has a "No Blacks Allowed" sign. The parents and the teacher know of it, but they decide it violates the law and demand equal service. Should the lake owner now be exempt from the law? The child stays away based on the signs, but the parents sue. There are other swimming pools and recreation parks that might not discriminate. Should the right to discriminate based on religious conviction trump the right against discrimination?

Case 3. A man in North Carolina owns four rental houses. He has strong religious beliefs against racial intermarriage. He rents one of his houses to a university professor. The landlord knows that the professor is married and that his wife will be joining him later. It turns out she is black and from Africa. At the end of the lease term the landlord tells the professor that he has decided to take the house off the market. That is false. The ruse is discovered when the professor's students apply to rent the house—as testers. Should the landlord's religious beliefs exempt him from damages or other relief under the Civil Rights Act of 1866, an act that would otherwise prohibit such conduct? Would such conduct be more excused if the landlord met the couple at first and refused to rent on the spot? After all there are undoubtedly other houses, and some landlords would not discriminate. Suppose the landlord puts a notice on his website and a sign on the door. Does that fix the problem?

All these examples involve for-profit commercial activity. In none of these cases would the religious objector be entitled to an exemption under current law. For most of us, our intuition would be that that result is right as a matter of sound public policy and should not be changed by statute. In the cases above, if we apply (or try to apply) Professor Laycock's balancing approach, treating race as he would sexual orientation, the religious objector wins, at least if other alternatives are available. But the result seems wrong. Looking for why it is wrong helps understand problems with the proposed exemption test for discrimination against gays and with its application by Professor Laycock.

Here are the things that are balanced when we treat race as Professor Laycock would treat sexual orientation (at least for the married or marrying): the minor inconvenience of having to go the back of the store with your young child to get your ice cream cone if you are black, balanced against the owner being coerced into violating deeply held religious and moral objections to integration. The description of the interests is radically incomplete. In the Laycock description transposed to race, we have a minor inconvenience on one side and the strong and grave interest against violating one's deeply held religious beliefs on the other. Being served ice cream at the back of the store, being barred from swimming at a particular pool because you are a black child, and being unable to rent a nice and convenient home are all examples of this sort of "minor inconvenience," and according to this approach, they should all fail to overcome the "strong interest" in preventing the coercion of believers to violate deeply held religious beliefs. (Of course, the alternative "no delay of the sin" approach, taken literally, could produce a result favorable to the victim of discrimination.)

A problem with balancing is how one describes and values the interests. If Professor Laycock has not inflated the religious interest, he has deflated both the interest of the victim of discrimination and the social interest in rooting out discrimination. The interest supported by the broad antidiscrimination law is not preventing a minor inconvenience, such as getting an ice cream cone at the back rather than the front of the store. (The back of the store alternative is admittedly very close at hand.) Instead, it is the interest in eliminating a racial caste system that has systematically degraded the rights of a whole people across a wide spectrum of interests—personal liberty, safety, equality in criminal justice, equality in opportunity, opportunity to participate in the political process, to name a few. It is the interest in not putting a group of people in an inferior and less protected class. And it is the interest in preventing a grave insult to human dignity, regardless of whether this insult arises from a "minor inconvenience," or from pervasive discrimination, or even from the threat of physical violence. For marrying gays, Professor Laycock leaves psychological damage out of his description. That is what Martin Luther King, Jr. called "the 'ultimate tragedy of segregation'—the psychological damage that white supremacist ideology had inflicted on those blacks who had internalized its lessons."[79]

Those of us who have not been discriminated against based on sexual orientation may underrate the harm and see it as mere minor inconvenience, as opposed to, say, a basic assault on the human dignity of the person discriminated against. We may overlook the effects of the discrimination in legitimizing a cruel caste system. Indeed, under the exemption system, it is possible that discriminating against gays will become more fashionable, a badge of religious honor. Professor Laycock's signs might proliferate.

The law sends messages. The antidiscrimination law sends a message that the racial caste system, or a similar one based on sexual orientation, is wrong and illegal. Applying the law to particular acts of discrimination emphasizes the message. The message sent by allowing religious exemptions is that discrimination is wrong and illegal—except when it is right and legal. It is illegal and wrong unless your deeply held religious beliefs support the caste system and, by one version, unless the victim of discrimination can find a convenient alternative. The right to discriminate can convey a message (at least in certain circumstances) that it is right to do so.

General application is important. What would the result have been in the segregated South if exemptions based on religious convictions had been in place? The result would have been even worse if all "moral" objectors to integration were also included. Of course, Professor Laycock's caveat might have helped if no one would serve blacks. But the force of the law would have been greatly diminished, and problems of proving a case would have been increased. Gays have also suffered from pervasive prejudice and a caste system. They have long been treated as a disfavored group, and discrimination against gays has been considered acceptable and proper.

Many gays are afraid to identify themselves for fear of discrimination. But the more gays identify themselves, the more people will learn that gays are our children, our relatives, our friends, and our colleagues. That helps to break the caste system that puts gays in a special and disfavored class. So, general protection against discrimination helps to dismantle the caste system and to allow gays to come out, which further dismantles the caste system. Generally banning discrimination in housing, employment, commercial transactions, and public accommodations is important for that purpose. Exemptions undermine it.

The approach of some religious conservatives seems to suggest that because gays may be legally married in some states, they (or at least gay couples) must be open to discrimination by religious discriminators in those states (or, perhaps, in all states with antidiscrimination laws that cover gays). This will reinforce the caste system, encouraging self-deception and dissemblance by gays and making it more dangerous and painful for gays to come out. Our common basic interest in truth and honesty supports dismantling this caste system.

As a practical matter, employment discrimination is probably the most pressing problem. Employment is particularly crucial in these dismal times, when there is so little current interest in alleviating the plague of unemployment and when losing a job may consign a person to being without one for a very long time and perhaps to even being homeless. Lots of jobs come from small employers. For an individual denied a job because of sexual orientation or discharged because of it, the effect may be devastating. Housing would be next as a pressing problem. Public accommodation is less likely to be a pervasive problem. Most ice cream parlors will not check for sexual orientation, and merchants who behave that way (or who post Laycock signs) are likely to lose more than just the patronage of gays. Perhaps the problem would be self-limiting.

VI. Legally Required Exemptions and Public Policy: Various Scenarios

A. Hypothetical 1: Public Policy

At one time, of course, the court gave heightened scrutiny to neither race nor gender and had not found the interest in antidiscrimination laws to be compelling. In the eyes of the Supreme Court, women and blacks were given no more, and indeed less, protection than the court gives gays today. Back then, as a matter of legislative policy, and faced with laws addressing public accommodations, equal housing, or equal employment, should the legislature have provided exemptions for race and gender discrimination when the violation was based on religious or moral principles? If the answer is no, why should discrimination based on sexual orientation be different today? Suppose exemptions were provided. How would allowing a religious or moral objection for race discriminators in the 1960s have affected the effort to uproot the racial caste system?

B. Hypothetical 2: In 1920, a State with a Religious Freedom Restoration Act Bans Discrimination Based on Race in Public Accommodations, Housing, and Employment

Think about an imaginary state that, in 1920, had a religious freedom restoration act, as well as a state law that banned racial discrimination in a commercial context—including housing, employment, and public accommodations. These hypothetical laws were passed before the US Supreme Court gave racial classifications substantially heightened scrutiny and before it found racial antidiscrimination laws supported by a compelling state interest. Assume that in 1920 the state constitutional law is where federal constitutional law was in 1920 as to race.

The state RFRA provided that the state government should not substantially burden a person's exercise of religion, even if the burden results from a rule of general applicability, except where the burden is in furtherance of a compelling governmental interest and is the least restrictive means of furthering that interest. Would the state RFRA test have protected religiously motivated race discriminators in the commercial sphere? Should it have? In short, should our imaginary early state RFRA have protected religious discriminators if race was treated no more protectively, and indeed even less protectively, than the court treats sexual orientation today?

If the state RFRA trumped state antidiscrimination laws, the effect would be to substantially weaken the antidiscrimination law. The legislature's general ban on racial discrimination by merchants would be effective only to the extent that the state court decided the interest was compelling or decided that applying the law in a commercial context did not substantially burden the exercise of religion.

C. *Hypothetical 3: Smith Comes Out the Other Way*

Suppose *Smith* had come out the other way. What about state laws that banned discrimination based on race, gender, and sexual orientation? Would religious discriminators be entitled to a *federal* constitutional exemption from the law?

After many years of a far different approach, the court held race to be a suspect class and gender to be a quasi-suspect class. In addition, the court ultimately held that the interest in rooting out race and gender discrimination is compelling.[80] In contrast, the court has not yet found the state interest in rooting out private discrimination based on sexual orientation to be compelling.[81] So today, the ban on race and gender discrimination would be safe from religious exemptions—providing the court did not upset precedent by holding that banning race and gender discrimination serves a compelling state interest.[82]

If *Employment Division v. Smith* had come out the other way, the fate of a law banning discrimination based on sexual orientation in provision of public commercial services would depend on the answers to two questions. The law would fall only if (1) the law substantially burdened a person's exercise of religion, and (2) if the ban on discrimination based on sexual orientation did not serve a compelling state interest.

In this alternate constitutional universe (where *Smith* came out the other way), suppose that a landlord who owns rental houses and an apartment house has strong religious objections to homosexuality. A married gay couple applies to rent the house or to get an apartment. The landlord says renting to the gay couple will substantially burden his exercise of religion. In our alternate universe, would the landlord be likely to prevail in the courts? Should he prevail? If he were to prevail, it is hard to see why, as a constitutional matter, the court would allow discrimination against married gays, but not against single gays.

D. *Hypothetical 4: Today, RFRA Still Limits Congress. Assume Congress Bans Discrimination against Gays in Housing, Employment, and Public Accommodations.*

Since the RFRA still limits Congress, and if Congress bans discrimination against gays in housing, employment, and public accommodations, religious discriminators who are merchants or landlords would likely claim a RFRA exemption. Although the federal Religious Freedom Restoration Act was unconstitutional as applied to the states, it is alive and well as applied to the federal government. Would the federal RFRA limit a later amendment to the 1964 and 1968 antidiscrimination acts by providing an exemption in the case of religious discriminators? Should the RFRA protect religiously motivated merchants who discriminate against gays in public accommodations, housing, and employment? If so, a law that was enacted to protect a member of a minority religion in the exercise of the rites of his church will have proved a Trojan Horse. The legal issue would be whether the government has a compelling state interest in eliminating discrimination against gays and whether a ban on discriminating against gays in commercial settings substantially burdens the merchant and landlord's exercise of religion. Either way of upholding the law is defensible—finding a compelling interest or no substantial burden on free exercise. But it is not hard to imagine judges ruling the other way. If so, a well-intentioned law designed to protect core religious practices may produce unacceptable results.

E. Current State Antidiscrimination Laws in a State with a State Religious Freedom Restoration Law

The same sorts of questions arise under current state laws.[83] Some states have RFRAs and have antidiscrimination laws that cover sexual orientation. Should state RFR laws be interpreted to protect religiously motivated discriminators in the public, commercial sphere? Is such discrimination an exercise of religion; is the interest in preventing discrimination compelling?

VII. Caveats

A. Balanced Compromise?

Perhaps a general national ban on discrimination against gays in employment (with an exception for businesses with, say, five or fewer employees) would be a trade worth making. The same would be true for exempting landlords who rent apartments in their residences, for example. Statutory exemptions without expansion of coverage are a one-sided deal. There is no reason to think that religious and moral exemptions will stop the holy war against gay marriage. In fact, "[29] states have constitutional bans on same-sex marriages, and [12] have laws against it."[84] In any case, religious conservatives would be most unlikely to support either gay marriage or broader antidiscrimination statutes covering gays even with exemptions for small establishments or with religious exemptions. Supporting exemptions from laws that already protect gays, without in any way broadening such protections, is unbalanced. On the other hand, the New York law, with its exemption for churches, is an example of a pragmatic compromise.

B. Limited Exception for Churches

Churches will need to be allowed to choose their pastors, ministers, rabbis, and religious teachers. Otherwise they might be unable to teach their doctrines, a result that would implicate both free speech and free exercise of religion. Ministers may decide who they will marry. Many state laws have such exemptions in place, exemptions that accord with constitutional requirements. There is no reason to think gay marriage can or should change things.

C. The Patronage Trap: The Church as a Provider of Government Services

Churches may be able to use their political power to get government social service jobs transferred to the churches and still funded by the government. If so, employees should not lose their jobs, nor should future employees be denied employment based on sexual orientation, or religion for that matter, whatever the views of the church. If the church elects to provide a formerly public function and be funded by public funds in doing so, its claim of a right to discriminate should be denied.

D. Free Speech Issues

The civil rights struggle of the 1960s achieved immense gains without denying free speech to opponents of racial equality. Gays have also made substantial progress under a free speech regime.[85] Proposals to limit speech on matters of public concern because the speaker opposes gay equality raise the gravest First Amendment concerns. For many reasons beyond the scope of this essay, that is a route to be avoided.[86]

E. The Abortion Analogy

One analogy suggested by advocates of exemptions is to the conscience exemptions provided in terms of assisting with an abortion. To me, interracial marriage is the better analogy. In any case, the suggestion should not reassure the supporters of gay rights. The right to an abortion has been shrinking continually under a sustained, unremitting assault. Recently several states have banned abortion after 20 weeks, in some cases having unwise and cruel effects on women's health.[87] The conscience exemptions did not stem the assault on abortion. As a pragmatic matter, they are not an encouraging model for gay equality and liberty. Professors Lupu and Tuttle discuss the abortion conscience exception in their article on same-sex family equality.[88] Interested readers can pursue problems with the analogy there.

CONCLUSION

The best way to think about the claim that gay marriage requires expanded exemptions from existing laws for religious discriminators is in the larger context of both race and gender discrimination and in the larger context of discrimination against gays outside of gay marriage—as well as in the case of discrimination against people in same-sex marriages. The racial analogy may help some see why the harms of discrimination against gays are substantial and why broad exemptions are problematic. If so, this essay will have been a modest success.

NOTES

1. "Same-Sex Marriage and State Anti-Discrimination Laws," The Becket Fund for Religious Liberty, January 2009.
2. Civil Rights Act of 1964, Pub. L. No. 88–352, §§ 201–07, 78 Stat. 241, 243–46.
3. Ibid. § 703, 78 Stat. at 255–57.
4. 388 U.S. 1, 12 (1967).
5. Ibid., 6 n. 5.
6. Emp't Div., Dep't of Human Res. of Oregon v. Smith, 494 U.S. 872, 889 (1990).
7. See Perez v. Lippold, 32 Cal. 2d 711, 731–32 (1948).
8. Civil Rights Act of 1964, Pub. L. No. 88–352, 78 Stat. 241.
9. Jones v. Alfred H. Mayer Co., 392 U.S. 409, 413 (1968). "[The Civil Rights Act of 1866] bars all racial discrimination, private as well as public, in the sale or rental of property, and that . . . statute, thus construed, is a valid exercise of the power of Congress to enforce the Thirteenth Amendment."
10. Title VII of the Civil Rights Act of 1964 only applied to employers who had 25 or more employees. § 703, 78 Stat. at 253.
11. 42 U.S.C. § 1982 (2006).
12. According to the Department of Housing and Urban Development website, "[i]n some circumstances, the Act exempts owner-occupied buildings with no more than four units, single-family housing sold or rented without the use of a broker, and housing operated by organizations and private clubs that limit occupancy to members." "Fair Housing—It's Your Right," US Department of Housing and Urban Development, accessed February 7, 2012, http://portal.hud.gov/hudportal/HUD?src=/program_offices/fair_housing_equal_opp/FHLaws/yourrights.

13. Religious Freedom Restoration Act of 1993, Pub. L. No. 103–141, 107 Stat. 1488 (1993).
14. See, for example, Conn. Gen. Stat. Ann. § 52–571b (West 2009). For a more detailed look at issues caused by state RFRAs, see Christopher C. Lund, "Religious Liberty after Gonzalez: A Look at State RFRAs," *South Dakota Law Review* 55 (2010): 466.
15. The Declaration of Independence, para. 2 (1776).
16. On the significance of the Preamble for constitutional analysis, see Harold Anthony Lloyd, "'Original' Means Old, 'Original' Means New: An 'Original' Look at What 'Originalists' Do," *National Lawyers Guild Review* 67 (2010): 141. Lloyd notes the framing and aspirational language of the Constitution's Preamble.
17. See, for example, G.T. Gillespie, *A Christian View on Segregation* (Greenwood, MS: Educational Fund of the Citizens' Councils, 1954), 8–10. Gillespie cites several passages from Genesis, along with Leviticus 19:19 and Deuteronomy 7:3, to support segregation.
18. U.S. Const. amend. XIII, § 1.
19. U.S. Const. amend. XIV, § 1.
20. U.S. Const. amend. XV, § 1.
21. U.S. Const. amend. XIX.
22. U.S. Const. amend. XXIV, § 1.
23. *The Civil Rights Cases*, 109 U.S. at 9; *Cruikshank*, 92 U.S. at 548; *Prigg*, 41 U.S at 608.
24. See, for example, Civil Rights Act of 1866, 42 U.S.C. § 1981 (2006), declaring that people born in the United States are citizens—regardless of race, color, or previous condition of slavery or involuntary servitude—and granting such citizens full and equal enjoyment of all laws and provisions for the security of person and property as enjoyed by white citizens); Don't Ask, Don't Tell Repeal Act of 2010, Pub. L. No. 111–321, 124 Stat. 3515. The act repealed Don't Ask, Don't Tell, which allowed gays to be discharged from military service if their sexual orientation was discovered.
25. Civil Rights Act of 1964, Pub. L. No. 88–352, 78 Stat. 241.
26. 42 U.S.C. §§ 1973–1973aa –6 (2006).
27. Civil Rights Act of 1968, Pub. L. 90–284, §§ 801–819, 82 Stat. 73, 81–89.
28. Equal Pay Act of 1963, Pub. L. No. 88–38, 77 Stat. 56.
29. § 702, 78 Stat. at 255.
30. See, for example, Cal. Civ. Code § 51 (Deering Supp., 2011), which banned discrimination because of sexual orientation (along with race, sex, etc.) in public accommodations; Cal. Gov't Code § 12940 (Deering Supp., 2011), which banned discrimination because of sexual orientation (along with race, sex, etc.) in employment; Cal. Gov't Code § 12955 (Deering Supp., 2011), which banned discrimination because of sexual orientation (along with race, sex, etc.) in housing.

31. See Juan Williams, "The 1964 Civil Rights Act—Then and Now," *Human Rights Magazine* 31.3 (Summer 2004), http://www.americanbar.org/publications/human_rights_magazine_home/human_rights_vol31_2004/summer2004/irr_hr_summer04_1964cra2.html.
32. In the mid-1980s, as I recall, I appeared before the North Carolina House or Senate Judiciary Committee regarding N.C. Gen. Stat. § 14–177.
33. This example is based on an interview I conducted with the married couple shortly after the events, as well as a review at that time of the transcript of the preliminary hearing and other sources. See Michael K. Curtis and Shannon Gilreath, "Transforming Teenagers into Oral Sex Felons: The Persistence of the Crime against Nature after *Lawrence v. Texas*," *Wake Forest Law Review* 43 (2008): 160–61.
34. See N.C. Gen. Stat. § 14–177 (2009); see also State v. Whiteley, 616 S.E.2d 576, 580–81 (N.C. App. 2005), which argued upholding the "crime against nature" statute as facially constitutional, and holding that it was improper to give a jury instruction regarding whether there was consent for the sexual acts, as no consent is required under the statute.
35. Teenagers are another matter. See Curtis and Gilreath, "Transforming Teenagers," 156.
36. 494 U.S. 872 (1990).
37. Ibid., 890.
38. Ibid., 874.
39. Ibid.
40. Reynolds v. United States, 98 U.S. 145, 162 (1879). Mormon religious belief in a duty to marry multiple wives was insufficient to void conviction under the Morrill Anti-Bigamy Act of 1862.
41. See, for example, Sherbert v. Verner, 374 U.S. 398, 401–02 (1963). Denial of employment compensation based on religious belief against working on Saturdays unconstitutionally burdened the free exercise of religion. Cf. Wisconsin v. Yoder, 406 U.S. 205, 234 (1972). Here was an exemption for Amish children from having to go to school beyond the eighth grade.
42. Religious Freedom Restoration Act of 1993, Pub. L. No. 103–141, §2, 107 Stat. 1488, 1488.
43. Ibid., § 3, 107 Stat. at 1488.
44. City of Boerne v. Flores, 521 U.S. 507, 508–09 (1997).
45. See Max Blumenthal, "Agent of Intolerance," *Nation*, May 16, 2007, http://www.thenation.com/article/agent-intolerance.
46. Loving v. Virginia, 388 U.S. 1, 3 (1967).
47. W. Chester & Phila. R.R. Co. v. Miles, 55 Pa. 209, 215 (1867).
48. Ibid., 213. Fay Botham surveyed court cases relying on religion to oppose race mixing from 1867–1964. Botham, *God Created*, 155–61.
49. See, for example, Naim v. Naim, 197 Va. 80, 87 S.E.2d 749, 752, 756 (1955), which upheld the antimiscegenation statute and voided an interracial marriage, using the language from the Pennsylvania case; Harris v. City of Louisville, 165 Ky. 559, 177 S.W. 472, 477 (1915), which upheld

a residential segregation statute; Berea Coll. v. Commonwealth, 123 Ky. 209, 94 S.W. 623, 627–28 (1906), which required segregation of a private college; Bowie v. Birmingham Ry. & Elec. Co., 125 Ala. 397, 27 So. 1016, 1018–20 (1900), which upheld segregation in transportation; Green v. State, 58 Ala. 190, 194, 197 (1877), which upheld a conviction for interracial marriage; State v. Gibson, 36 Ind. 389, 404–05 (1871), which upheld the same.

50. *Naim*, 87 S.E.2d, 752.
51. Botham, *God Created,* 156.
52. Dailey, "Sex, Segregation, and the Sacred"; see also Bill J. Leonard, "A Theology for Racism: Southern Fundamentalists and the Civil Rights Movement," *Baptist History and Heritage* 34 (1999): 49.
53. Dailey, "Sex, Segregation, and the Sacred," 125 (quoting Theodore G. Bilbo, *Take Your Choice: Separation or Mongrelization* (Poplarville, MS: Dream House Publishing Co., 1947), 109).
54. Ibid.
55. Ibid.
56. Ibid., 130–33.
57. Ibid., 126.
58. See, for example, Michael Kent Curtis, *Free Speech, "The People's Darling Privilege": Struggles for Freedom of Expression in American History* (Durham, NC: Duke University Press, 2000), 224–26; see also William Ellery Channing, *Slavery* (Boston: James Munroe and Co., 1835), 8–11, 110–13; Paul Finkelman, *Defending Slavery: Proslavery Thought in the Old South: A Brief History with Documents* (Boston: Bedford/St. Martin's, 2003), 13.
59. See, for example, Matthew 7:12 (NAS). "In everything, therefore, treat people the same way you want them to treat you. . . ." For a discussion of biblical passages commonly treated as about homosexuality in context, see Jack Rogers, "What the Bible Says and Doesn't Say about Homosexuality," in *Jesus, the Bible, and Homosexuality: Explode the Myths, Heal the Church* (Louisville, KY: Westminster Knox Press, 2009). See also ibid., "Real People and Real Marriage."
60. See, for example, Leviticus 25:44 (NIV): "Your male and female slaves are to come from the nations around you; from them you may buy slaves."; 1 Peter 2:18 (NIV): "Slaves, submit yourselves to your masters with all respect, not only to those who are good and considerate, but also to those who are harsh."; Genesis 9:20–27 (the curse of Ham); see also Finkelman, *Defending Slavery*, 31–33, which cites Bible passages accepting slavery.
61. The Lutherans now ordain gay ministers based on the same criteria as heterosexual ministers. See Michael Luo and Christina Capecchi, "Lutheran Group Lifts Limits on Gay Clergy," *The New York Times*, August 22, 2009, A9. Presbyterians likewise allow openly gay people in same-sex relationships to be ordained as ministers, elders, and deacons. Laurie Goodstein, "Presbyterians Approve Ordination of Gay People," *The New York Times*, May 11, 2011, A14.

62. See, for example, Bradwell v. Illinois, 83 U.S. 130, 141 (1873) (Bradley, J., concurring). "The natural and proper timidity and delicacy which belongs to the female sex evidently unfits it for many of the occupations of civil life. . . . [T]he domestic sphere . . . properly belongs to [women]. . . . The paramount destiny and mission of woman are to fulfill the noble and benign offices of wife and mother. This is the law of the Creator."
63. Robin Wilson, Charles J Reid, and Douglas Laycock each lay out variations of a plan to incorporate religious exemptions into hypothetical laws recognizing gay marriage in *Same-Sex Marriage and Religious Liberty: Emerging Conflicts*, ed. Douglas Laycock, Anthony R. Picarello, Jr., and Robin Fretwell Wilson (Lanham, MD: Rowman & Littlefield Publishers, Inc., 2008), 98, 186, 193.
64. Laycock, Picarello, and Wilson, *Same-Sex Marriage*.
65. Douglas Laycock, "Afterword," in ibid., 189.
66. Ibid.
67. "Same-Sex Marriage," Becket Fund, 2.
68. See, for example, "Suicide Risk and Prevention for Lesbian, Gay, Bisexual, and Transgender Youth," *Suicide Prevention Resource Center* (2008), 20–22, http://www.sprc.org/library/SPRC_LGBT_Youth.pdf.
69. 494 U.S. 872 (1990).
70. "Same-Sex Marriage," *Becket Fund,* 2.
71. Laycock, "Afterword," 198.
72. Ibid., 198–99.
73. Ibid., 199.
74. Ibid.
75. Ibid., 200.
76. 20 U.S.C. § 4071 (2010).
77. Laycock, "Afterword," 189, 190–91. For a trenchant critique of the Laycock and Wilson approach and their analogies and a careful discussion of how to balance religious concerns and gay marriage, see generally Ira C. Lupu and Robert W. Tuttle, "Same-Sex Family Equality and Religious Freedom," *Northwestern Journal of Law and Social Policy* 5 (2010): 274 –306.
78. Compare W. Va. State Bd. of Educ. v. Barnette, 319 U.S. 624, 635–42 (1943), which recognized the difference between religious exemptions from generally applicable laws and free speech rules that protect all, with Minersville Sch. Dist. v. Gobitis, 310 U.S. 586, 594–95 (1940), which refused any religious exemptions from a generally applicable law.
79. Michael J. Klarman, *From Jim Crow to Civil Rights: The Supreme Court and the Struggle for Racial Equality* (New York: Oxford University Press, 2004), 163.
80. See, for example, Grutter v. Bollinger, 539 U.S. 306, 327–28 (2003); Roberts v. U.S. Jaycees, 468 U.S. 609, 623 (1984).
81. Cf. Boy Scouts of Am. v. Dale, 530 U.S. 640, 648 (2000), which held the First Amendment freedom of association allows the Boy Scouts to exclude a gay scout leader from membership because his presence "affect[ed] in a significant way the group's ability to advocate public or private viewpoints."

But cf. *Lawrence*, 539 U.S. at 573–75; *Romer*, 517 U.S. at 631, which used heightened rational basis review.

82. See, for example, *Roberts*, 468 U.S. at 623; *Grutter*, 539 U.S. at 327–28.
83. For a more detailed look at state RFRAs, see Lund, "Religious Liberty."
84. Nicholas Confessore, "Beyond New York, Gay Marriage Faces Hurdles," *The New York Times*, June 27, 2011, A1.
85. See Michael Kent Curtis, "Be Careful What You Wish For: Gays, Dueling High School T-Shirts, and the Perils of Suppression," *Wake Forest Law Review* 44 (2009): 437–49.
86. See ibid.
87. See Erik Eckholm, "Several States Forbid Abortion after 20 Weeks," *The New York Times*, June 26, 2011, A10.
88. See Lupu and Tuttle, "Same-Sex Family Equality," 20–22.

CHAPTER 5

Accommodation as Establishment: State Sponsorship of Religious Pilgrimages in Nigeria

Simeon O. Ilesanmi

Introduction

Since its existence as a territorial unit of the international community, Nigeria has wrestled with the challenge of the perceived dissonance between its avowed political and legal norms and their equitable application to the diverse and competing spheres of culture and society. With its origin as a modern nation-state in the arbitrary colonial amalgamation of socially disparate and culturally unaffiliated peoples, it has sought to define a new cultural identity, through constitutional and democratic avenues, which would prevent the identification of the state with any one of the cultural segments within it. Even during the intermittent interregna of military regimes, a semblance of constitutionalism was always maintained by promulgating edicts and co-opting judicial functionaries so as to douse, even if unsuccessful, the impression that military rule is irreconcilable with the rule of law. Notwithstanding the abysmal performance of its rulers, past and present, the belief remains strong among Nigeria's citizens that the country's political and economic renaissance lies in an unyielding commitment and genuine fidelity to democratic values anchored in constitutional practice. The preamble to the 1999 Constitution, not unlike its predecessors, boldly declares the constitution as the supreme law of the land and its provisions as having "binding force on all authorities and persons throughout the Federal Republic of Nigeria."[1]

Moreover, contrary to popular belief, these modernist sentiments did not derive from the colonial transplantation of European Enlightenment philosophy, neither are they dysfunctional imitations of Western constitutional orders; rather, they are partly rooted in the endogamous triple religious heritage of the country[2]—Islam, Christianity, and traditional religions—whose adherents, according to one scholar, "are hard to distinguish on the subject of democracy."[3]

Yet, the relationship between religion and the Nigerian state remains, at best, ambiguous and, at worst, ominous. Arguably the fastest growing industry in the country, religion has also "always formed a shadow over the Nigerian federation, and has, since May 1999, not only formed a darker shadow over the polity, but even threatened to eclipse it."[4] Muslims, Christians, and adherents of the traditional religions are divided over the limits, if any, that should be imposed on their freedom, and the scope of responsibility they should have in shaping political life, broadly construed. Their disagreement remains the single most important issue in Nigeria's postcolonial history and is rendered more complex by other streams of pluralism that are latent in the country, including ethnicity, class, and region. In addition, the absence of common symbols of discourse deriving from the indigenous traditions with which to think and speak as Nigerians about the meaning of political reality and responsibility, coupled with the frequent eruption of civil tumults in the country, complicate the task of articulating an account of the proper relation between religion and the state.[5]

The coalescence of these conflicting signals—on the one hand, a commitment to the rule of law and, on the other, the "divergent epistemic notions of democracy that are disputed on cultural grounds"[6]—creates the need to reexamine the integrity of Nigeria's evolving experiment regarding the constitutional status of religion. It is not enough that a country declares an adherence to a constitution, written or unwritten, it is also necessary to inquire about the motivational rationale behind that commitment. As Richard Joseph rightly observes, "many contemporary dictatorships have constitutions which serve more to camouflage the exercise of power than to guide and determine it."[7] Ernst Troeltsch has suggested that any regulative policy of the state regarding its official position on religion must be guided by "the inner position of society vis-à-vis the religious life generally."[8] David Martin specifies this principle more clearly as referring to the "objective patterns—or frames—of religion-society relationships," by which he means the number and variety of religious confessions in a society, on the one hand, and the degree to which that circumstance is, as a matter of degree, rigid or flexible, on the other.[9]

A central argument of this chapter is that the motivational rationale behind the current constitutional definitions of religion in Nigeria lies in the wide acknowledgment of the normative importance of the country's contextual plurality. To the extent that this is true, Nigeria can be said to have distinguished itself from other similarly situated postcolonial states that opted for a different constitutional direction. In order to avoid the charge of what one scholar characterized as "intra-imperial isomorphism" in their national constitutions, which refers to the act of imitating and reproducing the putatively secular constitutional models of the former colonizing powers, countries such as Pakistan, Malaysia, and Tunisia, among others, "either: (a) explicitly name a specific religion as the official state religion, (b) make reference to a specific religion as providing certain legal principles, (c) have some kind of provisions which directly elevate a particular religion or (d) have some combination of these."[10] However, in so doing, these countries undermined the process by which a sociologically diverse society can become a democratic, pluralist polity.[11]

Generally speaking, "a pluralistic polity is one in which the collectivity is divisible along the axes of self and other, whether in terms of recognition of ethnic, cultural or religious differences, or of an individualism revolving around a multiplicity of values and objectives."[12] Of pluralism and constitutional government "in our time, it can be said that, like love and marriage in an old sweet song, 'you cannot have one without the other.'"[13] In the absence of some kind of pluralism, modern constitutionalism would make little, if any, sense. Their interdependence is a reflection of their common association with certain normative presuppositions from which they derive their valence and identity. These include "the idea of the legal subject, the inviolability without due process of the sovereignty of the subject, the separation of powers in the state, the presupposition of innocence and the impartiality of the operators of the system, and the necessity for the judiciary to remain an arbiter between the powerless individual and the all-powerful state."[14] In short, pluralism is the primary reason for embracing constitutionalism and the end that this ideal is intended to serve. "In a completely homogenous society, with a commonly shared secular or religious conception of the good, constitutionalism would be superfluous, as the governors would be identified with the governed, the law makers with those subject to laws, and as the organically cohesive polity would delimit a normative realm relying on duties rather than on rights."[15]

However, the linkage between constitutionalism and pluralism is neither merely conceptual nor accidental; it arose out of historical experience and judgments about the most desirable way to handle the phenomenon of *difference* in human society. Differences of world views, religious convictions, and conceptions of the good had been used in the past—as they are still being used now—as justifications for persecution and discrimination. Constitutionalism reflects a deep political and moral orientation, construed in the West as political liberalism, that a certain set of institutional checks and balances needs to be created to mitigate the tendency of persons and groups to unleash evils against others on the basis of identity difference. I shall characterize this as the negative function of constitutionalism. There is also its positive function, arising from the same orientation, which is instantiated in the two realities that liberalism fosters: "cooperation between persons and groups of diverse normative persuasions, and the freedom of the same persons and groups to pursue their normative agenda."[16] Constitutionalism therefore has a dual relationship to pluralism: on the one hand, the reality and awareness of plurality or difference prompt a reflection upon how best to curb its deleterious effects; on the other hand, the response itself is designed to delimit the scope of pluralism without erasing it.

The current official status of religion in Nigeria seems to have been guided by these substantive normative and procedural perspectives on constitutional democracy and its pluralist inflection. It is a complex and arguably ambiguous status, given the multiple references to religion in the constitution. The two prominent ones are the non-adoption of religion and the free exercise clauses in sections 10 and 38(1), respectively.[17] In theory, Nigeria operates a federal system that presupposes a relative autonomy and interdependence of the national, state, and local government levels or "a dynamic process of cooperation and shared action"[18] among all three; in practice, the country actually has one national constitution. Accordingly, these regulative principles apply to both federal and state governments, thus making unnecessary the device of the doctrine of incorporation typically used in other jurisdictions to extend the application of federal law to the states.[19]

Most commentators have limited their discussion of religion-state relations in Nigeria to the import of these two provisions and how they interact with each other. A standard interpretation of the non-adoption clause, for example, is that it confers a secular status on the Nigerian state and restricts religion to the private realm. This interpretation accords lexical priority to the non-adoption norm over the free exercise principle, seeing the institutionalization of secularity as a precondition for a legitimate exercise and enjoyment of religious freedom. In his plea for what he calls the "the politics of the public sphere," which "presumes basic secularity and the relationality of religious *truths*," Ebenezer Obadare asserts that Nigeria's goal of becoming "an all-inclusive political community" would be undermined and its democratic aspirations frustrated if "polarized religious and ideological persuasions" are not held to "an integrative social vision."[20] Similarly, Jibrin Ibrahim calls for an overlapping consensus among Nigeria's social forces on the sanctity of "a domain of the profane that cannot be subsumed by the religious domain, irrespective of the level of religiosity in question."[21] One is reminded of a similar argument made by Philip Kurland, commenting on the relationship between the establishment clause and the free exercise clause in the First Amendment to the US Constitution, that "the clauses should be read as stating a single precept: that government cannot utilize religion as a standard for action or inaction because these clauses, read together as they should be, prohibit classification in terms of religion either to confer a benefit or to impose a burden."[22]

On the opposite side are those who contend that attributing secularity to the Nigerian state, on the basis of section 10, would contravene the free exercise norm, which guarantees a zone of freedom to every citizen for maximal expression of their religious or nonreligious fundamental beliefs. The latter view contends that the logic of secularity entails certain philosophical assumptions about the relationship between the individual and the state, private and public, spiritual and temporal, which are incompatible with the orthodoxies of certain religious traditions. The complementary aim of the non-adoption and the free exercise provisions, it is contended, is to protect freedom of religious beliefs and actions.[23] Although the secularists use the metaphor of separation, the anti-secularists emphasize accommodation, to articulate their respective visions of the proper relationship between religion and the Nigerian state. Each side seems entrenched in its position and the impasse created by their mutual rigidity has unfortunately fueled the impression that "religion is an anomaly, requiring exotic constitutional treatment different from anything else."[24] They both overlook the fact that "the Constitution expresses special concern for religion because of and to the extent that religious difference inspires inequality in stature and reward, and accordingly, that the constitution's fundamental religion-specific goal is that of opposing discrimination."[25] Although each view contains an important partial truth that accounts for its attraction, each fails to recognize the partial truth in the other view. Each view, therefore, is inadequate to the task of offering a morally defensible interpretation of the religion provisions in the Nigerian Constitution or providing guidance on how religious beliefs, practices, and institutions should be properly related to the Nigerian state.

I defend a third view, anchored in the notion of equal liberty, which I argue is what is envisioned in the nondiscrimination principle found in section 42 of the constitution, according to which

> A citizen of Nigeria or a particular community, ethnic group, place of origin, sex, religion or political opinion shall not, by reason only that he is such a person, (a) be subjected either expressly by, or in the practical application of, any law in force in Nigeria or any executive or administrative action of the government, to disabilities or restrictions to which citizens of Nigeria of other communities, ethnic groups, places of origin, sex, religious or political opinions are not made subject; or (b) be accorded either expressly by, or in the practical application of, any law in force in Nigeria or any executive or administrative action, any privilege or advantage that is not accorded to citizens of Nigeria of other communities, ethnic groups, places of origin, sex, religious or political opinions.

Rather than engage in an abstract discussion of the idea of equal liberty or a sweeping assessment of the goodness of religion in general and its optimal role in public life, I will focus on one example of religion-state entanglement that raises the issue of distributional fairness and underscores the mediating role of the nondiscrimination principle vis-à-vis the norms of non-adoption and free exercise. Government involvement in pilgrimage, at both federal and state levels, offers an opportunity to examine the utility of these principles as frameworks for handling Nigeria's own burden of democratic governance. To keen observers of Nigerian affairs, the pilgrimage issue seems the least candidate to test the practical value of constitutional prescriptions in setting the proper boundary between the secular and the sacred or to adjudicate conflicts that routinely erupt between the two spheres. For over two decades, Nigeria has been engulfed in the inferno of sharia controversy in all its multiple dimensions; the most recent is the adoption of this religious law by ten northern Nigerian states and the push by some Muslim constituencies to extend its influence and application to the southern part of the country. Although the furor surrounding the issue seems to have subsided a bit, no one doubts its possible eruption at any opportune moment in Nigeria's kaleidoscopic political milieu. More important, we should want to know why a characteristically volatile Nigerian political terrain has experienced minimal, if any, controversy on account of government sponsorship of pilgrimage, a sponsorship that involves not just huge financial expenditure but also the use of government resources, including personnel, property, time, and the unquantifiable imprimatur of the symbolic support of the state.

It can be surmised that the absence of an effective legal channel through which civil disagreements can be justly resolved is one among many reasons that Nigerians have not bothered to challenge the government for its involvement in what is ostensibly beyond its allotted responsibility. This does not mean that there are no judges and lawyers in Nigeria; in fact, the doctrine of separation of powers is writ large in the country's governmental structures. However, the judiciary has functioned more like an extension of and sometimes a lackey for the executive and legislative branches than an independent coequal branch. Although the symbolisms may be similar, the actual jurisprudential impact of the Supreme Court of Nigeria has been relatively minimal, compared with the role such institutions play in other democracies, notably the United States, where the court's decisions have "directly impacted the way people express themselves religiously on a daily basis and shaped [their] understanding of what it means to live in a democracy with substantial religious diversity."[26] But because of the fascist and autocratic tendencies of Nigerian governments, military and civilian, the nation's high court has been reluctant to issue authoritative pronouncements in "most of the leading cases that questioned some of the established norms of the Nigerian political system."[27] To have done so would have meant career suicide, if not literal death, for the judges concerned. Thus, for guidance on religion jurisprudence, whether about pilgrimage or other subjects, we will have to look elsewhere for "the 'lively sparks' that might ordinarily be expected from the judiciary in a complex and highly segmented nation-state like Nigeria."[28] It is to the analysis of these sparks that I now turn.

Pilgrimage Tradition in Nigeria: An Unequal Religious Requirement

Pilgrimage has been described as a journey undertaken by a person or group of persons to a sacred place, as an act of religious devotion. It is an integral part of the complex reality of religious life, existing at the intersection of myths, doctrines, and ritual. At one level, it resembles such mundane human activities as tourism, in that "both are born from a desire to travel, to head into an unknown, foreign place where one might experience new sights and sounds and tastes and smells, and ultimately to be corporeally inspired by some transcendent locale."[29] However, journeys undertaken for religious purposes possess certain characteristics that are lacking in other kinds of peripatetic adventures, including but not limited to "the existence of *sacred place* or pilgrimage center, *journey* to this place individually or in a group, with the hope of obtaining some *material or spiritual* benefits."[30] Although all three elements—the presumed supernatural power inherent in the pilgrimage site, the numinous quality of experiencing a temporary exile, and the economy of rewards—jointly imbue pilgrimage with a compelling rationale, its main attraction lies in the construction and preservation of sacred geography and the impact this has on the pilgrim's self-understanding and identity. The notion of sacred space "implies a hierophany, an opening to the holy or divine, a place where communication with sacred power is made possible."[31] Mircea Eliade, a historian and phenomenologist of religion, refers to such places as *axis mundi*, the center of the world. It is the point around which, symbolically speaking, the world rotates.[32] Examples of such places include the birthplace, location of life events, or tomb of a holy person, as well as natural objects like rivers, mountains, caves, islands, and strange features of the landscape that are believed to incarnate the spirit or radiate spiritual magnetism. Moreover, because sacred place "represents not only an 'opening' to heaven but also a reproduction, on the human scale, of the cosmos or of Creation itself," that is, "an *imago mundi*, an image of the original world order,"[33] every encounter with it induces expectations of unparalleled divine favors or even miracles. In short, the religious quality of pilgrimage makes it a potentially transformative journey for those who undertake it.

Every year thousands of Nigerians participate in this kind of journey. The destinations may vary, but the motivation and objectives are comparable. The tradition of going on pilgrimage predated the arrival of Islam and Christianity in Nigeria and remains an integral part of indigenous cultural life. The shrines of Oshun in the southwestern city of Oshogbo and of Arochuckwu in eastern Nigeria are examples of sacred sites that annually attract pilgrims seeking different kinds of divine favors and blessings.[34] The myths and symbols connected with these shrines are "expressive of the human search for the ultimate."[35] Similarly, every Christmas, members of the Celestial Church of Christ, an African initiated denomination, make pilgrimages to the holy city of Imeko, where the church's founder, Prophet Oschoffa, was buried. The church's constitution describes the Christmas pilgrimage as "a 'convocation' of members," ordained by the Holy Spirit, obligatory for consecrated evangelists of the church, and undertaken "in expectation of the blessing of anointment."[36] Prophet Oschoffa underscored the significance of the choice of this location in a message he reportedly received in a vision in 1973 and relayed to his members that "Mecca would be closed, that Jerusalem would cease to be in its accustomed place, and that God had chosen Imeko as the New Jerusalem."[37] This is precisely what Imeko has become, "a sort of Rome or Vatican in the heart of the African bush,"[38] according to one scholar, and the same can be said of Oshun and Arochukwu shrines. All of these signify the attempt to affirm the possibility of encountering the divine within the geographical boundary of Nigeria and to demystify the privileged status that seems to have been ascribed to the birth places of the two so-called world religions in the country. This attempt at recognizing the legitimacy of local pilgrimage centers is in consonance with earlier efforts by theologians and others to develop and prescribe normative agendas aimed at responding to the sociocultural and political contexts and concerns, spiritual and material, of Nigerians.

However, like much else about Nigeria and perhaps the whole of Africa, local interests and initiatives have never been able to completely resist the allure of outside alternatives and possibilities; in fact, in every instance of competition between the local and the foreign, it is the latter that tends to dictate the terms of the engagement, which not only assures its victory but also perpetuates the pernicious myth of the inherent inferiority of indigenous worldviews vis-à-vis outside cultural contenders. Thus, in what would undoubtedly be a disappointment for people like Prophet Oschoffa, Mecca has not been closed and Jerusalem remains in its accustomed place. Both locations continue to draw Nigerian pilgrims and are believed to bestow far greater spiritual benefits and social prestige than any other recognized local sacred sites. Constitutionally, it is within the right[39] of these Nigerians to choose any locations, foreign or local, as the places to fulfill what they understand to be the injunctions of their faith. What is at issue, then, is not that they prefer Mecca, Jerusalem, or other holy sites outside of Nigeria to local options, but that they enlist government support for their religious journeys. Whether or not such support constitutes an illicit boundary crossing or a permissible aid intended to remove a burden impeding the free exercise of religion is a question that the Nigerian state must confront.

Aside from legal and political considerations, another reason for addressing this question has to do with the ambiguous theological status of pilgrimage across the spectrum of religious traditions, especially the two that are dominant in Nigeria. Islam and Christianity may share a common Semitic origin, but their belief systems are defined by radically different doctrinal content. Islam is organized around five pillars of faith, one of which is the *hajj* or pilgrimage to Mecca, which every adult Muslim who is in a position to do so is required to perform at least once in his or her lifetime. Muslim authorities generally agree on the following requirements of eligibility for the hajj: (1) one must be a confessing Muslim who (2) has reached the age of puberty, (3) is of rational and sound mind, (4) is a freed man or woman, and (5) has the physical strength and health to undertake the rigors of the journey.[40] Islamic law also provides that a pilgrim "must possess sufficient means not only to cover the expenses of the journey but also to make provision for his dependents while he is away. This provision includes the payment of school fees for the children and the feeding of the family."[41] In addition, the pilgrim "must be sure of security of life; that is, that there is nothing on the way, such as war, epidemic, flood, that can threaten his life."[42]

The duty to perform the hajj rests on the authority of the Koran and the recorded practice of the prophet Muhammad (*sunnah*), as these are interpreted by the orthodox schools of Islamic law. Although the Islamic tradition acknowledged the Abrahamic origins of hajj sites and rituals,[43] the privileged status that Mecca has historically enjoyed is defended on the basis of scriptural evidence found in Surah 3:90–91, declaring that

> The first House of Worship founded for mankind was in Mecca. Blessed and guidance to mankind. In it are evident signs, even the Standing Place of Abraham; and whoever enters it is safe. And the pilgrimage to the temple is an obligation due to God from those who are able to journey there.

Islam prescribes other spiritual journeys, but when these are not made to Mecca and fall outside the designated pilgrimage season—the last month of the Islamic calendar, *Dhu al-Hijjah*—they are considered mere "visits" (*ziyaras*) that can never substitute for a hajj no matter how many times they are repeated. According to one scholar, "no combination of *ziyaras* can equal a hajj, even if their destinations include the prophet's mosque in Medina, the tombs of the most venerated imams in Iraq and Iran, or the final resting places of the thousands of saints and martyrs all across Asia and Africa."[44] The emergence of Mecca as the preeminent sacred city in Islam is further bolstered by Muhammad's farewell hajj performed there in 632 AD, an event that laid the foundation for what would subsequently be known as the hajj rites, a body of liturgical practices that took between one to two centuries after the prophet's death to evolve into a definitive form.[45]

Thus, although there are traditions of pilgrimages in other religious traditions, the hajj is in a class by itself. As already indicated, it is obligatory, not voluntary, and has to be performed in a single location, at a specific time, and in a prescribed manner. It is not an exaggeration that Muslims view it as the most important of Islam's five pillars and the crowning spiritual achievement of their lives. "When Muslims undertake the hajj," Bianchi explains, "they are reenacting decisive acts of monotheism's two greatest prophets—the very first and the very last. The drama reminds pilgrims of their bonds with Muslims around the world and with the millions of pilgrims who preceded them over fourteen centuries."[46] Being firmly rooted in scripture, combined with an unswerving focus on a single city, the hajj enjoys, as it always did, an "exalted religious status" that is "distinguished by unparalleled cosmopolitanism and continuity."[47] The director and head of department of Operation, Planning, Research and Statistics for the Muslim Pilgrims Welfare Agency in Kano, Nigeria, sees the "spirit of submission to God" and nourishment of spiritual joy, which the hajj makes possible, as among the reasons it has acquired this status.[48]

Just as in Islam, the image of Christian life on earth as *peregrinatio*[49] has played an important role in Christianity; however, the meaning and importance of pilgrimage is not explicit in this religion. Christian pilgrimage tradition has its origin in the Jewish antecedents, where a relatively simple practice of visiting sites linked to a marvelous event in the life of an individual Israelite or in the collective history of the community evolved into an elaborate event culminating in a sacred journey to Jerusalem. But early Christianity was ambivalent about the Jewish conception of the land as holy, in part because of the concern that it might encourage the localization of the divine as well as the internal disagreement within the tradition on the value of pilgrimage and sacred geography for the formation of Christian identity and assurance of salvation. In fact, four different approaches to pilgrimage are discernible during the formative centuries of Christianity, namely: "rejection, apathy, vacillation, and adjustment of one's stance as a result of social relationships, ecclesiastical crises, or theological controversies."[50] Jerome articulates one of these positions when he claims, following Paul, that if God is present everywhere, then he cannot be restricted to the holy spaces of Palestine. Similarly, Augustine asserts that believers were aliens in this world, journeying always regardless of their actual destination, and that their souls, rather than the physical Jerusalem, should be understood as God's temple where genuine hierophany can truly be experienced. Noting that *peregrinatio* and *peregrinus* do not always designate a physical journey but include a sense of spiritual exile and wandering, Augustine proposed a broader theological system that placed more emphasis on the spiritual aspects of Christian identity.[51]

Even theologians who attached some spiritual value to pilgrimage disagreed on the sites that should be privileged for encountering the divine. For example, Gregory of Nyssa flatly rejected the importance of Jerusalem as a pilgrimage site, promoting in its stead (like Prophet Oschofa of Nigeria) his own diocese of Cappadocia. At the same time, Cyril of Jerusalem sought to elevate Jerusalem relative to Caesarea through promotion of Jerusalem's holy sites. His appeal was to all Christendom, holding that Christian identity was tied to the sacred space of Jerusalem. To appreciate what was at stake at this period, one has to pierce through the veil of theological rhetoric and place the disagreement in the context of a complex world of power relations between bishoprics and efforts by bishops to control their congregations. As Bitton-Ashkelony observes, correctly it seems, "the debate at the end of the fourth century centered not merely on the religious function of the holy places but rather on the extent to which a local leader could build on the local territory of divine grace in order to transform it into a territory of power."[52] The tenor of the debate may have changed since, but the substantive issue about the extent to which a contingent practice could be elevated to a binding theological principle remains unresolved. From the beginning of the religion and before it became a major cultural presence in Nigeria, Christianity has never spoken with one voice on pilgrimage. Local church leaders who resisted its centralization in Jerusalem were motivated not only by a genuine belief in the ubiquitous presence of God, but also by the awareness of the social, economic, and political benefits that would accompany the recognition of a place as a pilgrimage location. Shrines in Lourdes, Fatima, and the Basilica of the Virgin of Guadalupe are among the Christian sites that today compete with Jerusalem for millions of pilgrims every year.

Government and Pilgrimage: A Reward for Good Behavior

Modern Nigeria came into existence in 1914 when the colonial governor-general, Lord Lugard, amalgamated the then northern and southern protectorates. Before then and for much of the colonial period, pilgrimage was largely regarded as a private religious affair, and those who undertook it did so as an act of piety that justified the huge personal sacrifice and financial expenditure committed to it. Not surprisingly, it received minimal, if any, emphasis in the doctrinal teachings of the Christian missionaries, both foreign and local, and remained a dormant aspect of the church's devotional life until the early 1980s. Among Muslims, for whom pilgrimage is a doctrinal requirement, official meddling was virtually nonexistent or mitigated by contextual constraints where it was found. In fact, until the advent of modern transportation facilities, only a few Muslims were able to make the hajj by land routes to Mecca, and among these were local rulers who went, not as representatives of political kingdoms, but in their capacities as believers.[53] To the extent that we can speak of official policy on pilgrimage in precolonial Nigeria, it was one of benign indifference. Religion in general, and pilgrimage in particular, enjoyed relative independence from political manipulation, even if those who managed the affairs of the various kingdoms were expected to be religiously attuned as a matter of cultural legitimacy.

Colonialism changed the paradigm of jurisdictional autonomy that had characterized religious life and practice, though it would be an exaggeration to blame outside intrusion for all of Nigeria's contemporary ills. Yet, there is some justification in the claim that "contentious issues in the Nigerian State and Constitution are traceable to Nigeria's colonial history and promises to remain an aspect of future Nigerian politics."[54] Much has been written about the system of indirect rule imposed by the colonial government, which involved, in some significant ways, restrictions on religious proselytizing across regional boundaries. The government's justification for this arrangement was to allow maximum freedom for each religion in the area where it was dominant—Christianity in the south and Islam in the north—while also reducing to the barest minimum any incidents of interreligious conflicts and the attendant disruption of political order.[55] But the paternalism undergirding this *cuius regio, eius religio* principle was anything but benevolent; the public face of religion and the ordering of its internal life were now subject to government regulations, and the interests of the state, not of religion, would determine what kinds of regulations to impose.

The official policy on pilgrimage during this period illustrates the precarious position of religion. After their conquest and reconstitution of the Sokoto caliphate, the spiritual headquarters of Nigerian Muslims, the colonial government did not encourage pilgrimage, fearing that contacts with the wider Islamic world that pilgrimage afforded would spur resistance sentiments in the pilgrims when they returned home. This was a period of intense reform and anticolonial, even jihad, activities in many Muslim societies, notably Sudan, the pathway for many Nigerian pilgrims, so the colonial government had reasons to be concerned. Those who led these movements tended to have a religious reawakening after visiting Mecca and Medina not just for the hajj but also to study, and "such student pilgrims sometimes carried a spirit of Islamic revivalism back to their homelands."[56] In the 1950s however, with the impending independence of Sudan (1956), the close educational links between Sudan and Northern Nigeria, and the well-established relationship with the traditional leadership class in the region, the British colonial government came to regard pilgrimage as less threatening. This lead to a policy reversal in a way that stripped pilgrimage of its religious essence: it was now seen as a major reward for the "good behavior" of Northern Emirs.[57] Of course, what counts as good behavior is almost always what benefits the state. Successive governments in postcolonial Nigeria have retained this patrimonial principle, conditioning their interaction with virtually every organ of civil society upon the surrendering of the right to critical vigilance in exchange for the largesse of the state.

"Pilgrimage as a reward" has grown beyond the lifting of travel restrictions to an all-inclusive package of government generosity, at both federal and state levels, that has at its core the establishment in 2006 of the National Hajj Commission of Nigeria (NAHCON), Nigerian Christian Pilgrims Commission, and similar bodies in each of the 36 states of the federation.[58] The legal status and functions of the two commissions are essentially similar, so a focus on one of them would suffice for our purpose. The NAHCON is administered by a Chairman and nine other members, three of whom are on full-time appointment, and the others are part-time. The Nigerian president not only appoints the chairman, but he also designates which members "are to serve on full time basis and those that are to serve on part-time basis."[59] The government provides the Commission with a building, which houses its various departments; pays the Chairman and the NAHCON's members "such remuneration and allowances as he may from time to time determine"; and determines eligibility for participation in the government pension program.[60] Also serving on the NAHCON are representatives from each of the following government ministries: Aviation, Foreign Affairs, Internal Affairs (Immigration), Finance, Health, and Central Bank of Nigeria.[61] There are 12 enumerated functions of the commission, the most pertinent of which are as follows:

- organizing and coordinating the movement of persons from Nigeria to Saudi Arabia, and for providing accommodation, transportation, and health, financial, security, customs, immigration and other services related to the performance of the hajj;
- establishment and management of pilgrims camps and related facilities, equipment and such other necessary materials;
- conducting educational and enlightenment campaigns on hajj and umrah in all the states of the federation and the Federal Capital Territory; and
- regulating and controlling in and outside of Nigeria all matters concerning the welfare of Nigerian pilgrims.[62]

Although each individual pilgrim, Muslim or Christian, is expected to pay his or her way to the Holy Land, only few actually do so because of the subsidies provided by the federal and state governments. The state governments are especially known for engaging in competition as to which of them is most generous in funding pilgrimages. In 2010, the Zamfara state government in the north proudly reported that it "had approved free feeding of its pilgrims during their five days' stay in Munna and Mountain Arafat in an effort to subsidize expenses and provide good food for the pilgrims."[63] The Oyo state government gestured a similar posture at the 2011 inauguration ceremony of the Pilgrims Welfare Board (Christian Wing), promising that pilgrims to the Holy Land will not be neglected, and that "when the welfare of people on pilgrimage to Jerusalem will be mentioned nationwide, Oyo State will receive unrivaled mention and celebration."[64]

Considering that Muslims and Christians are only a part of the Nigerian population, admittedly a substantial part,[65] and that not all Nigerians are religious, it is necessary to ask whether these extensive involvements of the government are justified in light of the relevant religion provisions in the Nigerian Constitution.

ASSESSING STATE SPONSORSHIP OF PILGRIMAGES IN NIGERIA

Of the three religion provisions already identified, it is the non-adoption and the nondiscrimination norms that offer the greatest challenge to the government policy and practice of sponsoring pilgrims to the Holy Lands. The free exercise provision appears not to be offended, not only because of the inclusive conceptualization of religious freedom in the Nigerian Constitution as encompassing the freedom "to manifest . . . [one's] religion or belief in worship, practice and observance," but also because the constitution construes this right as an entitlement that citizens have rather than as a restraint against the government. Unlike the language of the free exercise clause in the US Constitution, which imposes a restraint on the government regarding the permissible scope of its action toward religion (a negative right construction), the construction of the right in the Nigerian context is in positive language. The difference between the two approaches is that positive rights "require other people to act positively—to 'do something'—whereas [negative rights] require other people to refrain from acting in certain ways—to do nothing that violates the rights."[66] Although one presumably confers benefits, the import of the other is to prevent harm. So conceived, it is no wonder that Nigerian Muslims and Christians see the involvement of their government in pilgrimage as a logical entailment of their constitutional right. Fulfillment of the right is more than simply granting a normative space or a value zone within which people of different faiths and of no faith can carry out the dictates of their conscience. It includes the provision of what is necessary (e.g., financial and bureaucratic support) for the removal of any obstacles, such as financial handicaps, against compliance with these dictates.

This interpretation would be unproblematic but for the other two strictures imposed by the constitution on the conduct of the government. The first bars the government from adopting any religion as state religion. The key word here is "adopt," ordinarily understood to mean, *inter alia,* "to affiliate, attach to anyone," "to treat as favorites," "to take or receive as one's own (that which is not so naturally)," "to choose and follow."[67] Thus, what has to be determined is whether government provision of funds and other forms of assistance toward pilgrimages constitute an adoption of religion within the meaning of the constitution. Since the Nigerian courts have yet to consider this question, it might be useful to seek guidance from pronouncements from other jurisdictions facing similar problems. One pervasive concern in establishment litigation in the United States is the degree of assistance governments may offer to religious organizations. Typically, this has involved religious groups that supply services that nonreligious organizations also provide, such as hospitals, adoption agencies, soup kitchens, as well as financial aid to parochial schools. In all these cases, the ultimate beneficiaries of the aid or assistance are either the clients served by the agencies or the students who attend parochial schools, not the religious organization themselves, although they function as intermediaries through which the objects of the aid are transmitted. The constitutionality of such aid has often hinged on this distinction between the beneficiaries and the administrators of the aid. The defining characteristic of the former is their status as citizens, and their needs are legitimated by this grammar of membership in a political society. Although the aid administrators also share this common identity of citizenship, it is also within their democratic right to rely upon and be public about their religious values when they seek to participate in society through various avenues of service. The only caveat is that "political participation through service" cannot become a pretext for religious proselytization.

This argument is at the heart of the three-pronged *Lemon* test under which a challenged law or policy is valid only if it (1) has a secular purpose, (2) does not have a primary effect that advances or inhibits religion, and (3) does not foster an excessive entanglement.[68] Despite a sustained judicial onslaught against the *Lemon* test, the Supreme Court has not explicitly renounced it, nor has it officially been replaced by any other tests. On the contrary, its elements are routinely invoked by jurists and, as one scholar observes, "cases decided under *Lemon* are treated as authoritative."[69] Although the Nigerian Supreme Court is not bound by the jurisprudence of the US Supreme Court or its pronouncements on the First Amendment establishment clause, it seems reasonable to suppose that similar considerations will bear on the Nigerian Supreme Court and its subordinate courts when dealing with the non-adoption clause in section 10 of the 1999 Constitution. More important, the elements of the test resonate with the prevailing sentiments in Nigeria about how to resolve the quandary of religion-state interactions.

Of the three, it is the first element of *Lemon* that Nigerians would find most controversial to use in assessing the constitutional propriety of government involvement in pilgrimage. The disagreement is not likely to be about "purpose," whether this denotes "the actual aims of those who perform an action, their 'subjective' purposes or aims . . . or some more objective standard of the significance of what the actors have performed,"[70] but about what the secular nature of the purpose connotes. Two standard sociological conceptualizations of secularity are worth retrieving here. The term was initially understood to mean "the retreat of religion from various public spaces: politics, science, art, the market" but later expanded to include "the notion of declining religious belief and practice, often thought to be an inevitable consequence of modernity."[71] In a society where this marginalized status of religion has become an empirical fact, a purpose that is secular would be one that reflects the character of that society. This hardly matches the picture of Nigeria's social and cultural reality. The country's more than 130 million inhabitants are almost equally divided between Islam and Christianity, with a tiny minority, about 10 percent, claiming to be adherents of the traditional religion or of no religion.[72] It is in light of this that many Nigerians, Muslims and Christians alike, dismiss the characterization of Nigeria as a secular state on the basis of the non-adoption clause in section 10 of the constitution.

The obvious reason for objecting to secularity is its inadequate description of Nigeria and its people, but suspicion about the term is much deeper. A secular state or a secularly motivated purpose, it is feared, will be callously indifferent[73] or even blatantly hostile to religion, which if permitted, would exacerbate Nigeria's problems of moral disorientation.[74] A Nigerian Roman Catholic theologian deems extreme a policy of "an impenetrable judicial wall of separation between church and state" and ridicules those who would support it as insane who have no interest in "the survival of the nation."[75] The threat to the social health of Nigeria is not religion but secularity, evident in the chronic vices of "moral depravity, corruption, oppression, infidelity and syncretism,"[76] which can be cured, according to a Muslim judge, "only by divine injunctions backed by those who govern."[77] On this reasoning, it is not enough simply to provide for the free exercise of religion, the state must also accommodate religious beliefs and practices in its legislative process and policy formulations.

What remains unclear from the argument of the opponents of a secular purpose doctrine is whether government funding of pilgrimage is a permissible accommodation of religion. Understood as "an area of allowable and, in some cases, compelled governmental deference to the religious needs of people holding a variety of beliefs,"[78] the concept of accommodation is a free exercise, not an establishment, doctrine. As such, what it calls for is "a delicate balance between government's duty to promote the cohesiveness necessary for an ordered society and its responsibility to honor the religious practices of citizens by refraining from unnecessary or burdensome regulation."[79] Were the Nigerian government to proscribe pilgrimage, it would clearly be imposing unnecessary and burdensome regulation on its overwhelmingly religious population, thereby abridging constitutional rights. However, its current mode of intervention in pilgrimage affairs is not proscription but positive assistance, and justifying this gesture under the rubric of accommodation stretches the meaning of the term beyond its legitimate bound. Such a subversive application of accommodation offers a recipe for "heightened civil strife, corruption of religion, and oppression of religious [and nonreligious] minorities."[80]

It can be argued that the Nigerian government sponsorship of pilgrimage, like other instances of its "appeasement of religion,"[81] such as the state funding of a national mosque and a Christian ecumenical center, is responsible for the perception that the Nigerian state "is not simply a policy-producing mechanism balancing different notions of equality against each other,"[82] but is "itself the greatest prize and resource, over which groups engage in a continuing struggle. . . . It is also a distributor of resources, which is nearly always done differentially."[83] As is often the case when free money is available, it does not matter that the largesse would be spent on frivolous projects or peripheral religious values. This is clearly the case with the Nigerian Christian elevation of pilgrimage to an important ritual practice. The former head of the Anglican Church in Nigeria, Archbishop Peter Akinola, admitted that "pilgrimage is unimportant in Christianity," but he justified his push for government sponsorship because "it was a vital step toward equality with Muslims."[84] Interestingly, Muslim politicians welcomed a resurgent Christian interest in pilgrimage because they hoped it would force Christians to "abandon their strict interpretations of secularism,"[85] since they now benefit from the same sort of aid the state had provided to Islam.

For both Christian and Muslim groups, pilgrimage has become less a matter of complying with a religious injunction than an avenue for political patronage. Their politicization of this ritual (which they wrongly believe is warranted by the principle of accommodation) also reveals their lukewarm commitment to the principle of religious disestablishment and the vision of living in a state where no religion is adopted as state religion. Neither side seems bothered by the demand of equity imposed by the pluralistic nature of Nigeria's religious composition. The justification for government support of pilgrimages offered by Christians—to achieve political parity with Muslims—ignores the fact that there are also Nigerians who adhere to the traditional religion and religions other than Christianity and Islam or to no religion at all and who do not receive similar funding from the government.[86] Similarly, the non-strict interpretations of secularity proposed by the Muslims and some Pentecostal Christians would only strengthen the already problematic ties between religion and the state, the kind of effect that *Lemon* fears would advance religion and foster an excessive entanglement between two functionally separate institutions.[87]

But funding is not the only way in which pilgrimages enjoy the support of the state. As already indicated, various government ministries and personnel, including state governors, are involved in their planning and operation, sometimes accompanying pilgrims to the ritual sites. The government is also responsible for the recruitment and compensation of the Pilgrims Commissions' staff at both federal and state levels. In addition, government buildings and web portals are used for disseminating not just logistical information about pilgrimages, but also for teaching about their spiritual benefits.[88] This explicit association of the accouterments of government with religious affairs raises their social significance and extends their influence beyond the ambit of spirituality. However, complaints about the misuse of public money would do a poor job of capturing what is constitutionally troublesome about this manner of government involvement in pilgrimages. To see the relevant harm here, it will be helpful to briefly review how the US Supreme Court has intervened in other cases of establishment litigation involving public exhibitions of religious symbols, such as the crèches, the Ten Commandments, and so on.

The *locus classicus* for thinking about the constitutional quagmire arising from public display or affirmation of religious symbols is the endorsement test developed by Justice O'Connor in the court's very first holiday display case, *Lynch v. Donnelly*. The case involved the display by the city of Pawtucket, Rhode Island, of a nativity scene or crèche in a park owned by a nonprofit organization and located in the city's shopping district.[89] Justice O'Connor said that the crucial question was whether the display amounted to an endorsement of religion (or of a particular religion):

> The Establishment Clause prohibits government from making adherence to a religion relevant in any way to a person's standing in the political community. Government can run afoul of that prohibition . . . [by its] endorsement or disapproval of religion. Endorsement sends a message to nonadherents that they are outsiders, not full members of the political community, and an accompanying message to adherents that they are insiders, favored members of the political community.[90]

There are several advantages of using this test for the discussion of the pilgrimage palaver in Nigeria over the elements furnished by the *Lemon* test. First, it avoids a language that significant segments of the Nigerian population find offensive to their moral and religious sensibilities, notwithstanding that their understandings of secularity or a secular purpose are theoretically stale and jejune. In his recent monumental book, Charles Taylor offers what I consider a more adequate account of secularity that, he claims, refers not merely to the dwindling of religion or even the functional separation of religion from state, science, and aesthetics. For him, the term connotes "a move from a society where belief in God is unchallenged and indeed, unproblematic, to one in which it is understood to be one option among others, and frequently not the easiest to embrace." Secularity is not just a net reduction in religious belief or practice, therefore, but a change in the very conditions of belief. "Secularity in this sense," Taylor writes, "is a matter of the whole context of understanding in which our moral, spiritual or religious experience and search takes place."[91]

Taylor's account of secularity is compatible with the main thrust of the endorsement test, which leads me to the second advantage of the test, namely, an emphasis on disparagement as the relevant injury suffered when government publicly endorses religious symbols. The injury arises because of what seems to be an utter disregard for what Taylor calls "the whole context" that shapes religious belief, experience, and practice. In a pluralistic context like Nigeria, the injury of being disparaged as a religious outsider can have repercussions beyond this sphere, even determining whether someone has a materially meaningful life or not. Preventing this injury or mitigating its effects requires, then, a rehabilitation of the most dormant of the religion clauses in the Nigerian Constitution, the nondiscrimination principle and its associated norm of equal liberty, and this I regard as another advantage for using the endorsement test. The intended goal of the test is *impartiality* in the way that citizens of a religiously pluralistic society are treated, such that no one would have any reasons to consider him or herself superior or inferior to others solely on the basis of religious identity.

But why should any one be concerned about being discriminated against or disparaged on the basis of religion? An answer to this question has to be sought in what Eisgruber and Sager call "four structural features of religion" and their effects on "the social meaning of religious displays."[92] The features are: (1) the comprehensiveness of religions—"large, expansive webs of belief and conduct"; (2) the tendency of religions to classify people as insiders and outsiders and sometimes undergirding the classifications with strict enforcement rules; (3) the reinforcing role of religious rituals (e.g., pilgrimage) "in signifying who is 'in' or 'out' of these comprehensive structures"; and (4) the fact that "the perceived stakes of being or without these structures of belief and membership are often momentous."[93] The upshot of this analysis is that because "religion plays a role in defining civic identity,"

> Public endorsements of religion carry a special charge or valence. Such endorsements signify who is 'in' or 'out' of competing large-scale social and ideological structures, and assign powerful and pervasive judgments of identity and stature to the status of being in or out. Religious endorsements valorize some religious beliefs and those who hold them, and thereby disparage those who do not share those beliefs.[94]

This is what is at stake in the unabashed involvement of the Nigerian government in pilgrimages. By lending the imprimatur of the state behind these ritual events, the government makes a preferential option for members of the two dominant religions in the country and treats as outcasts members of other religions or of no religions, as well as members of the favored religions for whom pilgrimage is a low priority requirement. Christians who return from pilgrimages acquire the title of JP (Jerusalem Pilgrim), which they proudly put in front of their names, and their Muslim counterparts are referred to as Alhajis (or Alhajas if they are women). These are designations that literally and symbolically enhance the social prestige of the bearers, providing them with a unique advantage to access and manipulate Nigeria's complex networks of political and economic power.[95] To stem the current tide, political and legal debate may have to be moved from the domains of the non-adoption and free exercise (accommodation) clauses and relocated at the heart of the nondiscrimination clause with its impartiality and equal liberty principles. As the Roman Catholic archbishop of Abuja and the immediate past chairman of the Christian Association of Nigeria (CAN) rightly puts it, "as long as there are pilgrimage commissions and for as long as government continues to support some pilgrimages, it must necessarily face the challenge of equity and fairness."[96]

CONCLUSION

This chapter has argued that the tendency by scholars to focus exclusively on the non-adoption and free exercises clauses in the Nigerian constitution as adequate mechanisms for the protection of the country's religious pluralism and the secular character of the state is mistaken. It contends that existing interpretations of both clauses have encouraged rigid ideological positions among religious and nonreligious partisans and have failed to grasp the real nature of the moral hazards that are inherent in a religiously pluralistic society. The chapter thus argues that a more adequate test for determining the extent to which the Nigerian Constitution takes cognizance of the country's religious pluralism is its articulation of the norms for opposing inequality and discrimination among the citizens.

By examining the involvement of the Nigerian government, at both the federal and state levels, in religious pilgrimages, the chapter demonstrates the precarious status of these norms and the imperative to defend their lexical priority over the other constitutional provisions on religion.

NOTES

1. Federal Republic of Nigeria, *Constitution of the Federal Republic of Nigeria* (Lagos, Nigeria: The Federal Government Press, 1999), §1(1).
2. See Olufemi Taiwo, *How Colonialism Preempted Modernity in Africa* (Bloomington: Indiana University Press, 2010).
3. Michael Bratton, "Briefing: Islam, Democracy and Public Opinion in Africa," *African Affairs* 102 (2003): 494.
4. J. Isawa Elaigwu, "The Shadow of Sharia over Nigerian Federalism," *Publius: Journal of Federalism* 33 (2003): 123.
5. See Ebenezer Obadare, "In Search of a Public Sphere: The Fundamentalist Challenge to Civil Society in Nigeria," *Patterns of Prejudice* 38 (2004): 177–97.
6. Rita Kiki Ediozie, "Democratization in Multi-Religious Contexts: Amina vs. The (Disunited) States of Nigeria," in *Local Institutions, Global Controversies: Islam in Sub-Saharan African Contexts*, ed. Kamari Clarke (New Haven: Yale University , 2007), 145–76.
7. R. A. Joseph, "National Objectives and Public Accountability: An Analysis of the Draft Constitution," in *Issues in the Nigerian Draft Constitution*, ed. Suleimanu Kumo and Abubakar Aliyu (Zaria, Nigeria: Ahmadu Bello University Press, 1977), 1.
8. Ernst Troeltsch, *Religion in History*, trans. James Luther Adams and Walter F. Bense (Minneapolis: Fortress Press, 1991), 109.
9. David Martin, *A General Theory of Secularization* (San Francisco: Harper and Row, 1978), 18–24.
10. Julian Go, "Modeling the State: Postcolonial Constitutions in Asia and Africa," *Southeast Asian Studies* 39, no. 4 (2002): 565.
11. As explained by Abdullahi An-Na'im, "the phenomenon of diversity is a permanent feature of all human societies everywhere, manifested in different forms and dynamics among them over time. . . . [But] pluralism is an ideology and system that accepts diversity as a positive value and facilitates constant negotiations and adjustments among varieties of difference without seeking or expecting to terminate any or all of them permanently." See Abdullahi An-Na'im, *Islam and the Secular State: Negotiating the Future of Shari'a* (Cambridge: Harvard University Press, 2008), 225.
12. Michel Rosenfeld, "A Pluralist Critique of the Constitutional Treatment of Religion," in *The Law of Religious Identity: Models for Post-Communism*, ed. Andras Sajo and Shlomo Avineri (The Hague: Kluwer Law International, 1999), 44.

13. Richard L. Sklar, "On the Study of Constitutional Government in Africa," in *Constitutionalism and Society in Africa*, ed. Okon Akiba (Aldershot: Ashgate Pub., 2004), 43–54.
14. Taiwo, *How Colonialism Preempted Modernity*, 3.
15. Rosenfeld, "A Pluralist Critique," 44.
16. John Kelsay, "Plurality, Pluralism, and Comparative Ethics: A Review Essay," *Journal of Religious Ethics* 24 (1996): 418.
17. Section 10 provides that "The Government of the Federation or of a State shall not adopt any religion as State Religion," and, according to section 38(1), "Every person shall be entitled to freedom of thought, conscience and religion, including freedom to change his religion or belief, and freedom (either alone or in community with others, and in public or in private) to manifest and propagate his religion or belief in worship, teaching, practice and observance." See *Constitution of Nigeria*, ch. II, § 10; ch. IV, §38.
18. Ranjit S. Sarkaria, foreword to S. C. Arora, ed., *Current Issues and Trends in Centre-State Relations: A Global View* (New Delhi: Mittal Publications, 1991), 3.
19. In the United States, for example, the Bill of Rights, by its express terms, applies only to the federal government. However, the First Amendment and most of the remaining amendments in the Bill of Rights apply to state governments today because of the judicially created "incorporation doctrine." Essentially, the doctrine incorporates the provisions of the Bill of Rights into the Fourteenth Amendment's "due process" clause by declaring that each of the rights was "fundamental" to the conception of due process of law. See the landmark case of *Gideon v. Wainwright,* 372 U.S. 335 (1963) for the Supreme Court's explanation of the doctrine; and for subsequent clarification, see *Pointer v. Texas,* 380 U.S. 400 (1965).
20. Obadare, "In Search of a Public Sphere," 179.
21. Jibrin Ibrahim, "The State and Religion in Nigeria: Forces and Dynamics," *Afrika Zamani* (1997), 5.
22. Philip *Kurland,* "Of Church and State and the Supreme Court," *University of Chicago Law Review* 29 (1961): 96.
23. This argument echoes Justice Brennan, concurring in *Abington v. Schempp*, 374 U.S. 203 (1963), that "the Establishment Clause [is] a co-guarantor, with the Free Exercise Clause, of religious liberty. The framers did not entrust the liberty of religious beliefs to either clause alone."
24. Christopher L. Eisgruber and Lawrence Sager, *Religious Freedom and the Constitution* (Cambridge: Harvard University Press, 2007), 17–18.
25. Ibid., 9.
26. Ronald B. Flowers, Melissa Rogers, and Steven K. Green, *Religious Freedom and the Supreme Court* (Waco, TX: Baylor University Press, 2008), 1.
27. Mojeed Olujinmi A. Alabi, *The Supreme Court in the Nigerian Political System 1963–1997* (Ibadan: Demyaxs Press Ltd, 2002), 229.
28. Ibid.

29. S. Brent Plate, "The Varieties of Contemporary Pilgrimage," *Crosscurrents* (2009): 263.
30. Edmund Emefie Ikenga-Metuh, "Pilgrimage in African Religion: A Quest for the Ultimate," *Dialogue & Alliance* 6, no. 4 (1992–93): 4.
31. James C. Livingston, *Anatomy of the Sacred* (Upper Saddle River, NJ: Prentice Hall, 1998), 43.
32. Mircea Eliade, *The Sacred and the Profane*, trans. W. R. Trask (New York: Harper & Row, 1959), 24.
33. Livingston, *Anatomy of the Sacred*, 44.
34. Jacob K. Olupona, "Orisa Osun: Yoruba Sacred Kingship and Civil Religion in Osogbo, Nigeria," in *Osun across the Waters: A Yoruba Goddess in Africa and the Americas*, ed. Joseph M. Murphy and Mei-Mei Sanford (Bloomington: Indiana University Press, 2001), 46–67.
35. Ikenga-Metuh, "Pilgrimage in African Religion," 4.
36. Andre Mary, "Pilgrimage to Imeko (Nigeria): An African Church in the Time of the 'Global Village,'" *International Journal of Urban and Regional Research* 26, no. 1 (2002), 113.
37. Ibid., 111.
38. Ibid., 112.
39. The two rights implicated here are the freedom of religion and freedom of movement. On the latter, see *The Constitution of Nigeria*, ch. IV, § 41.
40. David Edwin Long, *The Hajj Today: A Survey of the Contemporary Makkah Pilgrimage* (Albany: SUNY, 1979), 11; F. E. Peters, *The Hajj: The Muslim Pilgrimage to Mecca and the Holy Places* (Princeton: Princeton University Press, 1994), xxi–xxiv.
41. M.O.A. Abdul, *Islam as a Religion: Faith and Duties* (Lagos, Academy Press, 1971), 74.
42. Ibid.
43. Peters, *The Hajj*, 3–7.
44. Robert R. Bianchi, *Guests of God: Pilgrimage and Politics in the Islamic World* (Oxford: Oxford University Press, 2004), 40. Other scholars have offered a political explanation of Muhammad's choice of Mecca. According to the renowned Dutch Orientalist and colonial officer whose views shaped modern pilgrimage policy, the choice was a stroke of political genius that accomplished many goals simultaneously. By centering his new state in Mecca (the city he was forced to flee and conquer) instead of Medina (the city that gave him refuge), Muhammad won over his former enemies and consolidated Islam in Arabia. He also marshaled resources to launch a united force against the greatest military powers of his day, the Byzantine and Persian empires. When Muhammad instructed Muslims to pray in the direction of Mecca rather than Jerusalem, his community could make a double claim: they could be monotheistic without being Jews or Christians, and they could be universalistic without ceasing to be Arab. See G. W. J. Drewes, "Snouck Hurgronje and the Study of Islam," in *Bejdragen tot de taal-, land- en volkenkunde van Neerlandsch Indie* 113 (1957): 1–15.

45. Long, *The Hajj Today*, 9, 11.
46. Bianchi, *Guests of God*, 39.
47. Ibid., 40.
48. Kabiru Sani Hanga, "The Hajj Exercise in Nigeria: Challenges, Constraints, and Drawbacks" (Feb. 1999), at http://maisikeli.com/documents/The_Hajj_Exercise_in_Nigeria_Final_Document_.pdf.
49. This Latin term gives us the English *pilgrimage*.
50. Brouria Bitton-Ashkelony, *Encountering the Sacred: The Debate on Christian Pilgrimage in Late Antiquity* (Berkeley: University of California Press, 2005), 204–5.
51. Ibid.
52. Ibid., 64.
53. Dunama, the second Muslim king of Kanem in northeastern Nigeria, was said to have performed the hajj thrice during his reign in the twelfth century. He died in the Read Sea during his third pilgrimage. See O. E. Tangban, "The Hajj and the Nigerian Economy," *Journal of Religion in Africa* 21, no.3 (1991): 242.
54. Kelechi A. Kalu, "Constitutionalism in Nigeria: A Conceptual Analysis of Ethnicity and Politics," *West Africa Review* 6 (2004): 1.
55. See Ogbu U. Kalu, "Christianity and Colonial Society," in *The History of Christianity in West Africa*, ed. Ogbu U. Kalu (London: Longman, 1980), 182–86.
56. Nehemia Levtzion and John O. Voll, "Introduction," in *Eighteenth-Century Renewal and Reform in Islam*, ed. Nehemia Levtzion and John O. Voll (Syracuse: Syracuse University Press, 1987), 8.
57. John N. Paden, *Ahmadu Bello Sardauna of Sokoto: Values and Leadership in Nigeria* (Zaria, Nigeria: Hudahuda Publishing Co., 1986), 280.
58. These separate commissions were preceded by a common Nigerian Pilgrims Board serving both Muslim and Christian constituencies, and their state equivalents were known as Pilgrims Welfare Boards. The first of such boards was established by the Western Regional Government of Chief Obafemi Awolowo in 1958. See H. O. Danmole, "The Religious Factor in Nigerian Politics: Awolowo and the Muslims, 1957–1983," in *Obafemi Awolowo: The End of an Era?*, ed. Olasope O. Oyelaran, Toyin Falola, Mokwugo Okoye, and Adewale Thompson (Ile-Ife, Nigeria: Obafemi Awolowo University Press, 1988), 874–98.
59. National Hajj Commission of Nigeria (Establishment Act), *Official Gazette of the Federal Republic of Nigeria* 93, no. 66 (2006): A330.
60. Ibid.
61. Ibid., 4.
62. Ibid., 5–6.
63. "2010 Hajj: Zamfara Remits N1b to NAHCON," *Nigerian Tribune*, July 2, 2010.
64. "No Oyo Pilgrim Will Suffer Neglect—Ajimobi," *Daily Independent* (Oct. 13, 2011), http://dailyindependentnigeria.com/2011/10/13/no-oyo-pilgrim-will-suffer-neglect-%E2%80%93-ajimobi.

65. Census is a notoriously controversial subject in Nigeria, especially when it concerns religious data; however, Christians and Muslims are estimated to be about 40% and 50%, respectively, of the population. See *2008 Report on International Religious Freedom—Nigeria*, at http://www.state.gov/g/drl/rls/irf/2008/108385.htm.
66. Henry Shue, *Basic Rights: Subsistence, Affluence, and U. S. Policy*, second ed. (Princeton: Princeton University Press, 1996), 36.
67. Noah Webster, *Webster's New Unabridged Dictionary,* deluxe second ed. (1983), 26
68. *Lemon v. Kurtzmman*, 403 U.S. 602 (1971).
69. Kent Greenawalt, *Religion and the Constitution: Establishment and Fairness* (Princeton: Princeton University Press 2008), 352–53.
70. Ibid., 164.
71. Michael Warner, Jonathan VanAntwerpen, and Craig Calhoun, *Varieties of Secularism* (Cambridge: Harvard University Press, 2010), 8.
72. See Frieder Ludwig, "Christian-Muslim Relations in Northern Nigeria since the Introduction of Shari'ah in 1999," *Journal of the American Academy of Religion* 76 (2008): 602–37.
73. Koppelman identifies *callous indifference* as one of the four objections to the secular purpose doctrine. The other three are the *rubber stamp objection*, which "holds that nearly anything can satisfy the secular purpose requirement, because a secular rationale can be imagined for almost any law"; the *evanescence objection*, which claims "the 'purpose' that the rule seeks either does not exist or is not knowable by judges"; and the *participation objection*, which suggests that "the rule makes religious people into second class citizens by denying them the right to participate in the legislative purpose." See Andrew Koppelman, "Secular Purpose," *Virginia Law Review* 88 (2002): 88–89.
74. See Sam Amadi, "Religion and Secular Constitution: Human Rights and the Challenge of Sharia," (Unpublished research report paper on file with the Harvard Kennedy School Carr Center for Human Rights Policy, 2004), 10–11, available at http://content.hks.harvard.edu/carr/cchrp/research/reports.php.
75. Ikem B. C. Ngwoke, *Religion and Religious Liberty in Nigerian Law: From the Colonial Days to 1983* (Rome: Pontifica Universita Lateranense, 1987), 140–41.
76. Ibraheem Sulaiman, *The Islamic State and the Challenge of History: Ideas, Policies, and Operation of the Sokoto Caliphate* (London: Mansell Publishing Limited, 1987), 3.
77. Justice Sambo, "Draft Constitution Fails to Provide for Morality," *New Nigerian*, (Jan. 5, 1977), 7.
78. Arlin M. Adams and Charles J. Emmerich, *A Nation Dedicated to Religious Liberty: The Constitutional Heritage of the Religious Clauses* (Philadelphia: University of Pennsylvania Press, 1990), 58.
79. Ibid., 59.
80. Koppelman, "Secular Purpose," 88.

81. Amadi, "Religion and Secular Constitution," 13.
82. Federal Republic of Nigeria, *Report of the Political Bureau* (Abuja: Directorate for Public Enlightenment and Social Mobilization, 1987), 42.
83. Jibrin Ibrahim, "The Political Debate and the Struggle for Democracy in Nigeria," *Review of African Political Economy* 37 (1986): 45.
84. Bianchi, *Guests of God*, 214.
85. Ibid., 213.
86. See Idumange John, "Nigeria: Abolish State Sponsorships of Pilgrimages," *Sahara Reporters* (Feb. 2, 2010), at http://www.saharareporters.com/article/nigeria-abolish-state-sponsorship-pilgrimages.
87. See Lisa Newton, "Divine Sanction and Legal Authority: Religion and the Infrastructure of the Law," in *Religion, Morality, and the Law*, ed. J. Roland Pennock and John W. Chapman (New York: New York University Press, 1988), 179–200.
88. The Edo state government advertises the following as the benefits of Christian pilgrimage: "(1) To experience firsthand the land where our faith was born; (2) To connect us more intimately to our Christian faith; (3) To grow in deepest understanding of the scriptures; (4) It points us back to the miracles of Christ, e.g. Cana of Galilee, you will remember where Jesus turned water to wine; at Bethany, you will recall the miraculous raising of Lazarus from the dead; (5) It brings spiritual renewal and revival. The sacred places you will see, enter, and pray will help to renew your encounter with God and your experience with Him will become more intense than ever; (6) Holy Living: The exercise affects lives morally and spiritually. This builds up holiness because the Christian life is a call to holy living; (7) To witness the miraculous restoration of the nation of Israel." See *Information on Edo State Christian Pilgrims Welfare Board, Benin City*, at http://www.edostate.gov.ng/benefits
89. Lynch v. Donnelly, 465 U.S. 668 (1984).
90. Ibid., 688 (O'Connor, J., concurring).
91. Charles Taylor, *A Secular Age* (Cambridge: Harvard University Press, 2007), 3.
92. Eisgruber and Sage, *Religious Freedom and the Constitution*, 125.
93. Ibid. For a different account and much longer list of important features of religion, Robert Audi and Nicholas Wolterstorff, *Religion in the Public Square: The Place of Religious Convictions in Political Debate*, (Lanham, MD: Rowman & Littlefield, 1997), 5.
94. Ibid., 126.
95. See Joseph V. Hickey and William E. Thompson, "Politics and the Emergence of Alhajis among the Bokkos Fulani," *Journal of Asian and African Studies* 16 (1981): 212–22; Jeff Haynes, *Religion and Politics in Africa* (London: Zed Books, 1996), 79–103; Donal B. Cruise O'Brien, *Symbolic Confrontations: Muslims Imagining the State in Africa* (New York: Palgrave 2003), 1–29.
96. John Onaiyekan, Dividends of Religion in Nigeria (May 12, 2010) (unpublished manuscript).

Part 3

The Challenge of Islam

CHAPTER 6

Theocrats Living under Secular Law: An External Engagement with Islamic Legal Theory

Andrew F. March

I. The Classical Islamic Principle of Legitimacy and the Dilemma of the Minority Theocrat

The idea of a divinely revealed Law[1] has long been central to Muslim identity. As Islam developed and flourished for the vast majority of its history as the public religion of state power, doctrines of public law and political obligation, no less than matters of worship and ritual, have always been objects of intense practical concern. On this conception of religious morality, a political order is legitimate to the extent that it approximates an ideal legal order as expressed in the idea of *shari'a*, just as for a political liberal a political order is legitimate to the extent it approximates the terms of social cooperation as would be endorsed by parties contracting in ideal circumstances, whether something like the Original Position or an ideal speech situation.

Let us call this the "classical" Islamic theocratic principle of legitimacy, bearing in mind both that this is an ideal discourse not directly transferable to sociological, political, or anthropological experiences, and that what precisely constitutes the theocratic *shari'a* vision is often indeterminate or deeply contested even by Muslim jurists. For a fairly representative contemporary statement of the Islamic principle of political legitimacy for Muslim-majority societies, consider the reflections of contemporary Egyptian-Qatari scholar Yusuf al-Qaradawi:

> For Muslim societies, as Islam is a comprehensive system of worship (*'ibada*) and legislation (*shari'a*), the acceptance of secularism means abandonment of *shari'a*, a denial of divine guidance and a rejection of God's injunctions. It is indeed a false claim that *shari'a* is not suitable to the requirements of the present age. The acceptance of a legislation formulated by humans means a preference for humans' limited knowledge and experiences over the divine guidance: "Say! Do you know better than God?" (Q. 2:140).
>
> For this reason, the call for secularism among Muslims is atheism and a rejection of Islam. Its acceptance as a basis for rule in place of *shari'a* is clear apostasy. The silence of the masses in the Muslim world about this deviation has been a major transgression and a clear-cut instance of disobedience which have produced a sense of guilt, remorse, and inward resentment, all of which have generated discontent, insecurity, and hatred among committed Muslims because such deviation lacks legitimacy. . . . We Muslims believe that God is the sole Creator and Sustainer of the Worlds. One Who ". . . takes account of every single thing" (Q. 72:28); that He is omnipotent and omniscient; that His mercy and bounties encompasses everyone and suffice for all. In that capacity, God revealed His divine guidance to humanity, made certain things permissible and others prohibited, commanded people observe His injunctions and to judge according to them. If they do not do so, then they commit disbelief, aggression, and transgression.[2]

But what of societies where Muslims are a minority? Islamic jurists have traditionally given a variety of answers to this question, including that Muslims may not legitimately live in a land ruled by other than Islamic law, that Muslims may live in any land where they have the freedom to "manifest their religion," and that Muslims may live in non-Muslim polities but must aspire to as much self-governance as they can negotiate.[3] Islamic jurisprudence on the options for Muslims living as a minority community in a non-Muslim polity thus maps on to common models of living as a pious "theocratic" minority in a nonideal polity. Consider, first, four common such models.

1. *The Thin Social Contract Model, or "Loyal Resident Alienage."* On this model, the theocratic community understands that the wider public system of law and justice will not be its own, but theorizes certain minimal conditions whereby its own residence is legitimate from its own moral perspective, even without institutions of

self-governance. This model posits that when the wider community guarantees it certain rights of security and religious freedom, it will consent to obey laws that it does not necessarily regard as just from its comprehensive theocratic perspective. This is the dominant approach to the minority condition in mainstream *Sunni* Islamic jurisprudence.[4]

2. *The Internal Retreat Model.* This model is a diluted form of the Thin Social Contract Model. Perhaps because its presence in the alien polity is nonvoluntary, or because it cannot actively imagine the conditions of living independently, the theocratic community tacitly accepts the reality of the wider polity but directs all of its spiritual and political energies toward its own communal life. It does not actively seek to disrupt the wider politico-legal order, but neither does it seek to legitimate the politico-legal order even in a contingent way. Such communities do not necessarily seek to create de facto state forms within the wider state, but they exert great efforts to socialize their members into common norms and to regulate internal matters and disputes informally, without appeal to the wider legal system. This model of "partial citizenship"[5] is that adopted by the Amish, *Haredim*, and some fundamentalist Mormon communities, as well as ultra-pious Muslim *Salafis*.[6]
3. *The Self-Governance Model.* In this model, the theocratic community not only regulates its own internal affairs as much as possible informally, but it also seeks certain guarantees of its autonomy from the wider state. Such self-governance seeks to secure a form of legal pluralism, with communal control over as many areas as possible, from family and personal law to criminal law.[7] Variations on this model include the Ottoman Millet system and existing countries, such as India, Lebanon, and Israel, where family law is in the hands of religious authorities.[8] This is the dominant, mainstream aspiration within Islamic jurisprudence beyond the Thin Social Contract Model.[9]
4. *The Temporary Modus Vivendi Model.* This model is immanent within all three preceding ones. However, here the emphasis is less on stabilizing the theocratic community's relationship to the state than on seeking to bring about conditions more in line with the community's theocratic vision. Perhaps it anticipates becoming a demographic majority in the near future or somehow altering the balance of power with other communities. In contemporary circumstances, perhaps the society is divided not just between various religious communities but between religious communities and secular ones, and thus coalitions are sought with other theocrats to advance the cause of religion in general over secularism. Here theocrats might see themselves as

forming a pious opposition to the state with no permanent, principled commitment to self-restraint in implementing its own comprehensive theocratic system. Such might characterize the position of many nonviolent Islamist groups in secular Muslim states (the Qaradawi quotation from above), and to a certain extent some Evangelical Christian movements in the United States.

If these are the most common models for living within polities not governed by one's own theocratic vision, all with echoes in Islamic legal thought, I want to note two other important options.

5. *The Religious Integralist Model.* What has often been referred to as the problem of theocracy in recent political philosophy is not always theocracy in the strictest sense of the term. Many religious citizens and groups believe that their lives should be morally integral, with no radical break between their private and their political lives.[10] But the idea that one should seek an integrated religiously faithful path of behavior in all areas of life does not necessarily imply that one's religious morality consists in a comprehensive, pre-political legal *code*, which one must strive to obey. Thus, a fifth model for theocrats is to move beyond Law to another form of religious political ethics. Such a religious ethics need not be liberal or fully comfortable with secularism but is likely to be more open-ended and thus more easily placed into conversation with other ethical doctrines. This might be regarded as dissolution of the problem of theocracy, insofar as such religious ethicists merely want their religious perspective to be admissible in public deliberation and not authoritative because of its truth. This form of non-theocratic religious integralism does not require, but is compatible with, the idea of an "overlapping consensus" on the basic terms of social cooperation in a pluralistic society and is visible in the more recent approach to Islamic ethics of the well-known European Islamic public intellectual, Tariq Ramadan.[11]
6. *The Thicker Social Contract Model, or Overlapping Consensus.* A final model would be a doctrine of affirming the substantive justness or legitimacy of a politico-legal system not based on one's own theocratic doctrine, but without abandoning, dissolving or moving beyond the terms of that theocratic doctrine. Like the Thin Social Contract Model, the religious legal doctrine establishes moral standards for the alien legal system, but in a much more capacious way. It moves beyond the legitimate terms of residence to ask whether the substance of an alien conception of justice might be sufficiently just or legitimate.

Is the Thicker Social Contract Model possible? Is it possible for a religious endorsement of the substantive justness of certain liberal principles to emerge from a theocratic, *legal* tradition?

It is undeniable that there is a certain paradox, even absurdity, in discussing the legitimacy of non-Islamic law within Islamic legal discourse. If God has told us how he can be sovereign on earth through a revealed law, how can a person committed to this conception of legitimacy regard another form of law as just and legitimate? Islamic law is nothing other than a discourse about political legitimacy and political obligation. Either Islamic law is a positive law for Muslim societies, in which case it has no reason to discuss what laws other societies should apply to themselves, or it is a universal law coterminous with justice.[12] Either way, it would not appear that Islamic law is a likely source for other ideas on how a religiously diverse society should distribute rights and responsibilities. Furthermore, even where Muslim jurists might approach non-Islamic laws individually to examine their acceptability, this is likely to involve no deeper engagement with the underlying principles of reasonable moral pluralism and individual autonomy.

Thus, it seems that citizens of religiously diverse societies should be satisfied with one of the first four models of theocratic membership in non-theocratic polities, particularly the first two. Short of, in fact, ceasing to be theocrats *stricto sensu* and becoming "religious ethicists" (even integralist ones), there is by definition no way for theocrats to endorse the substantive justness of non-theocratic forms of rule, particularly secular ones and particularly where the subject of legislation is the distribution of religious freedoms.

However, I believe that there are serious costs to adopting a purely political or agonistic attitude of "containment" toward all theocratic fellow citizens. Moving beyond Law and seeking to ground an overlapping consensus only with religious ethicists is tempting but runs the risk of leaving behind many more conservative fellow citizens.[13] For certain religious citizens there may be no alternative to looking to revealed Law. Since it is the more conservative traditions and the believers who seek to follow them that are most likely to have principled objections to liberal citizenship, establishing consensus or congruence with them is also a greater priority.[14] If political liberalism aims at the widest possible support for a public conception of justice, then it makes sense that it would begin with the most enduring principled hindrances to that support. Furthermore, and perhaps most crucially, the belief that a genuine and reliable Islamic doctrine of support for political liberalism requires a radical reformist project in both substance and language runs the risk of creating the common impression that all other thinkers who do not assert a radical break with Islamic law are therefore incapable of engaging reasonably with non-Muslims.

It is at this impasse where this chapter enters. I outline here the possibility for a certain legitimacy of secular law and political justice from within Islamic legal/moral theory. I explore, specifically, the possibility for such legitimacy as emerging out of a long-term dialectical negotiation of the meaning and requirements of religious freedom resulting from the relatively sudden encounter with an exogenously determined liberal framework.

I argue that a particularly promising source of dialogue between liberal and Islamic moral theorists is provided by the Islamic legal theory of the "purposes of *shari'a*," which holds that divine law must be understood in terms of the promotion of universal welfare, achieved through the promotion and protection of five universal interests: life, religion, property, reason, and lineage. This model of dialogue between political liberalism and a theological doctrine of legitimacy identifies the moment of engagement (and possible reconciliation) as occurring not only at the first stage of justification (whereby parties recognize reasonable pluralism and agree to construct terms of cooperation on a fair basis) but also at a later stage when liberal terms of social cooperation can be evaluated on the basis of their substantive congruence with fixed points of religious morality.

II. The Promise of Purposivism: Maqasid al-shari'a in Reformist Writings

Classical Islamic law is based on two conjoined principles: divine sovereignty and divine omnipotence. The first principle is that God is the creator and master of all existence. He is free to command obedience and punish disobedience. The second important corollary of this principle is that God's power is unlimited, which means that his power to command certain acts and beliefs cannot be constrained by a prior, ontologically independent moral order. God does not just *reveal* morality to us; he *creates* morality—good and bad, obligatory and forbidden—*ex nihilo* in a state of perfect freedom.[15] God is under no moral or logical necessity to create a Law that is rationally beneficial to humans as they might perceive it. To foreshadow, though: *as it happens*, God has made provisions for man's well-being, including the Law itself, which exists to promote man's welfare. Man is assured that the requirements of the Law will not be greater than what he can bear, although this is not by logical necessity, only by God's good will and mercy and the assumption that a perfect being like God does not lie or act frivolously.

Islamic law, like any legal system, distinguishes between positive (applied) law (*fiqh*) and legal theory or jurisprudence (*usul al-fiqh*, the "sources of law"). The theory of the "purposes of the Law" (*maqasid al-shari'a*) is that all applied rulings (*ahkam*) of the Law, originally justified by the jurists through a painstaking hermeneutic study of the texts of revelation, can be shown to advance and protect a consistent set of human interests (*masalih*, sing: *maslaha*). Space does not permit a sufficient discussion of the origin and evolution of this theory; however, it suffices to note for now that this approach has traditionally been used by scholars to explicate the deeper wisdom (*hikma*) of the Law's rulings, to help in extending the Law to new circumstances and to help in adjudicating cases of indeterminacy or apparent conflicts between rulings.

I would propose as a term for this form of Islamic legal reasoning something like "complex purposivism." This is a method of legal interpretation and argumentation that makes central an appreciation of God's purposes behind legislating, in general, and the specific body of legislation he has revealed, in particular. However, this purposivism is complex because of the way in which it is constrained, not only by the letter of revelatory texts, but also by the accumulated tradition of positive legal rules, most of which crystallized before the advent of the theory of the *maqasid* (or, indeed, before "classical" legal theory itself) and thus acquired the status of authoritative and binding interpretations.

Today this theory is perhaps the most popular trend in Islamic legal and political thought, with dozens of books and doctoral dissertations written on the theory of the *maqasid* and its application in every possible area—from criminal law to the ethics of genetic engineering. It is a fully legitimate and popular discourse even among very conservative scholars.[16] However, the idea that *shari'a* should not be understood solely as embodied in specific rules (e.g., inheritance must be divided in this way) nor in terms of a painstaking, thorough extraction of those rules from the revelatory texts according to the methods of classical legal theory (*usul al-fiqh*), but rather defined in terms of the overall purposes (*maqasid*) for which God revealed the Law is often viewed as a panacea for modern reformers and pragmatists.[17] For those who want to establish Islamic legitimacy for new substantive moral, legal, and political commitments in new sociopolitical conditions, this idea allows Muslims to ask not whether a given norm has been expressly endorsed as compatible with the texts, but whether it is compatible with the deeper goods and interests that God wants to protect through the Law. Consider a few statements to this effect:

> Among the ways in which *maqasid* and *maqasid*-based thinking can serve the Islamic call and those engaged in it is by giving them greater flexibility and innovativeness in relation to the means and approaches

> which they employ. Things which can be classified purely as methods and means, including those which are mentioned explicitly in revelation, admit of change, modification and adjustment.[18]
>
> I understand Islamic law *to be* a drive for a just, productive, developed, humane, spiritual, clean, cohesive, friendly, and highly democratic society. . . . The validity of any method of *ijtihad* [juridico-ethical reasoning and argumentation] is determined based on its degree of realization of *maqasid al-shari'ah*. The practical outcome is Islamic rulings which are conducive to the values of justice, moral behavior, magnanimity, co-existence, and human development, which are '*maqasid*' in their own right.[19]

The attractiveness of the purposive approach to Islamic normativity is particularly stressed in the context of the Muslim minority condition. A prominent Islamic think tank, based in London and the Washington, DC area, The International Institute of Islamic Thought (IIIT), has an ongoing publication series in Arabic and English of prominent texts on the *maqasid* and a translation series of *maqasid* texts from Arabic to English (and other languages spoken by Muslim communities). The coordinator of this translation project declares that "knowledge of the *maqasid* is a prerequisite for any attempt to address and resolve contemporary issues challenging Islamic thought. Indeed such knowledge can help in the process of developing a much needed objectives-based *fiqh* [jurisprudence, or ethics] for minorities."[20]

In this vein, consider Tunisian/British Islamist activist Rashid al-Ghannushi's statements about political legitimacy and participating in non-Islamic governments:

> An Islamic government is based on a number of values which if accomplished in their totality would result in a perfect or near-perfect system. But it may not be possible for all such values to be implemented, and therefore some must suffice in certain circumstances in order for a just government to exist. A just government, even if not Islamic, is considered very close to the Islamic one, because justice is the most important feature of an Islamic government, and it has been said that justice is the law of God.[21]

Ghannushi's argument, based on his understanding of the theory of the *maqasid*, holds that the Muslim's duty is "to work towards preserving whatever can be preserved of the aims of *shari'a*" understood broadly as the five basic human interests of life, religion, property, intellect, and lineage. This emphasis on the ultimate purposes of divine Law serves to deflect attention from both particular, technical rulings of Islamic law and the un-Islamic forms of behavior permitted in non-Muslim states. Instead, non-Islamic governments can be seen as *sufficiently* just because of the general human interests that they protect (such interests include for Ghannushi, both in Muslim majority and minority political contexts, "independence, development, social solidarity, civil liberties, human rights, political pluralism, independence of the judiciary, freedom of the press, or liberty for mosques and Islamic activities"), possibly resulting in a legitimate form of governance, which he calls "the government of rationale" as opposed to "the government of *shari'a*." The crucial measure of Ghannushi's doctrine of how to share political space with non-Muslims is how he addresses the question of social coalitions with non-Muslims. Here, he sides firmly with liberal secular groups over other non-liberal religious ones: "Can any Muslim community afford to hesitate in participating in the establishment of a secular democratic system if it is unable to establish an Islamic democratic one? The answer is no. It is the religious duty of Muslims, as individuals and as communities, to contribute to the efforts to establish such a system."[22] This goes for Muslim minorities in particular, who have no hope of establishing Islamic rule. "The best option for such minorities is to enter into alliances with secular democratic groups. They can then work toward the establishment of a secular democratic government which will respect human rights, ensuring security and freedom of expression and belief—essential requirements of mankind that Islam has come to fulfill."[23]

The centrality of the *maqasid* for theorizing an Islamic approach to the minority condition that is itself not "political in the wrong way" from an Islamic juridical perspective is stressed by the most prominent scholars to have written on both Islamic legal theory and the jurisprudence of Muslim minorities, such as 'Abd Allah Ibn Bayya,[24] Yusuf al-Qaradawi,[25] and Taha Jabir al-'Alwani.[26] The idea of the *maqasid* also figures prominently in thought of nontraditional scholars writing for a broader audience, such as Tariq Ramadan[27] and the American convert Umar Faruq Abd-Allah.[28]

This theoretical logic opens a crucial space for engagement on the part of the liberal political or legal theorist. Given that the Law exists to protect or preserve five primary purposes (life, religion, property, lineage, and reason), that Islamic scholars have often used the theory of the *maqasid* to justify a principled and purposive flexibility in legal reasoning, and that scholars concerned with the minority condition have declared an eagerness to turn to the theory of the *maqasid* to theorize a permanent Muslim presence in non-Muslim polities, it is natural to ask whether these general purposes of the Law can be attained in a secular liberal state, thus establishing a certain legitimacy for liberal justice.

Take two obvious examples: murder and theft. Classical Islamic legal theory accepted that the Koranic punishments for these crimes (retribution or blood money in the case of homicide; cutting off of hands in the case of theft) were the revealed methods for preserving the universal necessary goods of life and property. It is obvious that only the strictest theocrat would argue that non-Muslim laws, which also protect life and property without enacting the Koranic punishments, are insufficiently just and legitimate; they overlap sufficiently with *shari'a*.

For the Muslim or non-Muslim scholar interested in the long-term encounter between Islamic law and liberal justice, it is natural to ask a further question: Is the religious freedom offered by a liberal order sufficient for the *shari'a* purpose (*maqsad*) of "preserving religion" (*hifz al-din*)? Could it not be argued that liberal societies with extensive religious liberties offer robust provisions for the preservation of religion?[29] However, unlike homicide and theft, the distribution of religious freedoms is a much more complex and contentious matter and can obviously not be resolved in a cursory way by assuming that liberal religious freedom is sufficiently just and legitimate from an Islamic legal perspective, even in the minority condition.

III. Hifz al-Din in Majoritarian Islamic Legal Theory: The Philosophical Logic of "Preserving Religion" as Positive Religious Liberty

To this point, I have referred to the theory of complex purposivism as a framework that justifies legal change in reformist discourses. However, it should not be understood that the function of purposive (*maqasidi*) reasoning is to liberalize the *shari'a* by making it less restrictive on persons subject to it in all cases. In fact, the opposite is more likely, insofar as the mandate to "protect and preserve" various fundamental interests turns the jurist's attention away from the justification of rulings through reference to specific revelatory texts and toward the policy of "blocking the means" to the corruption of those interests. It is true that *maqasid*-reasoning opens the door to considering new means for advancing stable goals and interests, but it is also simply the case that the jurist now sees more things as harmful to reason, religion, and the other "universal necessary interests." If before the jurist clung to a narrow, formalist prohibition on alcohol based on the Koran, he now sees countless potential sources of harm to reason.[30]

In a sense, this does in fact make the Law less restrictive—less restrictive on those who seek to "command the right and forbid the wrong" rather than less restrictive on those who might seek to dip their toes in the waters of the wrong.

This is not the place for an expansive exploration of the Islamic juridical literature on "preserving religion" as an objective of the Law. I merely wish to note the way in which this discourse is most commonly used by traditionalist scholars not as a device for liberalizing the Law but rather as a way of demonstrating the underlying logic and wisdom of the traditional rulings of criminal and public law. As such these discussions tend to be an invaluable source for studying the philosophy of religious freedom in orthodox Islamic thought. This is a philosophy of a deeply communitarian, "positive" conception of religious freedom where "preserving religion" refers to fully realizing all of its possible objectives and removing any and all potential sources of harm. Or, in the words of the fourteenth-century scholar whose work is the *locus classicus* for complex purposive reasoning, Abu Ishaq al-Shatibi (d. 1388), "preserving religion involves calling to it with promises and warnings,[31] fighting those who resist it and those tumors who rot it from within, and repairing any accidental unforeseen defects."[32]

First, it is important to take note of the definition of religion adopted by the legal scholars. This definition of religion is the most expansive possible: "Religion consists of divine rules which God has revealed through prophets to guide mankind to truth in matters of belief and to good in matters of behavior and social relations. Religion constrains mankind by these rules and brings them into submission to their commands and prohibitions so that they may attain the happiness of this world and the next."[33] Complete, perfect religion is composed of four elements: faith (*iman*), external submission (*islam*), belief in right doctrines (*i'tiqad*), and works (*'amal*).

The jurists clearly specify the necessary human personal and social goods that are advanced by the various elements of religion, beginning with the metaphysical, or perhaps theologico-anthropological, claim that "since religiosity is part of innate human nature [*fitra*], all mankind must affiliate itself with some religion or another and opposing this innate nature is pure deviation."[34] The only question is whether it is the true one or one of the false ones. The only sense in which the jurists believe "preserving religion" to be one of the aims of the *shari'a* is insofar as it is understood that only Islam is recognized by God as the final religion valid for all time. The idea is thus that:

> Religion in the sense of divine revelation sent down through prophets is necessary to guide human minds to truth. Religion in the sense of belief in God is necessary for individual human life in order for the soul to find

> security and tranquility from the kind of anxiety and stress which can lead to a nervous breakdown or even suicide. It is also necessary for social life because it guarantees the establishment of legislation which protects social relations from all ills which might corrupt them. Religion in the sense of divinely legislated laws is necessary in order to provide rules of justice and equality between persons and to protect them from the traps of human whims and passions. Indeed, mundane interests alone suffice to prove the necessity of religion in the lives of individuals and societies.[35]

The jurists then divide the modes through which the *shari'a* protects the interest humans have in the integrity and flourishing of religion into the positive establishment of certain elements of religion (*al-hifz min janib al-wujud*)[36] and the removal of potential harms (*al-hifz min janib al-'adam*).[37] The former has a literal meaning of providing for the "existence," and the latter has a literal meaning of providing for the "absence." We may call them "positive preservation" and "negative preservation," respectively.

A single principle of religious obligation underlies all of these modes of preserving religion: the idea of "commanding the right and forbidding the wrong," the activist and interventionist conception of enforcing religious morality, which might be said to be *the* single principle underpinning all Islamic political, ethical, and legal thought. Strictly speaking, then, there is no separate, distinct branch of legal and ethical thought concerned with how Muslims are commanded to "preserve religion." Rather, the entire edifice of Islamic public and criminal law is what is meant by the obligation to preserve religion through the removal of specific harms; "preserving religion by 'providing for the absence' is simply to repel *everything which opposes religion in word and deed*."[38] "Preserving religion means salvaging it . . . from *anything* that might undermine and confuse beliefs and distort behavior."[39] The function of purposivism is thus primarily to explicate the wisdom and rationale of the rules, "revealing the perfection of Islamic law."[40]

IV. What Is Involved in Arguing to Modern Religious Liberty from the *Shari'a* Objective of "Preserving Religion"? An External Engagement

I introduced earlier the theory of complex purposivism as a potential device for creative, reformist Islamic thinking about norms and legitimacy in new conditions. The preceding section should convince us that, if what we mean by "reform" is something along the lines of modern human rights standards regarding freedom of religion and conscience, the move from the purposivism to "human rights" (in the modern liberal formulation) is hardly a slam dunk. I by no means wish to suggest that lurking behind the pious endorsement of the idea of "*shari'a* on the part of Western Muslims is the active desire to bring about the full scope of traditional *shari'a* punishments for apostasy, blasphemy, heresy, and sinful behavior. My point in introducing the preceding material is merely to highlight the problem of approaching the legitimacy of a secular liberal legal order via an interrogation of whether it "preserves religion." It is simply not the case that a long-standing Islamic jurisprudence of treating what we now call "negative liberty" as sufficient for the legal "purpose" of preserving religion lies ready and waiting for Muslim and non-Muslim liberals to point to and appropriate. Instead, we must view purposivism in Islamic thought as an opportunity for engagement and negotiation, rather than a lost tradition in need of rehabilitation (perhaps the way some Republican theorists have treated Cicero, Machiavelli, and Harrington). But that is precisely why I regard this as an important issue for active political philosophers.

Although there are numerous points of contact between Islamic law and political liberalism, for the purposes of this article I am concerned with the core question of religious freedom and individual autonomy. What political liberalism requires of *shari'a*-minded Muslims is affirmation of something like the following two principles:

- that Islamic conceptions of morality can only be cultivated and encouraged within Muslim families and communities though noncoercive means;
- that the public sphere in non-Muslim liberal democracies cannot be expected to accommodate all Islamic religious sensibilities by limiting freedom of expression.

This is the most familiar liberal conception of religious freedom, which inclines toward a negative conception of liberty. For purposes of simplicity, I refer to it throughout this article (following Constant and Berlin) as "modern religious freedom." I do not mean to suggest that all modern thinkers have endorsed this conception, that persons contesting or rejecting it are therefore "antimodern," or even if they were that the designation "antimodern" is a final and dismissive moral judgment. I also do not mean to suggest that the specific boundaries and distributions of religious liberties in a secular society is an easy matter, or a settled one, even for persons interested in defending a liberal, negative, "modern" conception of religious freedom. Nonetheless, I think the broad outlines are clear enough and, importantly, probably shared even by many persons presently interested in critiquing secularism and liberalism. By "modern religious freedom" I mean the following general ideas:

- Religious communities do not determine the civil rights of their members.
- Religious communities cannot be *guaranteed* protection from public criticism of their beliefs, from "moral injury" inflicted by the disapproved behavior of others (including blasphemy or mockery), or from the exit of individual members from the group.
- "Religious freedom" cannot be interpreted as the right of a religious community to fully and successfully realize its entire conception of the good without regard for the preferences of those who dissent from the interpretation of that conception.
- Religious freedom implies a right not only to reject one's own religion in favor of another but to reject religion altogether.

I believe that almost all of the disputed areas of the application of free religious practice—including the rights of religious groups to discriminate within their own institutions, the right to religious dress in schools, the right to parallel religious schooling, the right to religious arbitration of civil contracts and the issue of offensive speech—fall within this broad understanding of the "(religious) freedom of the moderns."

We know from above that Islamic positive law as prescribed for Muslim majority societies is strictly at odds with this liberal conception of justice, rights, and religious freedom. However, we also know that certain reformist and pragmatic Islamic thinkers, who are committed simultaneously to the broad idea of a *shari'a*-based solution to the legitimacy of the minority condition and to a creative and pragmatic understanding of what such a solution involves substantively and methodologically, have pronounced the theory of purposivism as their preferred model for how to approach non-Islamic political orders (and, indeed, even the reform project in Muslim-majority societies[41]).

What I am proposing here is thus an understanding of purposive reasoning as a *framework of argumentation* about the relative legitimacy of various legal and political institutions in non-Muslim liberal democracies, given that even very conservative Islamic jurists (including those contributing to the "jurisprudence of Muslim minorities") regard the Muslim presence in Europe and North America as a social phenomenon requiring original, creative jurisprudence.[42] The plausibility of this is demonstrated also in the way that jurists speak of the jurisprudence of the minority condition as itself having certain purposes that are served and advanced by certain conceptual tools from classical legal theory.[43]

For all of these writers, the tools provided by classical legal theory include the theory of purposivism conjoined with other tools, such as Islamic legal maxims, which stress ease and facilitation (*taysir*) in enforcing the Law. "This jurisprudence must balance between looking at individual texts on the one hand, but also at the spirit of Islam, the goals of *shari'a*, the universal purposes (*al-maqasid al-kulliyya*), and the general goals."[44]

However, it appears that to this point such scholars have not mobilized these jurisprudential tools for a *general theoretical inquiry* into what kind of conception of religious freedom in the West could be regarded as sufficient (if not ideal) for the goal of preserving religion. Here, again, is where there is room for the non-Muslim political or legal philosopher to engage with her Muslim fellow citizens.

What might be the components of such a framework of argumentation that is cautiously and critically open to Western legal frameworks while using the theory of purposivism to structure Islamic moral inquiry and political action? Most obviously, this would be a framework that would begin by taking seriously the distinctions between different types of *goals*, *agents*, *means*, and *obstructions* as part of a process of unpacking the cohesive and integral logic of "preserving religion"-as-positive-liberty elaborated earlier.

- Clear *goals* belonging to a moral obligation to "preserve religion" could include ensuring access to knowledge of Islam, perpetuating religiosity across generations, the construction of the religious institutions of a Muslim civil society (mosques, publishing houses, centers of research, seminaries, lobbying groups), minimizing social costs for living a Muslim life and for converting into Islam, enlarging the ranks of Muslim communities, and Islamizing presently non-Muslim states and societies.
- Purposive (*maqasidi*) legal-ethical reasoning would have to identify when preserving religion is the obligation of various kinds of *agents*, including individual Muslims, individual non-Muslims, Muslim communities and civil society institutions, non-Muslim communities and civil society institutions, and the non-Muslim state.
- There would have to be serious theoretical distinction between various *means* for advancing these goals, including coercive laws, persuasion, proselytism, Islamic religious schools, direct action, political participation, methods of social pressure, and violence.
- Finally, a strong theory would have something to say about the different kinds of *obstructions* to preserving religion that Muslim minority communities might theoretically face, including the mere

> fact of a dominant non-Muslim culture, the "moral injury" of others acting in alien and disapproved ways, the temptation of social and personal freedoms, the lack of communal control over the circulation of information and beliefs, direct efforts of other groups to "seduce" (*fitna*) Muslims away from Islam, laws which limit communal or family control over the education and rights of members, laws which limit the right to worship and behave Islamically in public, hostile representations or descriptions of Islam and Muslims in non-Muslim media, and coercive state laws that force Muslims to declare abandonment of Islam.

An intellectually serious account of whether the *shari'a* "purpose" of preserving religion can be attained within non-Muslim societies might proceed by imagining all of the possible ways in which religion might *not* be preserved in a non-Muslim society (from a society that merely protects Muslim apostates to one that actively persecutes Muslims merely for proclaiming belief in Islam), by positing a principled "minimum" which falls short of full self-governance on majoritarian *shari'a* lines but also represents a coherent account of fair religious liberty, by ranking and prioritizing various components of the communal "preservation of religion," by interrogating existing legal and political arrangements according to those standards, and then by considering how different *means* of advancement and resistance are appropriate for different kinds of obstructions.

A framework of this kind might replicate the classical dichotomy between how a non-Muslim environment sets out to provide "positive" protections for religion (*hifz min janib al-wujud*) and remove "negative" ones (*hifz min janib al-'adam*). By way of positive provision (*wujud*), liberals and Muslims might agree that a religiously diverse society ought to provide equal access to the public sphere, representation in media outlets and access to the institutions of state. Areas where the state *allows* groups and communities to provide for their own institutions might also fall under the rubric of positive provision (*wujud*), and thus liberals and Muslims might agree that Muslim communities ought to be allowed to create religious schools; proselytize; enjoy full rights of speech and dissemination, subject only to the same restrictions as other groups; and build mosques (including with minarets!), seminaries, and research centers.

By way of restrictions or removal of harms (*'adam*), liberals and Muslims might agree that in a religiously diverse society where Muslims are a minority there should be no coerced public declarations of controversial metaphysical views in shared institutions, no faith tests or requirements of religious homogeneity for public officials, and no punishment for conversion out of the majority religion into Islam. Areas where the state *allows* groups and communities to respond to harms might also fall under the rubric of negative provision (*'adam*), and thus liberals and Muslims might agree that Muslim communities ought to be allowed to publicly dissuade individuals from leaving their religious community; impose nonviolent deterrent punishments, such as boycotts or exclusion from institutions, on apostates and sinners; arrange internal institutions, such as mosques and seminaries, on hierarchical and authoritarian grounds; or publicly condemn dissenters, sinners, and heretics even in theologically harsh terms.

However, here is exactly where such a framework will inevitably come into contact with any kind of liberal secular one, as from an Islamic perspective "preserving religion" is a concept much better suited to a form of (semi-)sovereignty. By way of positive provision (*wujud*), Muslims thus might argue that in order for religion to be genuinely preserved the state must provide them with mandatory religiously homogenous schools to the exclusion of public education, legal recognition for the right of Muslim communal and religious leaders to represent exclusively all Muslims in dealings with the state, and full legal and political autonomy to apply Islamic law within the Muslim community, including criminal law. By way of restrictions or removal of harms (*'adam*), Muslims might argue that "preserving religion" requires that the non-Muslim state suppress all speech offensive to a Muslim sensibility, including novels, cartoons, and source-critical historical scholarship; prevent non-Muslims from actively proselytizing among Muslims; and create a common public space free of sexually immoral behavior. They might even argue that a commitment to religious freedom *requires* all of these things lest the "religious freedom" on offer be dismissed as an arbitrary, sectarian, liberal-secular conception of "freedom" no more justifiable than the one demanded by Islamic law.

Between these two extremes—perfect consensus and perfect antagonism—the kind of complex purposive framework I outlined is a likely candidate for structuring Islamic juridical thought on inevitable "hard cases" like schooling and offensive speech. Ideally, an Islamic juridical theory would be able to distinguish between, on the one hand, blasphemous or offensive speech that the state inscribes as part of its public language of justification or that public officials routinely feel free to engage in, from, on the other hand, offensive speech in civil society that the state merely refrains from suppressing and punishing. Moreover, a minoritarian Islamic juridical theory ought to be able to distinguish between various forms of political action in response to such speech: from protest to positive public representations of religion, to political bargaining, to murder. Similarly, such a theory ought to be able to distinguish the right to religious schooling from the right to restrict all community members to this form of schooling, and state regulations of religious schooling based on certain civic public interests from state regulations based on purely theological objections to Islamic teachings.

Indeed, there is evidence of the use and attractiveness of this form of argumentation by Islamic intellectuals. In addition to the above-quoted remarks by Rashid al-Ghannushi on the potential legitimacy and justness of certain non-Muslim legal systems, Tariq Ramadan has argued for the justness of present European positive law treatments of religious freedom. Using the language of Islamic legal theory, in particular the notion of purposivism, he writes that "the Islamic sciences were but a means for meeting Muslims' needs to protect their Faith, lives and religious practice."[45] In this context, he argues that European positive law provides a framework both for protecting religion and for negotiating the boundaries of religious practice. He also advances a hierarchy inspired by the theory of purposivism for evaluating the relative losses at stake in those *shari'a*-derived practices that are not protected.

Thus, "it is possible to assert that five fundamental rights are secured: (1) the right to practice Islam; (2) the right to knowledge; (3) the right to found organizations; (4) the right to autonomous representation; (5) the right to appeal to the law."[46] And, although "Muslims obviously cannot apply all the global principles and rulings prescribed by the Qur'an and the *Sunna* in the field of social affairs . . . it should be noted that the majority of [religiously prohibited activities] *are not imposed* on Muslims but are rather *legally allowed* . . . [and thus] the abode of Europe appears as a space within which Muslims can live in security with some fundamental rights both acquired and protected. As a minority in a non-Muslim environment they are able to practice and to respect the more important rulings of the Islamic teaching."[47]

The purpose of my presentation here of a possible framework for Muslims (and non-Muslims) to use Islamic legal theory to endorse secular positive law based on a liberal conception of religious freedom is not to suggest that the only intellectually serious use of the theory of the *maqasid* will exactly replicate the kinds of distinctions and evaluations that liberal theories of religious freedom make. Rather, what I would like to suggest is that if we are interested in the views of more conservative and traditionalist believers toward religious freedom and public space in a religious and morally diverse society, in addition to already semi-secularized "post-legal" Muslims, then we ought to look to the theory of purposivism as a flexible, complex form of legal/moral argumentation that has the capacity to provide for an Islamic response to the modern liberal conception of religious freedom, which is somewhere in between enthusiastic full endorsement and a mere agreement to obey the law out of unfortunate social and demographic necessity (*darura*, in Islamic legal terms).

V. Conclusion: Implications for Political Philosophy and Public Discourse

In an important article on Rawls's idea of the overlapping consensus, Kurt Baier argued that an overlapping consensus can occur to a varying extent on three dimensions: (1) the level or degree of specificity, (2) the extent of support among the population, and (3) the intensity of agreement by those not opposing the regime.[48] In this article I have only focused on the issue of formal doctrinal grounds for affirming or rejecting an overlapping consensus and left the issue of popular opinion and feeling entirely to the side. However, even when studying formal doctrine, one can appreciate that agreement or disagreement can occur at various levels of specificity, breadth, and depth.

Some approaches to the minority condition prefer a piecemeal consideration of every possible aspect of social life in the West. Here there may be numerous *specific* points of convergence and divergence between political liberalism and Islamic ethics that occur against a backdrop of mutual unintelligibility.[49] In contrast, some approaches prefer to begin with a broad statement of a post-legal humanist Islamic ethics that may have the breadth required by an overlapping consensus, but is not in a strong position to speak to specific questions emerging from the more mainstream Islamic legal tradition. My own interest in Islamic legal theory and particularly the doctrine of the *maqasid al-shari'a* is motivated by my belief that it is the most likely source of an Islamic minoritarian political ethics that is not only *specific* in application and *broad* in its consideration of social conditions but also *deep* in the range of answers it can give in response to objections emerging out of orthodox Islamic legal and theological debates. The theory of the *maqasid* is attractive because it is a coherent and elaborate theory, a strong edifice with deep roots in classical Islamic law, as opposed to a tacit or "decisionist" shift in emphasis, or a mere citation of numerous Koranic verses that seem conducive to legal change in a liberalizing direction.[50] It is both intellectually respectable and morally appealing to a conservative Muslim conscience.

More importantly for comparative ethical and philosophical purposes: *this is a rights-based approach to political morality*. Islamic complex purposivism connects with deep metaphysical claims, but methodologically is not a form of reasoning directly from a universal conception of the self or of the good. Rather, it is a potentially rigorous model for how to think about balancing various claims in society. Thus, although there is still plenty of room for deep disagreement with liberalism, using complex purposivism as a field of argumentation does not require that we establish a prior consensus on the self or the value of individual autonomy.

Instead, we begin with a rough consensus on the most important social and political interests a system must protect (life, property, lineage, reason, and religion) and argue from there. The theologico-political problem (metaphysical disagreement about the self and the good) does not go away, but neither does it entirely frustrate moral dialogue from the outset. Given the well-known problems about arriving at a prior consensus with deeply religious fellow citizens on the burdens of judgment or the precise meaning and value of being a "free and equal citizen," the availability of a theocratic vision that plays out at the intermediate level of prioritizing the protection of such social goods as life, property, lineage, reason, and religion is a source of great optimism.

In fact, I would suggest (I cannot do more than that here), that the preceding discussion about the special nature of the minority condition for Islamic political ethics and the promises of complex purposivism for theorizing a flexible approach to Islamic legal commitments, allows us to imagine a more general Islamic endorsement of *political constructivism* as a procedure for a deeper justification of the terms of social cooperation in a diverse society. Very briefly, we have seen four stages of thought about the minority condition that seem to approximate the procedure of political constructivism.

1. Stage One: The minority condition and the *contingent suspension of shari'a* rules.
2. Stage Two: The permissibility of *contracts* with non-Muslims as a way of establishing rights and obligations.
3. Stage Three: Testing contracts against *fixed points of Islamic morality*, such as the nonnegotiable requirements of protecting and preserving life, religion, property, lineage, and reason.
4. Stage Four: Searching for *reflective equilibrium* between the terms of life in a non-Muslim polity and the aims and desires of Islamic morality based on the use of complex purposivism.

However, as seen throughout this chapter, for those who approach Islamic ethics with an interest in the possibilities of some kind of dialogue with political liberalism (or some other non-Islamic moral doctrine), much more is needed than complex purposivism (the theory of the *maqasid al-shari'a*) alone. The Islamic moral theorist needs some *good* reason to balance the harm of allowing nonideal behavior with other benefits. Many simply accept that living as a minority imposes this unfortunate fact on Muslim minorities, but this approach is clearly "political in the wrong way" as it refuses to normalize or normativize such realism. Thus, an important area for scholarly research, as well as civic dialogue, is to closely follow the internal arguments and sources of motivation for combining a recognition of reasonable moral pluralism in a diverse society with the jurisprudential logic of the theory of the *maqasid al-shari'a*.

Nonetheless, the lack of such an account of reasonable moral pluralism in a permanently diverse society at this stage should not result in excessive pessimism or skepticism. Although reasonable pluralism is conceptually and philosophically prior to all other arguments in Rawls's theory, and recognizing the fact of reasonable pluralism is one of the necessary conditions of a reasonable doctrine, it need not be historically or chronologically prior in the case of any given non-liberal religious community. If the theory of the "purposes of the Law" enables a temporary end run around the question of the reasonableness of non-Islamic views by making non-Islamic laws "legitimate enough," it is still possible for *shari'a*-minded Muslims to gradually come to see the condition of pluralism as permanent and reasonable. This is certainly how many Christians came to terms with pluralism and tolerance, and it is consistent with Rawls's account of the move from a constitutional consensus to an overlapping consensus.

Thus, an awareness of the tools, language, and inherited doctrines of Islamic jurisprudence should at the very least impose on the non-Muslim interlocutor a measure of patience and flexibility in evaluating some of the outcomes of this encounter. Short of denouncing Koranic punishments, there may be many ways for an Islamic thinker to balance membership in the epistemic community of Islamic jurists with openness to the legal institutions of diverse, secular societies.

Imagine, for example, a conservative jurist considering the problem of religious freedom in the West from the perspective of Islamic legal theory. Suppose he or she advances something like the following position: Revelatory texts call for a set of punishments for moral crimes (*hudud*) that attained the status of near universal consensus from an early point in the history of Islam. Later Islamic legal theorists masterfully showed how all of the many individual rulings of the Law can be shown to advance a consistent set of human interests, the most important ones being the preservation of religion, life, property, lineage, and reason. Through this theory we gained a finer appreciation for which rulings of the Law are ends in themselves and which are merely the most ideal means for advancing them. Today in the West, we are confronted with a social, political, and legal situation unprecedented in the history of Islam. Without a doubt, our overall objective is to preserve the religion, life, property, lineage, and reason of Western Muslims. As for religion, the necessary and indispensible rights (*daruriyyat*) that we must secure are the rights to manifest our religion and educate our children into it in a condition of freedom and security from repression and intimidation. If these conditions are not available then Muslims must not live in such a land. Once these are secured, further important needs (*hajiyyat*) for preserving religion include the rights to openly call others to Islam, spread accurate knowledge of Islam, build mosques and other sacred spaces, enable Muslims to interact in the public sphere without engaging in forbidden acts, and create institutions of Islamic learning at all levels. As to the canonical criminal punishments (*hudud*), we do not deny that they are part of *shari'a* but we need not regard them as indispensible to living a good Islamic life and preserving our religion as the *shari'a* intends.

I believe there is space for a political liberal to appreciate the distinction between "we need not regard these punishments as indispensible to living a good Islamic life and preserving our religion as the *shari'a* intends" and "given our unfortunate demographic position, we need not insist on implementing these punishments *for the time being*." True, we prefer a less ambiguous shared condemnation of the very idea of punishing someone for revising their conception of the good. But that preference need not force us to adopt an antagonistic stance toward fellow citizens raised and living in a traditionalist religious community seeking to balance multiple commitments.[51] The structure of the theory of the *maqasid* provides such fellow citizens with both substantive and also linguistic flexibility, which we are well advised to recognize.

I would like to draw attention to a final implication of this case study. The question of the compatibility of constructivist methods and revealed moralities is not only a matter for the armchair. I would suggest that ultimately it can only be resolved empirically, that is, through examining the specific encounter between particular religious commitments at particular moments in time and a particular secular legal order. There is no a priori solution, no single argument or proof of the fairness or unfairness of the political liberal attitude to religion from the standpoint of all actually situated citizens. This chapter is not meant to refute religious arguments against liberalism, or historicist arguments for liberalism's arbitrariness. Rather, it is meant to show that no such skeptical arguments may be regarded as having force on theoretical or logical grounds alone. The theocratic challenge to political liberalism is not static or perennial. Theocratic conceptions of legitimacy often invoke a different temporal horizon and a rather different final arbiter. But the most enduring such conceptions endure precisely because of their ability to embed themselves in the lifeworlds and consciousnesses of their adherents, who themselves do not live only in the temporal horizons of theocracy. An appreciation for the capacity of theocratic doctrines to change and evolve is crucial for liberal political philosophers interested in public philosophy as a civic activity. However, doing that well involves not only good will and an appreciation that heteronomous, religious citizens may also live good lives, but also, I suggest, a sympathy for theocratic doctrines as *traditions* that rely in large measure on integrity and continuity. We need not regard these semipublic theocratic doctrines as having a right to immunity from criticism or investigation, but if we choose to engage with them we should do so with the same measure of seriousness we would approach any other expert discourse.

NOTES

1. In this chapter, I will use "Law" as synonymous with the idea of *shari'a* or an ontologically real morality created by God. It refers both to the very concept of a Divine Law and also Islamic scholars' conception of *shari'a* as something perfect and integral despite human's fallible and contingent understanding of it.
2. Yusuf al-Qaradawi, *Al-Hulul al-mustawrada wa-kayfa janat 'ala Ummatina* [Imported Solutions and How They Have Wronged Our Nation] (Beirut: Mu'assasat al-Risala, 1971), 113–14. All translations from Arabic in this article are mine.
3. For a presentation of all of these views, see Khaled Abou El Fadl, "Islamic Law and Muslim Minorities: The Juristic Discourse on Muslim Minorities from the Second/Eighth to the Eleventh/Seventeenth Centuries," *Islamic Law and Society* 1 (1994): 141–87.
4. See Andrew F. March, "Islamic Foundations for a Social Contract in Non-Muslim Liberal Democracies," *American Political Science Review* 101 (2007): 235–52; more generally, see *Islam and Liberal Citizenship: The Search for an Overlapping Consensus* (Oxford: Oxford University Press, 2009).
5. Jeff Spinner-Halev, "Cultural Pluralism and Partial Citizenship," *Multicultural Questions*, ed. Christian Joppke and Steven Lukes (Oxford: Oxford University Press, 1999), 65–86.
6. For a statement of this attitude toward non-Islamic polities, which overlaps with the Thin Social Contract Model but stresses the need for strict voluntary adherence to Islamic norms while living in exile, see 'Abd al-Mun'im Mustafa Halima (Abu Basir al-Tartusi), "*Man dakhala diyar ghayr al-muslimin bi-'ahd wa aman ma lahu wa ma 'alayhi*" ["The Rights and Responsibilities of Those Who Enter Non-Muslim Lands under a Contract of Mutual Security"]. Available at: http://www.abubaseer. bizland.com.
7. Lucas Swaine's proposal of "semi-sovereignty" for theocratic communities in liberal states is an exemplar of this model. See Lucas Swaine, "How Should Liberal Democracies Treat Theocratic Communities?" *The Liberal Conscience: Politics and Principle in a World of Religious Pluralism* (New York: Columbia University Press, 2006), ch. 3.
8. On the Indian case, see S. N. Balagangadhara and Jakob De Roover, "The Secular State and Religious Conflict: Liberal Neutrality and the Indian Case of Pluralism," *Journal of Political Philosophy* 15 (2007): 67–92.

9. See Abou El Fadl, "Islamic Law and Muslim minorities."
10. See, in particular, Swaine, *The Liberal Conscience.* See also: Nancy Rosenblum, *Obligations of Citizenship and Demands of Faith* (Princeton, NJ: Princeton University Press, 2000); Robert B. Thigpen and Lyle A. Downing, "Rawls and the Challenge of Theocracy to Freedom," *Journal of Church and State* 40 (1998): 757–73. For a discussion of the potential legitimacy of global human rights regimes from Confucian and Islamic integralist (as opposed to theocratic) perspectives, see Joshua Cohen, "Minimalism about Human Rights: The Most We Can Hope For?" *Journal of Political Philosophy* 12 (2004): 190–213.
11. Tariq Ramadan, *Radical Reform: Islamic Ethics and Liberation* (New York: Oxford University Press, 2009). On Ramadan's move from a more traditional legal perspective (referred to below) to a "post-legal" theological ethics, see Andrew F. March, "Law as a Vanishing Mediator in the Theological Ethics of Tariq Ramadan," *European Journal of Political Theory*, 10, no. 2 (2011).
12. Strictly speaking, classical interpretations of Islamic law regarded non-Muslim political space as lawless. Non-Muslim societies and polities may have conventions, which are law-like, but because those *conventions* were man-made, those societies were beyond the space of the organization of social life according to divinely originating, and thus objective and just, laws. A good example of this is the Islamic jurisprudence of warfare, which only discusses the obligations of Muslims in wartime. There was no conceptual framework for even thinking about the obligations of non-Muslims in wartime, only their legitimate responses to the Islamic invitation to join the Abode of Islam. An exception would apply to Jews and Christians who are often spoken of having divinely revealed "*shara'i*'" (pl. of *shari'a*).
13. Indeed, in his only comment on the matter, John Rawls refers to a scholar, Abdullahi An-Na'im, who is well known to represent a highly controversial, highly innovative approach to the place of Islamic law within Islamic theology and ethics in "The Idea of Public Reason Revisited," *The Law of Peoples: With "The Idea of Public Reason Revisited"* (Cambridge, MA: Harvard University Press, 1999), 151. As Rawls notes, An-Na'im's views involved reversing the traditional understanding of the temporary and the eternal in the Koran and are regarded by many Sunni Muslims to be heretical. (His mentor and originator of this approach, Mahmud Muhammad Taha was hanged for apostasy.)
14. Such consensus might also be presumed to imply that liberal principles will be justified for persons with a less demanding or rigorous conception of religious obligation. In other words, evidence of congruence from within more conservative sources is very likely to suggest the fact of congruence from within less conservative ones (even if the "evidence," i.e., the precise arguments that happen to convince the conservative believer, cannot be presumed to sway the less conservative one).
15. It is thus common to speak of orthodox Islamic moral theology as "voluntarist" or "subjectivist" as opposed to "objectivist." Morality is voluntarist

or subjectivist in the sense of being willed by God *subjectively* as opposed to objectivist in the sense of existing apart from God's freely willed choices. On a voluntarist account, we simply do not know whether lying, for example, is bad. On an objectivist account, we assume that there are some acts that have an intrinsic moral attribute that even God cannot violate. See, for example, the essays in George F. Hourani, *Reason and Tradition in Islamic Ethics* (Cambridge: Cambridge University Press, 1985).

16. See David L. Johnston, "*Maqasid Al-Shari'a*: Epistemology and Hermeneutics of Muslim Theologies of Human Rights," *Die Welt des Islams* 47 (2007): 149–87, for a typology of various trends in the treatment of human rights in Islamic legal thought, which includes discussion of how "traditionalists" and "progressive conservatives" (two different groups for Johnston) use the *maqasid*.
17. "The approach to scriptural interpretation that proceeds from what classical jurists identified as the *maqasid al-shari'a* has acquired almost panacean expectations among modern Muslims. This is based on the belief that interpretations that are violent, intolerant or misogynistic, or culturally, economically or politically stultifying or ineffective are almost invariably grounded in a literalism that cannot stand in the face of appeals to the broader aims and objectives of the law." See Sherman A. Jackson, "Literalism, Empiricism, and Induction: Apprehending and Concretizing Islamic Law's *Maqasid Al-Shari'ah* in the Modern World," *Michigan State Law Review*, 2006, 1469–86, at 1470.
18. Ahmad al-Raysuni, *al-Fikr al-maqasidi* [Legal Purposive Thought] (Rabat, Morocco: Mansharat al-zaman, 1999), 129.
19. Jasser Auda, *Maqasid al-shari'ah as Philosophy of Islamic Law: A Systems Approach* (London: International Institute of Islamic Thought, 2008), xxii–iii, emphasis added.
20. Anas S. al-Shaikh-Ali, "Foreword" to Gamal Eldin Attia, *Towards Realization of the Higher Intents of Islamic Law*, trans. Nancy Roberts (London; International Institute of Islamic Thought, 2007), ix.
21. Rachid Ghannouchi, "Participation in Non-Islamic Government," *Liberal Islam: A Sourcebook*, ed. Charles Kurzman (Oxford: Oxford University Press, 1998), 92.
22. Ibid.
23. Ibid., 94. Occasionally scholars will go so far as to say that because of the freedom Muslims enjoy in the West and the proliferation of Islamic societies and foundations available to them, Western countries should be viewed as part of the "Abode of Islam" (*dar al-Islam*). See Salah 'Abd al-Razzaq, *Al-Aqalliyyat al-muslima fi'l-gharb: qadaya fiqhiyya wa humum thaqafiyya* [Muslim Minorities in the West: Juridical Issues and Cultural Concerns] (Beirut: Dar al-Hadi, 2007), 45, quoting a Moroccan scholar 'Abd al-'Aziz ibn Sadiq who based his position partially on Ghannushi's views.
24. 'Abd Allah Ibn Bayya, *Sina'at al-fatwa wa-fiqh al-aqalliyyat* [Producing Fatwas and the Jurisprudence of Muslim Minorities] (Jedda, Saudi Arabia: Dar al-Minhaj, 2007), 168–9, 181–2.

25. Yusuf al-Qaradawi, *Fi fiqh al-aqalliyyat al-muslima* [On the Jurisprudence of Muslim Minorities] (Cairo: Dar al-Shuruq, 2001), 36.
26. Taha Jabir al-Alwani, *Towards a Fiqh for Minorities: Some Basic Reflections* (Herndon, VA: International Institute of Islamic Thought, 2003), 13.
27. "The great responsibility of Muslims in the West is to give an adapted European shape to their identity . . . [k]eeping in mind . . . the three levels of *maslaha*, namely the [three levels of interests theorized to be the Purposes of Islamic law]. . . . Muslims, whether scholars or organization leaders, must provide European Muslims with the appropriate teachings and rulings to enable to protect and fulfill their identity"; Tariq Ramadan, *To Be a European Muslim* (Leicester: Islamic Foundation, 1999), 196. See also Tariq Ramadan, *Western Muslims and the Future of Islam* (Oxford: Oxford University Press, 2004), 161–3.
28. See Umar Faruq Abd-Allah, "Living Islam with purpose," available at http://www.nawawi. org/downloads/article6.pdf.
29. Jackson's article "Literalism, Empiricism, and Induction" is based on a similar investigation of the meanings and uses of one of the five daruriyyat, in his case the *maqsad* of preserving reason (*hifz al-'aql*). However, his purposes differ somewhat in that he begins with a frustration about the lack of boldness and creativity on the part of Islamic scholars who tend to limit their concern with "preserving reason" to a constant repetition of the prohibition on intoxicants. For Jackson (a believing Muslim), the concept has rich possibilities for Islamic opposition to all forms of false consciousness and other hegemonic ideas that have served to corrupt the minds of African Americans and colonized Muslims.
30. Attia, for example, notes that "*maqasid*-based thinking contributes to the expansion of the process of assessment in analogical reasoning [*qiyas*]." Using the example of the prohibition on wine being linked to the *maqasid* of preserving reason (*hifz al-'aql*), Attia notes that one possibility emerging from this is a "process of broad *qiyas* [whereby] we apply the legal prohibition to everything which negatively influences one's reasoning capacity even if it does not inebriate as drugs do. Indeed, we can expand it still further by applying the same prohibition to everything which harms the mind, including superstitions, magic arts, brainwashing operations, baseless imitation of one's forebears, and the like." See Attia, *Towards Realization of the Higher Intents of Islamic Law, 165–6.*
31. *Al-targhib wa'l-tarhib*: this common phrase means to "incite desire and fear," or to use the carrot and the stick. The idea here is that Muslim proselytizers should inspire desire for what God gives and promises and at the same time fear of his disapproval and punishment.
32. Abu Ishaq al-Shatibi, *al-Muwafaqat fi ̄ Usul al-fiqh* [Congruencies in Legal Theory] (Beirut: DarIhya al-Turath al-'Arabi, 2001), vol. 4, 23.
33. 'Abd Allah Muhammad al-Amin al-Na'im and Yusuf al-Bashir Muhammad, *Maqasid al-shari'a al-Islamiyya* [The Objectives of the Islamic Shari'a] (Khartoum: al-Markaz al-Qawmi li'l-Intaj al-Islami, 1995), 26.

34. Muhammad al-Yubi, *Maqasid al-shari'a al-Islamiyya wa 'alaqatuha b'il-adilla al-shar'iyya* [The Objectives of the Islamic Shari'a and their Relationship to the Revealed Proofs] (Riyadh: Dar al-Hijra, 1998), 192.
35. al-Na'im and Muhammad, *Maqasid al-shari'a*, 27–8.
36. A common approach is to view the "positive preservation" of religion as consisting of three broad fields of thought and action: (1) acting in accordance with it [*al-'amal bihi*], (2) judging in accordance with it [*al-hukm bihi*], and (3) calling others to it [*al-da'wa ilayhi*].
37. Jurists generally speak of four forms of preserving religion via the removal of harms: (1) jihad, (2) the killing of self-declared and self-obscuring apostates, (3) combating heretics and occultists, and (4) forbidding sinful behavior and punishing its perpetrators. The most common definition of jihad is something like: "Fighting unbelievers for the glorification of the word of God," and it can include both defensive and expansionist wars. (al-Na'im and Muhammad, *Maqasid al-shari'a*, 33; Ihmaydan, *Maqasid al-shari'a al-Islamiyya*, 106.)
38. Ibid., 206. Emphasis added.
39. Muhammad al-Tahir Ibn 'Ashur, *Treatise on Maqasid al-Shari'ah*, trans. Mohamed el-Tahir el-Mesawi (London: International Institute of Islamic Thought, 2006), 120.
40. Attia, *Towards Realization of the Higher Intents of Islamic Law*, 153.
41. Evidence for the capacity of *maqasid*-style reasoning to facilitate reforms of Islamic law, which we might justly refer to as "liberalizing," can be found in two important areas: just war doctrine and treatment of the punishment for apostasy. In both cases, many jurists in the modern period have argued that the underlying purposes behind the traditional doctrines demonstrate that if those purposes can be achieved through other means, it is permissible to replace even doctrines that have grounding in revelatory texts. Thus, for many legal "modernists," the underlying purpose behind the jihad doctrine was not the eradication of disbelief or the universalization of Islamic legal order but the preservation of Islam in a hostile world and the spreading of the Islamic mission (*da'wa*) to new communities. Such modernist jurists argue that in the contemporary period, Islam is no longer in danger of eradication, and that where the right to proselytize is protected, there is no need for aggressive warfare. Similarly, many scholars argue that the original purpose of the capital punishment for apostasy was solely to protect the community from outright armed rebellion (*fitna*). Where apostasy is merely a matter of private conscience and is not linked to a general rebellion against the state and the social order, there is no justification for executing the apostate. See, for example, S.A. Rahman, *Punishment of Apostasy in Islam* (New Delhi: Kitab Bhavan, 1973).
42. Because these populations are largely the result of immigration over the past 50 years jurists do not tend to treat them the way they might treat "native" Muslim minorities in such countries as India, Israel, or various African countries, where juridical reflection tends to focus on communal self-governance.

43. For example, 'Abd Allah ibn Bayya along with Qaradawi, the most prestigious senior scholar writing on this topic, posits that the very idea of a minoritarian jurisprudence has the objectives (*maqasid*) of (1) preserving religious life at the group and individual levels, (2) subtle and gradual missionary activities, (3) civil interaction with the Other, and (4) good relations between the individual and the group. (Ibn Bayya, *Sina'at al-fatwa wa-fiqh al-aqalliyyat*, 168.)
44. Qaradawi, *Fi fiqh al-aqalliyyat al-muslima*, 36. See also Ibn Bayya, 169 and 'Abd al-Razzaq, 15.
45. Ramadan, *To Be a European Muslim*, 131.
46. Ibid., 135–7.
47. Ibid., 139–40, emphasis in original.
48. Kurt Baier, "Justice and the Aims of Political Philosophy," *Ethics,* 99 (1989): 771–90 at 776–7.
49. For example, all but the most radical Islamic scholars hold that all Muslim residents of non-Muslim polities are under strict obligations of mutual security with those polities. This is an important ethical attitude, but it does not suggest any affirmation of the principles by which that polity happens to govern itself.
50. For example, American Muslim writer and activist Maher Hathout offers a fully liberal account of religious freedom inclusive of non-Muslims, but he only mentions the five interests that form the *maqasid* as an afterthought once he has already proven his case via a long list of Koranic verses. Maher Hathout, *In Pursuit of Justice: The Jurisprudence of Human Rights in Islam* (Los Angeles: Muslim Public Affairs Council, 2006), 146.
51. I have in mind here some of the encounters between figures such as Tariq Ramadan and various non-Muslim Europeans, including Nicolas Sarkozy, where Western Muslims are called upon to denounce Islamic legal rules in very public ways and in a language supplied entirely by the non-Muslim interlocutor.

CHAPTER 7

The Just War Argument in Islam (Who's Up? Who's Down?)[1]

John Kelsay

Introduction

The relationship between the rule of law and the rule of God has never been simple. This is so in part because of the way the latter lays claim to the former. For any community in which the rule of God implies obedience to divine directives—or, to put it another way, in which the ultimate standard of righteousness is connected with God's law—the divine standard constitutes a measure against which any human claims may be evaluated.

Thus, even in a presentation like that of Thomas Aquinas (and thus of Roman Catholicism), the sense that various types of law exist in a complementary relation cannot eliminate the potential for conflict.[2] In Thomas' model, the eternal law provides the whole of which natural, divine, and human law form parts. Describing eternal law as that wisdom by which God directs all things, Thomas makes it a grand category, in some sense beyond human comprehension. We know the eternal law "in part," and thus Thomas speaks of the natural law as the knowledge appropriate to human reason, as it participates in the eternal law. Properly understood, natural law involves an apprehension of the basic precepts and goods that govern practical reason.

In this, the natural law is complemented by divine law, which is inclusive of norms revealed in scripture and the teaching of the universal church. Again, a proper understanding of divine law does not place it in conflict with natural law. The two are complementary, and the division of labor between them is a matter of God's wisdom, or of the directives of eternal law.

When we come to human law, something else is possible, however. Human law signifies the norms by which communities attempt to govern themselves. Such standards ought to be consistent with the natural law and respectful of the divine, but they are not always so. Some inconsistencies occur because of difficulties in applying the natural law. As Thomas has it, the more we move toward particular judgments, the frequency of disagreements and mistakes increases. As well, when it comes to divine law, humans can commit several kinds of errors. They may try to enforce aspects of the divine law that are best left to God. Alternatively, human beings may be ignorant about particular aspects of divine law, in which case it is possible that they behave in ways that suggest disrespect. In any case, when Thomas echoes Augustine's statement that "an unjust law seems to be no law at all," he points to the possibility of conflict. And the conflict may be construed as between human law and divine law, or at least a rule of law and the rule of God. Questions about what to do in such cases follow, and it is important to say that there is no one set of means to be employed—some cases legitimate active resistance, while others are better addressed through that peculiar silence we might describe as "omitting" to obey the law. For Thomas, the most general norm governing the choice of means seems to be that we must weigh the impact of active or passive disobedience on the common good.

The history of religions is filled with examples of groups whose behavior rests on a claim of inconsistency or conflict in these matters. When we talk about the relationship between law and religion, it is important to recognize this. The issue is particularly important as we move into the second decade of the twenty-first century. For part of the reason for conversations like the one that took place at Wake Forest in the spring of 2010, which are reflected in the essays included in this collection, is the sense that conflicts of the type suggested in the Thomistic account are very much with us.

In the case I shall outline, the focus is on the way Muslims are adjudicating such a claim. More particularly, the claim arises in and around the activity of the type of militancy for which al-Qaeda presents a standard example. Practically speaking, this claim becomes important because Usama bin Ladin, Ayman al-Zawahiri, and others argue that a conflict between existing systems of law and the authority of God requires that

Muslims take up arms.[3] Hence (and as the title of this essay suggests), the discussion among Muslims may be characterized as an argument about just war.

I take it that this debate between Muslims reveals something about the potential for conflicts between the rule of law and the rule of God. The current argument is of more than abstract or merely historical interest, however. Thus I want to go beyond simply describing the contours of the just war argument in Islam, to ask about the impact of the various positions. The part of my title that asks "Who's Up? Who's Down?" is intended to signal this.

First, since we are assessing a variety of just war arguments, the questions of "Who's up? Who's down?" might suggest something along the lines of the Paris Hilton review: Who's hot? Who's not? In this case, we would be thinking of the momentum associated with various trends or schools of Muslim thought.

Then again, we might think of ourselves in a kind of courtroom role. Here, assessing the variety of thinking among Muslims would involve judgments as to who has the better arguments. So we might imagine Ayman al-Zawahiri, Yusuf al-Qaradawi, and a host of other interpreters engaged in a grand debate regarding the practical import of Islamic sources. They articulate their views in front of us; we interrogate them about their appeals to the Koran and the sunna or exemplary practice of the Prophet, and we judge the winner. "Who's Up? Who's Down?" becomes "Who's right? Who's wrong?"

Of course, we cannot just focus on one or the other of these possibilities. Given an interest in current affairs, we have to do a little of both. We want to know who has the better argument, in terms of Islamic sources; we also want to know who is hot, in the sense of momentum among Muslim populations. It goes without saying that the better argument does not always have momentum. At the same time, I think we should say that one part of making a good argument in Islam has to do with articulating a fit between historic precedents and current circumstances. In this sense, momentum and accuracy can and should go together. In the following pages, I shall comment first as to "who's right?" Then I shall proceed to "who has momentum?" From that point, I will move to some brief conclusions regarding the import of this conflict for thinking about the rule of law and the rule of God.

Who's right? Who's wrong?

In a book published in 2007, I describe a grand argument taking place among Muslims.[4] The occasion for the argument is the claims of al-Qaeda, or more broadly, of various groups who are either affiliated with al-Qaeda or might be described as "like-minded." We may describe these as Islamists, jihadists, or militants—for my purposes, any of these will do. For the sake of the argument, what is important is the substance of a position, which includes the following claims: (1) that Muslims have a duty to establish a particular kind of government, namely government by divine law; (2) that encroachments on historically Muslim lands by the United States and its allies constitute a failure on the part of Muslims to fulfill this duty, as well as an obstacle to Muslim performance; (3) that armed force is necessary to rectify the situation; (4) that resorting to armed force is the right and duty of any and all Muslims, wherever they are situated; and (5) that such force may be directed at any and all targets, including those ordinarily considered civilian. Many readers will be familiar with this argument; in a nutshell, it is stated in the 1998 World Islamic Front *Declaration on Armed Struggle against Jews and Crusaders*. Bin Ladin and Zawahiri signed that document; they and others have enlarged on and defended it in a variety of statements. Today, we may find it rehearsed on websites and Internet chat rooms around the globe.

There are two types of argument by which Muslims challenge this position. The first stays largely at the level of tactics and might be classified as a "conduct of war" argument. Here, the focus is on the saying of the Prophet: "When you fight, make a just war. Do not cheat or commit treachery. . . . Do not kill children. . . . "[5] In other reports, we are given to understand that the exemplary practice of the Prophet involves an attempt to distinguish between combatants and noncombatants, and that the latter category typically includes women, children, the old, the lame, religious specialists, and others. In historic *fatawa* or responses of jurists to questions about the conduct of fighting, we understand that obedience to the Prophet requires a good faith effort in this regard. Muslim scholars admit that there are situations in which an otherwise legitimate attack will bring about harm to noncombatants. In some cases, such harm may be excused. In other cases, the harm may be so extensive as to be disproportionate; in those cases, a jurist like al-Mawardi, from the eleventh century CE (fifth century AH) says that the Muslim fighters should withdraw and wait to fight another day. Others have a higher threshold in this regard.[6] The point, however, is that no one thinks that indiscriminate or total war can be justified. Thus the argument: Insofar as militant pronouncements advocate a practice of indiscriminate targeting, they are wrong, on Islamic grounds.

The targeting issue is the most prominent line in the conduct of war criticism of militant claims. I think the reason for that is obvious. The requirement that Muslim fighters distinguish between combatants and noncombatants is one of the best-established precedents in the juridical discussion of *ahkam al-jihad*, the judgments pertaining to armed struggle that make up the Muslim analogue to just war tradition. Other war conduct criticisms relate to the militant stipulation that the entire world is a battlefield, or that the right and duty to use lethal force belongs to any Muslim, anywhere. The Egyptian scholar Yusuf al-Qaradawi, for example, thinks that fighting is justified in cases of occupation, as in Israel or in Iraq; but he is on record as denouncing the 1998 bombings of US embassies in Kenya and Tanzania, as well as the 9/11 attacks in New York and Washington and the subsequent attacks in Madrid and London.[7] The Saudi dissident Muhsin al-Awaji presents a similarly interesting critique of militant tactics when he says that the notion of fighting as an individual duty means that an established government should recruit and send fighters to areas where Muslims are in danger. It does not mean, in other words, that anybody anywhere may pick up arms whenever it suits him or her.[8]

It must be said, however, that these criticisms of war conduct take place within a larger context of agreement about political goals. Al-Awaji, al-Qaradawi, and others agree with militant judgments on an overarching point; namely, Muslims have a duty to strive for the establishment of governance by divine laws. To get a more thoroughgoing criticism of militants, we must go to another set of interlocutors, who might be described as Muslim democrats. These are people who argue that a proper reading of the Koran, the example of the Prophet, and other authoritative sources lends itself to the following judgment: Muslims should work for the establishment of constitutional democracies, in which the rule of law establishes protections along the lines of international human rights standards. For these interpreters, the tactics advocated by militants are symptomatic of a larger difficulty, which emerges whenever the phrase "Islamic State" is identified with "a state in which Islam is the established religion." For Abdulaziz Sachedina, Khaled Abou El Fadl, and others, the Koranic dictum at 2:256: "there is no compulsion in religion" means precisely that Muslims, as others, should distinguish between the task of calling people to faith and the task of political governance. The idea that the state should protect an Islamic establishment, so that war making, police, and taxing powers are guided by religious interests, actually creates a context in which religious violence makes sense. For Muslim democrats (like the Protestant sectarians of old), the notion of promoting religion by means of the power of the state is a contradiction in terms. They thus criticize militancy in terms of its basic presuppositions, and they do so on Islamic grounds.[9]

Now, to the question "who has the better of the argument?" Anyone familiar with Islamic tradition will quickly perceive that Muslim democrats are pushing the envelope. Most historic Muslim writing thought of an Islamic state as one in which the sharia is established as the law of the land, enforced by a consultation between religious and political leaders, with Muslims as citizens of the first rank and non-Muslims living under Muslim protection. That sounds like the case for governance by divine law is pretty strong.

Nevertheless, familiarity with Islamic tradition also suggests that making judgments about the sharia is an art, in which one strives to establish a fit between established precedents and current circumstances. In that sense, imagination and creativity are important to Muslim practice. One line of democratic argument involves a contextual account of traditional views about religious establishment, the point being that what fits with one set of circumstances may not fit with others. In my estimation, Muslim democrats give a pretty good account. One cannot yet declare them winners of the debate, but they make a good case.

About Momentum

When we move from "Who has the better of the argument?" to "Who has momentum?" however, it seems that Muslim democrats lag behind. I say that with regret; I hope someone will give me reason to change my mind.[10] For now, though, this means that the real argument is between those who agree on the necessity of a specifically Islamic form of governance in which divine law is the norm for policy. Put another way, the truly important argument is not between Muslim democrats and Muslim militants, but it takes place within the camp of the latter. Here, there is general agreement on the point that current international norms are in conflict with the claims of God. Among militants, the argument is really about the means to be employed in altering this condition. When is fighting justified? In what circumstances? Who can authorize fighting? What targets are legitimate? These are the questions of the day. Most Muslims criticize al-Qaeda and similar groups with respect to one or more of these questions. When they do, the argument is that militancy does more harm than good, or that the indiscriminate tactics of militant groups ends up looking every bit as unjust as the policies militants say they oppose.

Most Muslims offer such criticism. Surely they are right in this, given the consistency with which interpreters of Muslim tradition have held that a legitimate jihad requires a good faith effort to distinguish between civilian and military targets. Once again, though, the question of momentum comes into play, and it seems one must admit that the militant position has considerable traction. This is especially so among younger Muslims. One example will suffice. In October 2007, *The New York Times* ran a feature under the title "An Internet Jihad Aims at US Viewers."[11] The article described a young man brought to the United States by his parents in childhood. He had recently become very serious about religion and told anyone who would listen that his goal in life was to be a good Muslim. The young man explained that through the Internet, he had discovered the words of the man he called "Shaykh" Usama bin Ladin. He read bin Ladin's messages in connection with a steady stream of stories, pictures, and other materials depicting Muslim suffering in Iraq, Afghanistan, Palestine, and other settings. The young man was inspired by al-Qaeda declarations. Fired by zeal, he undertook his personal form of struggle, which involved downloading and circulating a variety of militant texts, complemented by his own commentaries on the immorality of America, the decadence of Western democracies, and the need for resistance. As the story continued, it told of his parents' concern. Frustrated in their attempts to dissuade their son, they called in the imam from their mosque. The young man was not cowed by the leader's superior learning, however. He had learned from bin Ladin that there are good imams and bad imams, and the measure between these was a willingness to see that contemporary Muslims are called to participate in a global struggle. The young man's parents, and also his imam, seemed old and tired. Jaded by long years of struggle, they thought the point was to get along in this life and to let God sort things out in the next. The young man believed they did not understand that those who love this life end up compromising on God's commands.

In short, the young man featured in the *Times* story was convinced of the righteousness of al-Qaeda's cause. He was also intransigent. In 2007, he seemed to be impervious to argument. People wondered what would become of him.[12] The story is a familiar one. Although all instances are not related so compellingly or in such prominent sources, one can easily find multiple examples. On November 5, 2010, German police arrested an 18 year old for posting videos threatening terrorist attacks; the young man claimed to speak for the "German *mujahiddin*." In March 2010, Colleen R. LaRose, better known by her online alias "Jihad Jane," was arrested for participation in a plot to kill a Swedish artist whose depictions of the Prophet Muhammad she found objectionable. On November 3, 2010, the online service YouTube yielded to pressure from authorities in the United States and United Kingdom, removing some of a large number of videos featuring Anwar al-Awlaki, whose calls for armed resistance had been cited as a source of inspiration for an attempt on the life of a British legislator and for the failed attempt of Anwar Farouk Abdulmutallab (better known as the "Christmas Day bomber.") At an earlier point, videos featuring al-Awlaki, along with other material circulated by militants were cited in the taped "confessions" left by the perpetrators of the July 7, 2004, attacks in the London Tube.[13]

The list goes on. It is important to note that such militancy has deep, though controversial roots in the history of Islam. Early on, we have the example of *al-khawarij*, the secessionists who carried out a revolt in the late seventh and early eighth centuries. Muslim sources tell us that the group practiced *isti'rad*, a kind of religious execution by which they challenged ostensible believers regarding the quality of their practice of Islam. Death was the penalty for those whose answers were deemed unsatisfactory. In the standard accounts provided by Sunni or majoritarian scholars, the Kharijites came to stand for "excess in zeal"—for the type of people who are in one sense quite pious, who give Islamic reasons for their behavior and are clearly motivated by the desire for righteousness, but who end up doing more harm than good. In the contemporary just war argument, the Kharijites provide a standard reference for many scholars who wish to criticize the behavior of militants—in other words, bin Ladin (now deceased), Zawahiri, and those with them are described as *al-khawarij*, a charge they have denied. As Zawahiri in particular has it, those associated with al-Qaeda are not rebels. They are rather to be compared with those companions of the Prophet who fought in the spirit of the Koranic summons issued at 4:75: "Why should you not fight in the cause of God and of those who, being weak, are ill-treated and oppressed? Men, women, and children who cry: 'Our Lord! Rescue us from this town, whose people are oppressors! Raise up for us someone who will protect; raise up for us someone who will help!'" Faced with the advance of democracy—a system that Zawahiri describes as a moral abomination—those engaged in armed struggle are said to be fired by a zeal that stems from the example of the Prophet and his companions. From this point of view, those who participate in armed resistance are not villains; rather, they are defending the rights of God over against unjust legal and political arrangements.[14]

Such zeal is not only found in Muslim tradition, of course. As noted earlier, the history of religions is filled with instances in which individuals and groups claim that a religious vision warrants taking extraordinary measures. The phenomenon of militancy has roots that spread broad, as well as deep. The *Wisdom of Sirach* is an early Jewish text, written in 180 BCE. At chapter 44 and following, we read the words by which a familiar Anglican liturgy begins: "let us now praise famous men." The names recited are heroes in the national history. As we might expect, the author of *Sirach* gives Moses and Aaron pride of place, for their part in the formation of Israel. But then the recitation takes an odd turn. For we read of Phineas, son of Eleazar, who "ranks third in glory," right behind Moses and Aaron. Who is this man, and what deed deserves such recognition? He was "zealous in the fear of the Lord," says the writer. For a more complete account, we must turn to the book of Numbers, chapter 25. There, we read about Phineas, who saw evil in the Israelite camp and perceived a threat to the entire people. While others stood to one side, Phineas took a spear and killed the perpetrators of evil. His zeal for the Lord rescued the people, and makes him worthy of praise.

Around the time *Sirach* was composed, Judas Maccabeus (Judah the Hammer) lead an armed uprising, in which Torah-minded Jews fought against the forces of Antiochus Epiphanes. According to *I Maccabees* chapter 2, the uprising was inspired by the zeal of Phineas: when Mattathias, Judah's father, saw an ostensible Jew offering improper sacrifices, Mattathais "burned with zeal and . . . gave vent to righteous anger." He ran and killed the evildoer on the altar.

Mattathias and Phinehas took the law into their own hands. For this they are praised. Even so, subsequent generations of believers have done. My own connections are Presbyterian; when I read the story of Phineas, I behold in my mind's eye the torches of a thousand Scottish covenanters.

It may seem strange to go from the story of a young Muslim man in the United States to tales from ancient Israel, or to early Judaism and to Calvinism. The point, however, is that religious zeal is hardly new, nor is it a peculiarly Muslim phenomenon. To employ a familiar distinction, one might draw a line between "high intensity" and "low intensity" forms of devotion. There cannot be much doubt that the young Muslim in *The New York Times,* or in other examples mentioned, provided an example of high intensity religiosity. And that fact means that he was not susceptible to argument. "Who's right? Who's wrong?" with respect to the variety of Muslim just war arguments was not so important to him.

In my judgment, the momentum is with those like him—that is, with young Muslims whom we might understand as possessed by the zeal of Phineas. I say this, despite the often repeated claims of US policymakers that al-Qaeda is "on the run," its' leadership "decimated" by the use of aerial drones and other methods of counterterrorism. Similarly, it seems we have to acknowledge the momentum of the militant position, even in the face of (what some describe as) surprising ideological rifts within militant ranks.[15] There is, of course, some polling done by the Pew Foundation indicating a movement of Muslim opinion away from sympathy for militant claims and toward groups that advocate a different approach. But overall, the data collected by Pew through the years supports the judgment that people in historically Muslim countries typically express more suspicion and fear of the United States than of militant groups, seeming to believe either that the threat from the latter is overblown, or that those active in or supportive of such groups represent an understandable, albeit regrettably violent response to US hegemony.[16] As always in such matters, much depends on who is asked to respond, by whom, and how the questions are put. Given this, it seems more important to note that the historical and psychological roots of zealotry are broad and deep. This implies that as things settle in Iraq, or if progress is made in Afghanistan, there will remain other points of tension. As well, if militants divide on the question of tactics, that should not come as a surprise. It is of course true that the history of religions indicates that militancy can wax and wane. From my point of view, one of the more important tasks presented to scholars of religion in the present circumstance has to do with an attempt to understand the history of militancy. Not least, we want to answer the question raised by people like James Gelvin and Bassam Tibi: what is it about modernity (or, as Tibi puts it, the "open society") that lends itself to such forms of religious and political expression?[17]

In the just war argument taking place among Muslims, who is up, and who is down? I do not say that the militant position is correct, or that contemporary militants have the best arguments, based on Islamic sources. I do say that the militant position has momentum. And so far as I can tell, that means we will be dealing with the phenomenon for some years to come.

Concluding Remarks

Given this analysis, what is to be done? If the militant position has momentum, and a lack of susceptibility to argument and counterargument is one feature of its adherents, it would seem that the future promises more in the way of armed conflict.

I do think that all the evidence points in this direction. Nevertheless, the description of intra-Muslim argument presented here does suggest something important with respect to thinking about the conduct of fighting. For the disregard or elision of established norms regarding the distinction between civilian and military targets remains the weak point in the claims of al-Qaeda and related groups to the mantle of Muslim legitimacy.

Those who, like the young man whose story is outlined above, are willing to overlook this problem do so in part because they are convinced by the arguments of the late Usama bin Ladin regarding the current conflict. As bin Ladin had it, the requirement that Muslim fighters distinguish between targets is no small matter; it is, he admits, a requirement of the sharia.

Nevertheless, bin Ladin argued that the requirement is not absolute, in the sense that there are cases that demand something different. The present conflict is such a case. Pressed for reasons that justify this judgment, bin Ladin cited two: first, that when US and allied troops kill Muslim civilians, there is a requirement of justice by which an equal measure should be taken; second, that the procedures of democracy mean that all

US citizens are responsible for the behavior of their government, and are thus to be counted as combatants.[18]

It is worth pressing these reasons, as we think about the current conflict. It is true that US and allied troops have been criticized for causing civilian deaths in Iraq, Afghanistan, and other areas. It is also true that the stated policy of the United States and its allies has been and remains that such deaths are unintentional, the result of faulty intelligence, mistakes, or an example of the kind of collateral damage justified or excused by the rules of war—that is, an attack on a military target may be legitimate, even though some civilians are injured or killed in the process. In such cases, the questions that follow have to do with whether or not due care was taken to avoid or minimize harm to civilians, what level of collateral damage is proportionate to the military value of the intended target, and what sorts of compensation are due to the families of civilians who suffer harm. Perhaps the United States and its allies cannot expect to convince al-Zawahiri and others of their good intentions. The United States can try to address the concern through careful monitoring of tactics and procedures, however—a fact noted by General Stanley McChrystal when he assumed control of allied forces in Afghanistan in 2009 and again by General Petraeus when he assumed command in 2010.[19]

The point of such monitoring is to strengthen the allied claim to justice. The argument is not abstract. As McChrystal, Petraeus, and other advocates of the contemporary counterinsurgency strategy outlined in (for example) *The U.S. Army/Marine Corps Counterinsurgency Field Manual* have put it, victory in the conflict between the allies and groups like al-Qaeda will belong to those able to protect people on the ground, and thus to convince them that a better way is possible.[20]

As to bin Ladin's second argument, the weakness of the reasoning is established by, among other things, the failure to consider harm to children and others unable to vote. Perhaps more important, however, is a feature of militant war-fighting strategies that remains unaddressed in these remarks. The war-fighting doctrine of al-Qaeda has taken a far greater toll among civilians living in Iraq, Afghanistan, and other historically Muslim areas than in the United States or Europe. One can make a good argument that Muslim sources prohibit the kinds of attacks that took place on September 11, 2001. With respect to al-Qaeda's claim to wear the mantle of the Prophet, however, a more telling point would involve pointing to the lack of discrimination in targeting present in militant attacks in Baghdad, Kabul, and other places where Muslim civilians are killed.

One of the points made above suggested that intra-militant argument is strongest with respect to this issue. In this regard, it is interesting to note the various attempts of Mullah Omar to disassociate himself and his group (the largest of the various factions of the loose coalition known as the Taliban) from al-Qaeda's war-fighting strategy. "A Book of Rules" establishes norms intended to govern the actions of those claiming status as *mujahiddin* in association with Mullah Omar's leadership. Among other guidelines, the following are related to martyrdom or suicidal operations: a fighter should be well-trained; the target should be "major," that is, important to the cause; "the utmost steps must be taken to avoid civilian loss; and any operation must be authorized by a central command."[21]

"A Book of Rules" is intended to accomplish a number of ends. Most obviously, the document is an attempt to bring a loose and wide-ranging coalition under a central command. The passage just cited, however, is also an attempt to claim the mantle of Islamic legitimacy. No doubt, Mullah Omar understands the importance of this matter, even as General McChrystal and General Petraeus.

It is important to press this matter. When we speak about the rule of law, we have in mind a set of norms that will guide human beings in situations of conflict, as well as aiming at conflict resolution and ultimately at peace. In a context where militancy has momentum, and the proverbial "hearts and minds" seem closed, this one point may be the best tool available to us to narrow the breach through which young people enter the world of militancy, and thereby to address this contemporary case of conflict between the rule of law and the rule of God.

Notes

1. All citations from the Koran are informed by the translations of M.A.S. Abdel Haleem and Yusuf 'Ali, with my own alterations based on consultation of the original.
2. For what follows, see Thomas Aquinas' "Treatise on Law," from *Summa Theologica* I/2, questions 90–114.
3. Of course, since the time of the conference for which this paper was written, U.S. special forces killed Usama bin Ladin during a raid on his home in Abbottabad in Pakistan in May 2011. The argument to which he contributed continues, however, and I have chosen to add notes here and there to reflect changing conditions, rather than to engage in a more thorough rewriting of this essay.
4. John Kelsay, *Arguing the Just War in Islam* (Cambridge: Harvard University Press, 2007).
5. See the version in al-Bukhari's *Sahih*, Book 19, Number 4294. More generally on these matters, see Kelsay, *Arguing the Just War in Islam*, especially 97–124.
6. See al-Mawardi, *The Ordinances of Government*, trans. Wafaa H. Wahba (Reading, U.K.: Garnet Publishing, 1996), 32, 36. Cf. al-Shaybani

(d. 804/5), as translated in Majid Khadduri, *The Islamic Law of Nations: Shaybani's Siyar* (Baltimore: Johns Hopkins University Press, 1966), especially 101–102.

7. See Kelsay, *Arguing the Just War in Islam*, 125–54.
8. Ibid.
9. For Sachedina, see *Islam and the Challenge of Human Rights* (New York: Oxford University Press, 2009); idem, *The Islamic Roots of Democratic Pluralism* (New York: Oxford University Press, 2001). For Abou El Fadl, see *The Place of Tolerance in Islam* (Boston: Beacon, 2002). One should also consult the various work of Bassam Tibi, whose arguments in favor of "Islamic humanism" make a number of similar points, albeit by means of an appeal to Muslim philosophical traditions. See, among others, *Islamism and Islam* (New Haven and London: Yale University Press, 2012) and "Islamic Humanism vs. Islamism: Cross-Civilizational Bridging," in *Soundings: An Interdisciplinary Journal* 95/3 (2012): 230–54.

Given the discussion following the presentation of this paper during the Wake Forest conference, it seems appropriate to elaborate on some of the interpretive issues at stake in the criticism of militancy offered by Muslim democrats. In particular, a question raised regarding the "verses on fighting" in the Koran deserves mention. As one of those present put it, how is it possible to grant any legitimacy to the arguments of Muslim democrats in the light of Koran 9:5, which reads in part, "wherever you find the idolaters, kill them, seize them, besiege them, ambush them, unless they repent, establish right worship, and pay the obligatory tax . . . "?

In response, it is noteworthy that many, if not most militant discussions of fighting lean heavily on the verses of this sura or chapter of the Koran, along with chapter 8. Other "verses on fighting" (for example, 22:39–41 and 2:190–94, which justify fighting as a matter of communal self-defense) do not receive as much attention. The interpretive strategy expressed in the militant emphasis on chapters 8 and 9 leans on the notion of abrogation; that is, understanding the verses on fighting in such a way that (1) there is a trend by which the scope of fighting (in matters of conduct, as well as of resort to war) becomes more expansive, and (2) that the later verses cancel out or supersede the earlier. Since traditional accounts do support the first claim, so that the progression of verses tracks the increasingly intense conflict between the Prophet and his enemies in seventh-century Arabia. This strategy of interpretation makes possible a claim that fighting against those who do not accept Islam or (in the case of Jews, Christians, and others) signal subordination to Muslims by paying tribute is a perpetual duty, and that Muslims who fail to carry it out are guilty of disobedience to God.

The strategy of Muslim democrats challenges this approach at several points. First, the argument of Sachedina, Abou El Fadl, and others requires that readers of the Koran and other Muslim sources attend fully to context. Thus, a reading of 9:5 in the context of verses appearing immediately before and after clearly indicates that the idolaters are guilty of breaking a treaty. It is the latter fact, rather than their identity as idolaters, that justifies fighting against them. To put it another way, the reasons for fighting are moral and political, rather than pointing to religious difference per se.

As well, the democrats' argument suggests that abrogation is not in play with respect to the fighting verses. Here, Muslim democrats grant that the progression of verses tracks the intensification of hostilities presented in standard biographies of the Prophet. They do not grant that this progression indicates that earlier verses are cancelled by those that come later, however. Here, the appeal of Sachedina and others rests on the fact that the verses indicating the phenomenon of abrogation (for example, 2:106: "We do not abrogate any verses, without replacing it with another, better . . .") occurs in the context of polemics intended to justify differences between Muslim practices and those of Jews or Christians in matters like the direction of prayer, the time of fasting, and the conduct of the pilgrimage. The principle of abrogation is nowhere directly applied to fighting in the Koran, so that those who utilize it are "reading into" the text rather than engaging in true exegesis or "taking the meaning out of" the verses.

The point, again, supports the notion that Muslim democrats make a good argument. Whether they are right regarding verses of the Koran or other sources of authority in Islam is another matter. See the discussion in *Arguing the Just War in Islam*, 166–97.

10. At one point following the composition of this essay, it appeared to some that the various movements associated with the Arab Spring might provide such a reason. For my own ideas about that, readers may wish to consult "The Limits of the Arab Spring," published in the online version of *Dissent* (June 13, 2011). Cf. http://www.dissentmagazine.org/online_articles/the-limits-of-the-arab-spring.
11. Available at http://www.nytimes.com/2007/10/15/us/15net.html?_r=1&scp=1&sq=an%20internet%20jihad%20aims%20at&st=cse (accessed November 25, 2010).
12. As it turned out, Samir Kahn cut ties with his family, left the United States, and eventually was killed in a drone strike in Yemen in 2011.
13. For these stories, see "Germany: 18-Year-Old Faces Charges of Terrorism over Internet Videos," at http://nytimes.com/2010/11/06/world/europe/06briefs--GERM . . .; "Views of 'Jihad Jane' Were Unknown to Neighbors," at http://www.nytimes.com/2010/03/11/us/11pennsylvania.html?ref+coll . . .; and "YouTube Withdraws Cleric's Videos," at http://www.nytimes.com/2010/11/05/world/05britain.html?ref=youtube. . . . (all accessed November 25, 2010). Since the original composition of this essay, one should note al-Awlaki's death by a drone strike in Yemen (September 30, 2011). Lest readers think that the examples render the point out of date, however, consider the testimony of a British Muslim regarding his journey to take part in the fighting in Syria, specifically in connection with the al-Qaeda-related group known as "Islamic State of Iraq and Syria," available through the Middle East Media Research Institute as Report #5529 of the

Institute's Jihad and Terrorism Studies Project. Cf. https://www.linkedin.com/groups/AQ-SYRIA-UK-On-Tumblr-1271127.S.58095278060313I0848

14. On these points, especially with respect to the Kharijites, see Kelsay, *Arguing the Just War in Islam*, and literature cited there. Since the time of original composition of this essay, it seems worthwhile to note that the characterization of al-Qaeda as "on the run" or even "near collapse" occupied an important rhetorical space in the campaign to reelect President Barak Obama. One would think that the evidence from Mali, Syria, Yemen, and Kenya (that is, by the Somali-based group al-Shabab) suggests such claims were premature, at least.
15. Here I have in mind, for example, Lawrence Wright's discussion in "The Rebellion Within," from the June 2, 2008, issue of *The New Yorker* magazine.
16. For a recent example, cf. "Concern about Extremist Threat Slips in Pakistan," available at http://pewglobal.org/2010/07/29/concern-about-extremist-threat-slips-in-pakistan/ (accessed November 25, 2010).
17. See James L. Gelvin, "Al-Qaeda and Anarchism," *Terrorism and Political Violence* 20 (2008): 563–81; Bassam Tibi, "Political Islam as a Forum of Religious Fundamentalism and the Religionisation of Politics," in *Totalitarian Movements and Political Ideologies* 10/2 (June 2009): 97–120.
18. Among other sources, see bin Ladin's interview with John Miller of ABC from May 1998 at http://www.pbs.org/wgbh/pages/frontline/shows/binladen/who/interview.html; also, see bin Ladin's "Letter to America," as translated and published in *The Observer*, http://www.observer.co.uk/worldview/story/0,11581,845725,00.html.
19. Gen. Stanley McChrystal, "Commander's Initial Assessment," August 30, 2009, available at http://www.nytimes.com/2009/09/21/world/asia/21afghan.html?ref=asia (accessed November 25, 2010); cf. also "Petraeus Takes Command in Afghanistan, Pledging Victory," at http://www.washingtonpost.com/wp-dyn/content/article/2010/07/04/AR2010070402479.html (accessed November 25, 2010).
20. Petraeus wrote a foreword for this manual. See *The U.S. Army/Marine Corps Counterinsurgency Field Manual* (Chicago: University of Chicago Press, 2007).
21. See the translation at http://www.pbs.org/wgbh/pages/frontline/shows/network/alqaeda/manual.html (link accessed November 25, 2010).

CHAPTER 8

Veiled Women in the American Courtroom: Is the *Niqab* a Barrier to Justice?

Anita L. Allen

The United States is home to millions of Muslims.[1] American Muslims are "largely assimilated, happy with their lives, and moderate with respect to many of the issues that have divided Muslims and Westerners around the world."[2] Experts disagree about whether the number of US Muslims is closer to two million or to eight million, but no one doubts that Islam is now among the most practiced religions in the country. Like their Christians, Jewish, Buddhist, and Hindu counterparts, many Muslims are devoutly religious. Michigan has more Muslims than any other US state; in 2005 the Islamic Center of America, the largest of more than twelve hundred US mosques, opened in Dearborn, Michigan. The ethnic and national origins of US Muslims are diverse. Some of the millions of US families who practice Islam are recent immigrants from Africa, the Middle East, Europe, or Asia. Michigan has one of the highest concentrations of Muslims of Arab ancestry outside of the Arab world. However, about a third of US Muslims are long-time US residents and citizens.[3] Of these, some were born into families who practice Islam, others converted to Islam as children or adults. Among the indigenous US Muslim population groups are African American adherents, and most Black Muslim women adopt Islamic dress.[4]

Although most American Muslims dress in standard "Western" secular clothing, some US women who practice Islam dress modestly. A number wear hijab headscarves in everyday life and keep their arms and legs covered. A few wear the niqab. The niqab is a garment worn outside the home or in the presence of unrelated men that cloaks a woman's head and neck, leaving only her eyes exposed. A very few US Muslim women don the burka. The burka is a full body mantle worn outside the home, cloaking the woman's entire body and face. Although American women who visit Muslim countries—including former Secretary of State and former First Lady Hilary Clinton and Congresswoman Nancy Pelosi, have donned modesty headscarves to show respect, not everyone in the United States accepts the sight of partly or fully "veiled" women. For many US non-Muslims and many US Muslims, too, face covering symbolizes female oppression and subservience, religious extremism, and radical politics. Many women who wear headscarves report that they have experienced anti-Muslim discrimination, have been prohibited from wearing the veil in schools, and have even endured violent attacks.[5] Professor of Islamic Studies Aminah McCloud argues that African American women who wear the hijab attract more hostility than Muslim immigrants because, although many non-Muslim Americans may accept that immigrants dress differently, they may find it difficult to accept locals who wear headscarves.[6]

Governments around the world have banned or placed restrictions on wearing the burka, niqab, and hijab.[7] In 2009, Belgium banned the burka and niqab from its public streets, incurring the price of immediate criticism.[8] On the premise that Muslim modesty attire hinders communication or visual identification, in 2010 the Canadian province of Quebec introduced a bill requiring the removal of the niqab when seeking medical and other benefits or services from the government.[9] A year earlier, however, in a criminal case brought against Muslim men accused of raping a Muslim woman when she was a child, an Ontario court found that a judge could not deny the victim an opportunity to testify in court wearing her niqab, without first conducting a preliminary hearing to determine whether her professed religious beliefs and practices were sincere and deeply held.[10] In 2004, the French government banned the hijab from public schools.[11] The Senate approved by a great majority (246 to 1) a bill to ban full facial veiling from all public places.[12] Although the Council of State warned that banning the veil from public places violates the French Constitution and the European Convention for the Protection of Human Rights and Fundamental Freedoms, the bill was declared constitutional in April 2011.[13]

Debates around the niqab also preoccupy courts and the public in Muslim countries. In 2010, the Cairo Administrative Court upheld a ban on the niqab in university examination rooms.[14] But in 2007 the Supreme Administrative Court of Egypt found, on religious freedom grounds, that the American University of Cairo could not ban the niqab from campus. It was permitted, though, to require brief unveiling for verification of identity.[15] Turkey banned the hijab, niqab, and burka from its universities entirely; then it did an about face on the niqab for a time, after the more comprehensive ban, which had been upheld by the European Court of Human Rights in 2004,[16] led some girls to choose piety over education. When the Turkish Parliament reinstated the hijab ban, some university students took to covering their hijab-hooded hair with wigs.[17] Syria prohibited the wearing of the niqab (but not the hijab) in its universities.[18]

In the United States, there have been no sustained calls for local, state, or federal government to ban the hijab, niqab, or burka from public places or schools. In fact, in contrast to the overwhelming majority of Europeans that support a ban against wearing the niqab, 65 percent of Americans say they would oppose such a ban.[19] I argue that a ban against wearing Islamic garments in the United States would clearly cross into a zone of constitutionally protected freedom of religion and personal liberty. The First Amendment of the US Constitution protects freedom of religious belief and exercise: "Congress shall make no law respecting an establishment of religion, or prohibiting the free exercise thereof." Yet in the context of court appearances, court detention, drivers' license issuance, and air travel, US policymakers and courts have authorized laws and practices that interfere with Muslim women's free exercise of their religion, namely, the wearing of modesty attire that conceals the hair or face from view.

Does government have a right to demand that women take off their modesty clothing? The Ninth Circuit Court of Appeals has held that when a woman facing a parole violation charge for a misdemeanor offense is detained in a courthouse holding cell she can be required to remove her hijab for security reasons.[20] Noteworthy as a bellwether development because Michigan has the largest population of Muslims in the country, a recently adopted Michigan law allows judges to order Muslim women not charged with any crime to bare their faces in court or go home. Courtroom controls over attire are clearly warranted and necessary for the sake of security, order, and decorum. Yet banning from the courtroom the niqab head covering of a sincere, practicing Muslim woman, of whose identity the court is certain, is intolerant and risks running afoul of the First Amendment principle of religious free exercise and other federal laws.

THE MICHIGAN NIQAB CASE

Michigan District Judge Paul Paruk dismissed Ginnah Muhammad's lawsuit against a car rental company when she refused to unveil.[21] The rental company was seeking $3,000 to cover repairs on an automobile leased to

Muhammad, an African American Muslim. Muhammad said the car had been damaged by thieves. Although she wanted access to small claims court to litigate her claim, Muhammad did not wish to show her full face. She wanted to wear her niqab, as she did in daily life. Because she refused to uncover her full face in his courtroom, Judge Paruk dismissed Muhammad's case. The Michigan District Judges Association sided with Judge Paruk's decision to oust Muhammad. Civil liberties groups sided with Muhammad who believed, with many other devout Muslims, that the holy Koran requires women to cover their bodies in the presence of men outside their families. Although many practicing Muslims in the United States do not wear modesty attire, for those who do, the practice is central to their faith. When a judge demands that an otherwise orderly person with a valid legal claim remove religious attire or face dismissal of her suit, the judge unfairly and unreasonably burdens her right of religious free exercise.

The Supreme Court of Michigan sided with Judge Paruk. On June 17, 2009, by a five to two vote, the Supreme Court of Michigan adopted an amendment to Michigan Rule of Evidence 611.[22] The new rule, Michigan Rule of Evidence 611(b), provides that: "The court shall exercise reasonable control over the appearance of parties and witnesses so as to (1) ensure that the demeanor of such persons may be observed and assessed by the fact-finder, and (2) to ensure the accurate identification of such persons." This amendment would presumably allow a judge to ask a party or witness entering the courtroom wearing a ski mask, nylon stocking stretched over his head, or a Ku Klux Klan hood to remove it for the duration of the proceeding. Yet Michigan Rule 611(b) was not adopted in response to ski masks, stockings, or Klan hoods. It was adopted to provide positive legal authority for Michigan judges (like Judge Paruk), to order a woman wearing the niqab (like Ginnah Muhammad) to uncover her face or leave the courtroom. The niqab has been understandably reviled as a symbol of women's political oppression and subservience, but coercing a woman to remove an emblem of religious piety raises a specter of political oppression of another kind.

Other US states have laws giving judges authority to control attire. Oregon has such a law, Uniform Trial Court Rule 3.010(1), authorizing exclusion of persons attired in ways that detract "from the dignity of the court." Yet an Oregon woman successfully appealed her theft conviction on the ground that the judge refused to allow a defense witness to testify when he declined to remove what the appeals court termed his "religious headgear" in the courtroom.[23] The witness in question was the woman's husband, whom an appeals court held the presiding judge improperly excluded under a misapplication of Rule 3.010(1). This obscure Oregon case brings to mind Gandhi's historic encounter with a South African judge. Upon Gandhi's swearing in as the nation's first "colored" bar member in a highly publicized and long-awaited ceremony, the judge asked Gandhi to remove his turban, presumably out of deference to the court. Gandhi reluctantly caved in, believing he had bigger battles to fight. But most Americans who wear religious attire in everyday life are more like the Oregon man than like Gandhi: they have no bigger battles in view to salve their wounded dignity in the present.[24]

The niqab is an unusual garment in the United States, but it is worn by US women of varied ethnicities who practice Islam. Although uncommon, Muslim modesty dress has led to publicized and litigated conflicts between Muslim women and public authorities. A Florida woman clashed with the Florida motor vehicle authority.[25] Sultaana Freeman argued that state officials violated the Florida Constitution and the Florida Religious Freedom Restoration Act (FRFRA) when they revoked her driver's license because she refused to be photographed without her niqab. The FRFRA provides that "Government shall not substantially burden a person's exercise of religion even if the burden results from a rule of general applicability," unless Government demonstrates "that application of the burden to the person: (1) Is in furtherance of a compelling governmental interest; and (2) Is the least restrictive means of furthering that compelling governmental interest."[26] Under FRFRA, Florida was required to show that it had a compelling interest in photographing drivers and that denying Freeman a license altogether was the "least restrictive" means of furthering its interest. Freeman's lawsuit, filed on her behalf by the American Civil Liberties Union (ACLU) of Florida, cited Colorado, Indiana, and Nebraska cases in which courts had ruled that individuals with sincerely held religious beliefs are entitled to licenses without photographs.[27] Those cases involved members of Christian sects who interpret the Bible's second commandment against graven images to prohibit them from having their pictures taken. ACLU attorney Howard Marks, who argued Freeman's case before Ninth Judicial Circuit Court, suggested that the state was using her as a scapegoat in the "war against terror," when all she wanted to do was to be able to "drive her kids to the doctor or go grocery shopping."[28] Following the litigation Florida amended the law to exempt the requirement of a full-face photo from FRFRA.[29]

A devout Pennsylvania woman clashed with officials at the State Correctional Institution at Graterford, Pennsylvania, who refused to allow her to visit her imprisoned son unless she agreed to remove her veil.[30] The woman brought a lawsuit in federal court to enjoin the prison to allow visitation while veiled. The judge who heard her case determined that "requiring the plaintiff to remove her veil as a condition of her right to visit her son in prison constitutes substantially burdening her exercise of religion."[31] Pennsylvania, like Florida has a Religious Freedom Restoration Act statute.[32] The judge's constitutional analysis in the Graterford prison case conformed to a model Congress and several states courts have established for thinking about what it means to respect the fundamental right to practice one's religion. This model indicates that government may not interfere with persons' free exercise of rights other than to further its compelling, that is, urgent and important, interests. When the government's compelling interests require burdens on religious free exercise, as they will from time to time, those burdens should be minimized. In considering means to further its compelling interests, the government must select practical means that are the least restrictive of religious freedom.

Although the state has a "compelling interest in making sure that visitors to inmates are indeed the persons they profess to be," the burdens placed on the veiled woman must be the "least restrictive."[33] Rather than excluding the veiled mother from visits, the court found that the prison should inform her of the visitation times and dates when female corrections officers are on duty, so that she can briefly unveil to establish her identity prior to contact with her son.

Without anticipatory safeguards in place directing officials to accommodate religious attire as required by law, a woman's unwillingness to remove the niqab can have dire consequences. The consequence can be denial of access to an incarcerated family member, illustrated by the Pennsylvania Graterford prison case, or denial of access to civil court, illustrated by the Michigan case. To toss out Muhammed's lawsuit because she wore the niqab, rather than to seek to accommodate her faith and lawsuit, was to ignore the demands of deference to religion.

It could be argued that since Michigan Rule 611(b) permits judicial discretion without requiring a judge to order the removal of Muslim modesty attire, it is lawful. Ideally a judge would not use his or her "reasonable control" authority to exclude religious attire unless first determining that exclusion was necessary to further a compelling state interest. However the amendment was adopted in the context of a dispute over the niqab, precisely to authorize an interference with religious free exercise. Given the rule's genesis and doubtful constitutionality, it is not surprising that the Michigan Supreme Court decision to adopt it was not unanimous. Two judges, Chief Justice Marilyn Kelly and Justice Diane Hathaway, dissented from the decision to amend the state's evidentiary rules.

Reasonable Control of the Courtroom

The Michigan Supreme Court sought to give judges the right to exercise "reasonable control."[34] It is hard to argue against a judicial power labeled "reasonable control." In the past American judges have sometimes failed to exercise "reasonable" control over states of dress and undress in their courtrooms. In an extreme instance from the past, the New York judge who tried the infamous *Rhinelander v. Rhinelander* marriage dissolution case allowed the plaintiff wife to undress in front of a jury, putatively to buttress the claim that her wealthy white husband was not a victim of fraud.[35] Intimate letters revealed that Mr. Kip Rhinelander had seen Mrs. Alice Rhinelander nude in sexual encounters before marriage, and her lawyers argued he had to have known that she was "colored" when he married her, hence there was no fraudulent pretense of whiteness.[36]

More recently, judges have demanded that an African American attorney remove an African fabric kente cloth he said was required by his role as an officer of his church,[37] that a Jewish man remove his yarmulke skull cap,[38] and that a Roman Catholic priest serving as an attorney in a criminal matter appear in court in nonclerical garb to ensure a fair trial.[39] One judge erroneously ordered a new trial because a witness who was a Roman Catholic priest testified in a personal injury case wearing his clerical collar.[40] It is important to consider what kind of control over attire worn for religious purposes is truly reasonable, and specifically whether a society citing compelling state interests may justly restrict the wearing of face coverings that are commended by religion.

In a 1991 memorandum addressed to his state's judges, New Jersey Chief Justice Robert N. Wilentz directed judges he supervised not to restrict litigants or witnesses from dressing as they choose: "I do not believe we should try to influence how litigants or witnesses dress, absent something that approaches the obscene."[41] (Muslim modesty attire is, by US standards, virtually the opposite of obscene, since it conceals breasts, sex organs, and then some.) Furthermore, Justice Wilenz wrote, "I believe the fact finder, albeit the jury or the judge, should see the litigant or witness as the person wishes to appear and reach whatever conclusions flow from that 'fact.'"[42] Many jurists would find Wilenz's anything-short-of-obscenity standard, too permissive. But the United States and England share a legal heritage and a recent UK study calls for an open mind and case-by-case pragmatism in responding to religious attire.

Indeed the Equal Treatment Advisory Committee of the United Kingdom's Judicial Studies Board urged tolerance, sensitivity, and pragmatism in its 2007 guidelines for managing religious attire worn by parties, witnesses, judges, jurors, lawyers, and incidental courtroom staff: "There is room for diversity, and there should be willingness to accommodate different practices and approaches to religious and cultural observance."[43] The board found that although sensitive, well-explained requests that a woman remove her niqab will sometimes be warranted by the facts and circumstances at hand, "it is often possible," the board concluded, "to assess the evidence of a woman wearing a *niqab*." Judges sometime take evidence over the telephone and some judges are sight-impaired, hence the judiciary may not consistently presume that "the veil represents a true obstacle to the judicial task."[44] In sum, "In many cases, there will be no need for a woman to remove her niqab, provided that the judge is of the view that justice can be properly served."[45] A case in England provided an example of the way sensitivity and consideration can resolve more complicated situations. In this case, a fully veiled woman was required to testify in court. Her counsel ensured in advance that the judge presiding over the case would be a woman. The counsel was screened from the Muslim woman's view by a large umbrella and the courtroom was guarded to ensure that other men did not enter during her testimony. In this manner, the woman was able to testify without the veil.[46]

Tolerance, sensitivity, and pragmatism are not inherently inconsistent with the popular US emphasis on judges having control over their courtrooms. Judges should have substantial control over their courtrooms, including the power to ban clothing or nudity that disrupts, demeans, or trivializes the forum of justice.[47] Judges can exercise control and yet be highly tolerant of person's style and religious preferences. A New Jersey judge was reversed when he held a female attorney in contempt of court for wearing slacks and a sweater in court.[48] In the American northeast, slacks and a sweater are less formal professional attire than a black suit and tie. But, unlike Mickey Mouse ears, a Batman costume, a comically oversized sombrero, a pants and sweater outfit does not demean, trivialize, or disrupt a courtroom.

Women of Muslim faith wearing the niqab are neither disruptive nor an affront. They have a right not to be observed, so long as they can be seen, heard, and identified in other straightforward and appropriate available ways.[49] As a constitutional matter, respect for religious freedom demands that there should be a very strong presumption against religious clothing bans and a strict requirement of accommodation in those instances in which the state asserts a truly compelling interest in undressing its people. US courts should avoid the quick conclusion that the niqab is "a true obstacle to the judicial task."

The Wider Constitutional Context

The US Supreme Court has not directly addressed restrictions on Muslim headscarves or facial veils. In the past, the court has upheld laws aimed at compelling religious minorities to conform to a variety of majority practices. The court's stance has been that "[w]e have never held that an individual's religious beliefs excuse him from compliance with an otherwise valid law prohibiting conduct that the state is free to regulate."[50] In *Kelly v. Johnson* (1976), the court identified law enforcement as a realm of public service in which the state may dictate uniform dress and hairstyles.[51] In *Goldman v. Weinberger*,[52] the court upheld military policies limiting the right of an active duty Jewish rabbi and clinical psychologist to wear the yarmulke. However, the weight of the courts' decisions point to recognition of a constitutional right of minority group members to wear distinctive religiously inspired garb, as free exercise of belief, and to a strong presumption that they may do so in the courtroom and courthouse.

In the landmark US Supreme Court case, *Cohen v. California* (1971), the court threw out the disorderly conduct conviction of a California man who donned a jacket bearing the offensive words "F–k the Draft" in a courthouse corridor.[53] The decision was not unanimous, but the majority stressed that the First Amendment is not obliterated simply because a man uses a single crude expletive to express his political position on military conscription. The *Cohen* decision rested on the requirements of freedom of expression protected by the First Amendment. The First Amendment also protects the free exercise of religion. If the First Amendment protects tasteless jackets, it could be expected to protect tasteful modesty attire worn for religious purposes.

To an extent, government may restrict attire and even hairstyles, consistent with the First Amendment. But the court has never been understood to endorse blanket disregard for religious attire in the name of conformity. Thus in 2005, the US Office of Civil Rights announced plans to intervene on behalf of a Muslim girl suspended from school for wearing a headscarf. The Benjamin Franklin Science Academy had suspended an 11-year-old Muslim, Nashala Tallah Hearn. The girl had refused to remove her hijab headscarf in class. A school dress code forbade wearing hats, bandanas, and other head coverings in the classroom. Muslim civil rights groups and the US Justice Department Office of Civil Rights criticized the suspension, which was soon lifted.

The 2009 Supreme Court's decision in *Safford Unified School District v. Redding*[54] underscores the obligation of the state to recognize and respect female modesty. The case held that public school administrators violated a middle school girl's Fourth Amendment rights against warrantless search and seizure when they conducted a strip search to look for contraband ibuprofen. Prior to *Redding*, the court had held that a "special needs" exception to the Fourth Amendment warrant requirement permits public schools to conduct non-law-enforcement searches of children and youth in public schools to check for illegal drug use or possession of contraband.

But with the *Redding* decision, the court recognized modesty as a limit of privacy on school's right to conduct bodily searches of youngsters. *Redding* was not the first time the court acknowledged the importance of modesty. The first acknowledgment came in *Union Pacific Railroad v. Botsford*.[55] Citing the importance of modesty and privacy, the case had held that a woman who filed a tort action alleging physical injuries need not submit to a medical examination at the request of the defendant. The notion that tort plaintiffs need not undergo a professional medical examination is now obsolete, but the notion that women have a "right to be let alone" that permits them to keep themselves covered in public lives on. The privacy sentiment advanced in the *Botsford* case has been enduring: "No right is held more sacred, or more carefully guarded, by the common law, than the right of every individual to the possession and control of his own person, free from restraint or interference of others, unless by clear and unquestionable authority of law."[56]

Some US judges are persuaded that hijab is protected free exercise. Accordingly, in 2007 a woman in Galveston, Texas, was awarded $17,250, after she alleged that a security guard refused to allow her to enter the courtroom unless she removed her headscarf "worn in observance of hijab." [57] Her case led to official measures to remind local "judges to be sensitive to the constitutional rights of people in the courtroom and specifically noting that people who wear their religious clothing or head wear are not required to remove [it] upon entering the courtroom."[58] The religious free exercise clause of the First Amendment must surely require toleration of the modesty garments of Muslim women. But the hijab, which leaves a woman's face fully observable, is not niqab, which leaves only a woman's eyes in view. Is the difference constitutionally relevant?

A "Compelling State Interest"

Because religious free exercise is a fundamental constitutional liberty, and a liberty protected by religious freedom restoration statutes, the central question that must be addressed is whether the state has a compelling interest that warrants excluding niqab from the courtroom. Five main concerns—veracity, accountability, demeanor, identity, and fairness—have prompted courts to seek to exclude face-veiled women as parties and witnesses.

Government has a compelling interest in a judicial system governed by rules and procedures that enable those responsible for fact finding—judges, lawyers, prosecutors and juries—to assess the veracity of witnesses and parties. The government also has a compelling interest in holding accusers accountable for the statements they make and serious allegations of wrongdoing they levy against others. As for veracity and accountability, the niqab interferes with the obligation to confront those whom one has accused. Facing a niqab-draped woman satisfies the desire to look a person in the eye to compel accountability and thereby to assess veracity, but it frustrates the ability to ascertain veracity on the evidence of overall facial expression and body language.

Demeanor is evidence of truthfulness and also of mental and emotional fitness to stand trial. Demeanor is evidence of character and of whether a person is making a serious effort to pay attention and show respect to others in court. Government has a compelling interest in a judicial system in which participants act with rationality, civility, and seriousness. The sight of niqab-draped women invites inferences of femininity, modesty, and religiosity, but it blocks inferences of immaturity, indifference, anger, boredom, or contempt. Behind her veil, the Muslim party or witness might be sticking out her tongue, yawning, dozing, pursing or biting her lips, smirking, grinning, or frowning.

Although it may be easier to judge the veracity and demeanor of a person who is not wearing a veil than to judge the veracity and demeanor of a person who is, judges, lawyers, and juries nevertheless have significant bases for judgment. They can rely upon assessments of the veiled woman's tone of voice, choice of words, and the consistency and plausibility of her statements. They can judge the woman based on the look and movement of her eyes, her carriage, her gait, her posture, the manner in which she uses her hands. The assessment of demeanor does not depend upon seeing the face or entire face of the speaker. In fact, "[a]ccording to the empirical evidence, ordinary people cannot make effective use of demeanor in deciding whether to believe a witness. On the contrary, there is some evidence that the observation of demeanor diminishes rather than enhances the accuracy of credibility judgments."[59]

In *Morales v. Artuz*, the Second Circuit Court of Appeals considered whether the defendant's right to confront a witness was violated when the key witness testified wearing sunglasses so "dark . . . that you can't see through them."[60] The court held that the jury was still able to observe the witness's delivery, nervousness, and body language. The court explained that it was more important that the jury was able to triangulate the observed demeanors with the substance of the testimony, the witness's opportunity to observe, the consistency of the testimony, and whether the witness had any hostile motive. It could be argued that the right to confront one's accusers goes to core public values and undercuts the right to veil. But that right to confront accusers cannot be interpreted as a right to force a person, who is completely willing to appear in a courtroom and be questioned, to take off attire called for by her faith. The wearing of the niqab is a kind of personal religious conduct that courts must tolerate and accommodate.

As for identity, it is easy to verify the identity of a person whose full face is in plain view, but the female form behind the niqab could be almost anyone of similar weight, height, and color. There are plenty of ways a judge or other court personnel can identify a woman, short of asking her to appear for the duration of a trial unveiled. The guidelines of the Maryland state attorney general for meeting the identification needs of Maryland courts call for asking a woman wearing a modesty veil to momentarily remove it in the presence of a female security officer.[61]

In 2005 a New Zealand judge ruled that two Muslim witnesses testifying for the prosecution in a criminal procedure could not testify while wearing burkas.[62] This case presented two difficulties. First, the burka not only covers the face but the whole body; thus, the witnesses' body language would be difficult to assess beneath the burka. Second, in a criminal case, such as this one, testimony is more crucial than in a civil procedure. Namely, criminal cases depart from the relations between two parties and become a matter of public interest.

The public has the right to a transparent and open criminal justice system and has an interest in the conviction of criminals. On the other hand, part of the defendant's right to fair trial should allow him to cross-examine witnesses whose faces are uncovered. The judge in this case ruled that the court and litigants should be able to see the faces of witnesses. Otherwise, the court stated, how could they know "that the person re-entering the witness box today is the same person who was there yesterday?" The court added that even with visual identification, it is difficult to distinguish between people of similar build and facial characteristics. The court emphasized the significance of watching witnesses' faces while they are under cross-examination and the public's right to observe justice unfolding in the courts. Nevertheless, the court allowed for some accommodations for the witnesses. The court ruled that screens would be used to ensure that only the judge and counsel would see the witnesses' faces while they testified and that the court's staff would be composed entirely of women. The court also ordered that steps be taken to ensure that the witnesses would not be seen unveiled in the entrance to the courtroom or when they departed. The court specifically mentioned that the witnesses were allowed to express their religious views by wearing a hat or scarf that covered their hair.

Finally, as for bias, the niqab will seem extreme and exotic to some judges, jurors, parties, witnesses, attorneys prosecutors, and courthouse personnel. Ethnic prejudice and unfair bias may be amplified by the appearance of veiled women in a US courtroom.

The Constitution will not allow a blanket niqab removal policy based either on the need to judge demeanor or veracity, to identify, to compel accountability, or to identify and avert bias. If the state's interest in all of these is compelling, it may interfere with religious free exercise, but it must do so in the least restrictive manner.

NOTES

1. "Muslim Americans: Middle Class and Mostly Mainstream," in Pew Research Center [database online]. Available from http://pewresearch.org/assets/pdf/muslim-americans.pdf (last visited June 2, 2010). Pew describes its report as the "first ever nationwide survey to attempt to measure rigorously the demographics, attitudes and experiences of Muslim Americans" (3).
2. Ibid., 7.
3. The Pew Research Center Report estimates the number of US Muslims to be 2.35 million and states that "Roughly two-thirds (65%) of adult Muslims in the U.S. were born elsewhere," and "Among native-born Muslims, roughly half are African American (20% of U.S. Muslims overall), many of whom are converts to Islam." Other estimates of the proportion of African Americans that comprise the Muslim population range from 40 percent to 85 percent. African Americans are considered the largest group of non-immigrant Muslims in the United States. Karan Fraser Wyche, "African American Muslim Women: An Invisible Group," *Sex Roles* 51 (September 2004): 319–28.
4. Converts to Islam in the United States are "among the most enthusiastic about wearing traditional women's attire." Donna Gehrke-White, *The Face behind the Veil: The Extraordinary Lives of Muslims Women in America* (New York: Kensington Publication, 2006), 2–5. See also, Yvonne Yazbeck Hadda, Jane I. Smith, and Kathleen M. Moore, *Muslim Women in America* (New York: Oxford, 2006), 45 ("Most Muslim women who are black choose to adopt Islamic dress and Islamic names . . ."). As an aside, it has also been documented that African American women are known for their creativity in designing stylish garments that also attend to the modesty requirement. Ibid., 13.
5. Yazbeck Hadda, *Muslim Women in America*, 103–7.
6. Ibid., 59–60 (taken from Aminah McCloud, *African American Islam* (New York: Routledge, 1995).
7. I also address this question in Anita L. Allen, "Undressing Difference: The Hijab in the West," *Berkeley Journal of Gender, Law and Justice* 23 (2008): 208–24.
8. Yassin Musharbash, "It Makes No Sense to Ban the Burqa," in *Spiegel Online* [database online]. Available from http://www.spiegel.de/international/europe/0,1518,687105,00.html (last visited June 2, 2010); Reuters, "Muslim Woman in Italy Is Fined for Wearing Veil," *The New York Times*,

May 5, 2010, A12 (reporting that "a 26-year-old Tunisian woman has been fined for wearing a face veil while walking to a mosque in northern Italy").

9. Bill 94: An Act to Establish Guidelines governing Accommodation Requests within the Administration and Certain Institutions, available from http://www.assnat.qc.ca/en/travaux-parlementaires/projets-loi/projet-loi-94-39-1.html (last visited June 2, 2010).

   See also, Ian Austen, "Canada: Bill in Quebec Would Ban Veils in Dealings with Officials," *The New York Times*, March 25, 2010, A15.

10. R. v. S. (N.) (2009), 2009 CarswellOnt 2268, 95 O.R. (3d) 735 (Ont. S.C.J.).

11. Recently, an Israeli court held that a private Catholic school can ban a Muslim teacher from wearing the hijab. Dan Izenberg, "Court: Private School Can Bar Teacher from Wearing Hijab," *The Jerusalem Post*, September 5, 2010, http://www.jpost.com/Israel/Article.aspx?id=187073.

12. Elaine Ganley, "French Senate Passes Ban on Full Muslim Veils," *The Washington Times*, September 14, 2010, http://www.washingtontimes.com/news/2010/sep/14/french-senate-passes-ban-full-muslim-veils/.

13. Lizzy Davies, "Nicolas Sarkozy's Cabinet Approves Bill to Ban Full Islamic Veil," *The Guardian*, May 20, 2010, 23. Recent veiling legislation in Spain almost followed the French example. In 2010, the Senate approved a ban against wearing the burka in all public places. This bill was later rejected by a slim majority in the Parliament. However, the government announced it will introduce a different version of the bill later. Raphael Minder, "Spain's Senate Votes to Ban Burqa," *The New York Times*, June 23, 2010, http://www.nytimes.com/2010/06/24/world/europe/24iht-spain.html?ref=muslim_veiling (last visited July 18, 2010). See also, Alan Clendenning and Harold Heckle, "Spain Rejects Burqa Ban—For Now," *The Huffington Post*, July 20, 2010, http://www.huffingtonpost.com/2010/07/20/spain-rejects-burqa-ban_n_653254.html (last visited July 20, 2010).

14. Jaclyn Belczyk, "Egypt Court Upholds Niqab Ban for University Examinations" in *Jurist* [database online]. Available from http://jurist.org/paperchase/2010/01/egypt-court-upholds-niqab-ban-for.php (last visited June 3, 2010).

15. Ibid.

16. Leyla Sahin v. Turkey, Eur. Ct. H. R. (Application No. 44774/98, Nov. 10, 2005). The European Court of Human Rights heard the case of a Turkish university student woman who had objected to a ban on the hijab in schools, a policy the Turkish Parliament reconsidered in 2008 because it was effectively excluding non-secular women from getting a university education at all. Today headscarves that cover the neck, the chador, and the burka are banned on campus; however traditional scarves tied under the chin are allowed. The European Court of Human Rights heard another case regarding the veil in Dahlab v. Switzerland (2001) V Eur Court HR 449. Here, a schoolteacher was banned from teaching in a primary school because she wore an "Islamic headscarf," but the case was dismissed as

inadmissible. For a critique of these two court cases, see Carolyn Evans, "The 'Islamic Scarf' in the European Court of Human Rights," *Melbourne Journal of International Law* 7 (2006): 52–74. (Evans criticizes the court's reliance on stereotypes about Muslim women).

17. Matt Porter, "Headscarves in Turkey Wave a Red Flag" in *Global Post* [database online]. Available from http://www.globalpost.com/dispatch/study-abroad/100209/headscarves-turkey (last visited June 3, 2010).
18. The Associate Press, Syria: Islamic Scarf That Leaves Only Eyes Exposed Is Banned, *The New York Times*, July 19, 2010, A9.
19. Pew Research Center, "Widespread Support for Banning Full Islamic Veil in Western Europe, Most Americans Disapprove" in *Pew Research Publication Center Publications* [database online], http://pewresearch.org/pubs/1658/widespread-support-for-banning-full-islamic-veil-western-europe-not-in-america (last visited July 20, 2010).
20. Khatib v. County of Orange, 603 F. 3d 713 (9th Cir. May 3, 2010).
21. Muhammad v. Paruk, 553 F.Supp.2d 893 (E.D.Mich.2008).
22. Amendment of Rule 611 of the Michigan Rules of Evidence, available from http://courts.michigan.gov/supremecourt/Resources/Administrative/2007-13-08-25-09-Order.pdf (last visited June 3, 2010).
23. State v. Allen, 113 Ore. App. 306, 308 (Or. Ct. App. 1992).
24. Mohandas K. Gandhi, *Gandhi an Autobiography: The Story of My Experiments with Truth*, trans. Mahadev Desai (New York: Beacon Press, 1993).
25. Freeman v. State, 2003 WL 21338619 (Fla.Cir.Ct. Jun 06, 2003) (NO. 2002-CA-2828). Affirmed by Freeman v. Department of Highway Safety and Motor Vehicles, 924 So.2d 48, 31 Fla. L. Weekly D537 (Fla.App. 5 Dist. Feb 13, 2006) (NO. 5D03-2296), rehearing denied (March 29, 2006).
26. A federal Religious Freedom Restoration Act of 1993, 42 U.S.C. § 2000bb, was found unconstitutional as applied to the states in City of Boerne v. Flores (1997). The passage of federal RFRA was a response by Congress to Supreme Court free exercise decisions including Employment Division v. Smith, 494 U.S. 872 (1990). Prior to RFRA, the court had held that minority religions are not relieved from the force of laws of general application, such as the nation's polygamy and controlled substance laws. The *Employment Division* case upheld the denial of unemployment benefits to two Native American men who lost their state jobs because they had consumed sacramental peyote as part of a Native American church ritual. Florida has adopted its own version of RFRA that mirrors the federal statute, as follows:

    Fla. Stat. Ann. §§761.01–761.05 (1998)
    761.01 Short title.—This act may be cited as the "Religious Freedom Restoration Act of 1998."
    761.02 Definitions.—As used in this act:

    (1) "Government" or "state" includes any branch, department, agency, instrumentality, or official or other person acting under color of law of the state, a county, special district, municipality, or any other subdivision of the state.

(2) "Demonstrates" means to meet the burden of going forward with the evidence and of persuasion.

(3) "Exercise of religion" means an act or refusal to act that is substantially motivated by a religious belief, whether or not the religious exercise is compulsory or central to a larger system of religious belief.

761.03 Free exercise of religion protected.—

(1) The government shall not substantially burden a person's exercise of religion, even if the burden results from a rule of general applicability, except that government may substantially burden a person's exercise of religion only if it demonstrates that application of the burden to the person:

(a) Is in furtherance of a compelling governmental interest; and

(b) Is the least restrictive means of furthering that compelling governmental interest.

(2) A person whose religious exercise has been burdened in violation of this section may assert that violation as a claim or defense in a judicial proceeding and obtain appropriate relief. . . .

27. Quaring v. Peterson, 728 F.2d 1121 (8th Cir. 1984); Bureau of Motor Vehicles v. Pentecostal House of Prayer, Inc., 269 Ind. 361, 380 N.E.2d 1225 (Ind.1978); Dennis v. Charnes, 805 F.2d 339 (10th Cir. 1984).
28. John-Thor Dahlburg, "Court Battle over Veil Pits Religion against Security," *Los Angeles Times*, May 30, 2003, available from http://articles.latimes.com/2003/may/30/nation/na-veil30 (last visited June 10, 2010).
29. Section 332.051 reads as follow: "Notwithstanding chapter 761 or s. 761.05, the requirement for a fullface photograph or digital image of the identification card holder may not be waived."
30. Bint-Ishmawiyl v. Vaughn, 1995 WL 461949 (E.D. Pa. 1995).
31. Ibid.
32. 71 Pa. Stat. §2401–2407 (2002).
33. Ibid.
34. Amendment of Rule 611 of the Michigan Rules of Evidence, available from http://courts.michigan.gov/supremecourt/Resources/Administrative/2007-13-08-25-09-Order.pdf (last visited June 3, 2010).
35. Rhinelander v. Rhinelander, 219 N.Y.S. 548 (N.Y. App. Div. 1927), *aff'd* 157 N.E. 838 (N.Y. 1927).
36. Earl Lewis and Heidi Ardizonne, *Love on Trial: An American Scandal in Black and White* (New York: W.W. Norton, 2001).
37. Anita Womack, "Judge Tells Lawyer Not to Wear Kente Cloth in Court" *Times Daily*, May 23, 1992, http://news.google.com/newspapers?nid=1842&dat=19920523&id=iUweAAAAIBAJ&sjid=MscEAAAAIBAJ&pg=1385,3508784 (last visited June 3, 2010).
38. Close-It Enters., Inc. v. Mayer Weinberger, 64 A.D.2d 686, 407 N.Y.S.2d 587 (2d Dept. 1978).
39. La Rocca v. Lane, 77 Misc.2d 123, 353 N.Y.S.2d 867 (N.Y.Sup. Mar. 11, 1974), reversed on other grounds in La Rocca v. Lane, 47 A.D.2d 243, 366 N.Y.S.2d 456 (N.Y.A.D. 2 Dept. Apr. 07, 1975).

40. Ryslik v. Krass, 652 A.2d 767 (N.J. Super. Ct. App. Div. 1995).
41. *Ryslik*, 652 A.2d at 770.
42. *Ryslik*, 652 A.2d at 770.
43. Equal Treatment Advisory Committee (ETAC) of the Judicial Studies Board (JSB), available from http://www.judiciary.gov.uk/about-the-judiciary/training-support/judicial-college/how-the-judicial-college-is-governed/equal-treatment-advisory-committee/ (last visited June 10, 2010). Chapter 3.3 Religious Dress, 3-18/1.
44. JSB, 3-18/4
45. JSB, 3-18/6.
46. Caroline Bridge, "Case Reports: Practice: Evidence," *Family Law* 37 (2007): 986.
47. State v. Allen, 113 Ore. App. 306, 308 (Or. Ct. App. 1992).
48. *In re* De Carlo, 357 A.2d 273, 275 (N.J. Super. Ct. App. Div. 1976).
49. Aaron J. Williams, "The Veiled Truth: Can the Credibility of Testimony Given by a Niqab-Wearing Witness Be Judged without the Assistance of Facial Expressions?," *University of Detroit Mercy Law Review* 85 (2008): 273.
50. Employment Division v. Smith, 494 U.S. 872, 878 (1990).
51. Kelly v. Johnson, 425 U.S. 238 (1976).
52. Goldman v. Weinberger, 475 U.S. 503 (1986).
53. Cohen v. California, 403 U.S. 15 (1971).
54. Safford Unified School District v. Redding, 557 U.S. 364, 129 S. Ct. 2633 (2009).
55. Union Pac. R.R. v. Botsford, 141 U.S. 250 (1891).
56. Ibid., 251.
57. Boyd v. Texas, 301 Fed. App'x 363, 364–65 (5th Cir. 2008).
58. Ibid.
59. Olin Guy Wellborn III, "Demeanor," *Cornell Law Review* 76 (1991): 1075.
60. Morales v. Artuz, 281 F.3d 55 (2d Cir. 2002).
61. Office of the Attorney General, State of Maryland, May 27, 2009, "Constitutional Law-Free Exercise Clause—Whether Deputy Sheriff May Require an Individual Entering a Courthouse to Remove a Religious Face Covering for Security Purposes." 94 Md. Op. Atty. Gen. 81, 2009 WL 1648560 (Md.A.G.). Available from http://www.oag.state.md.us/Opinions/2009/94oag81.pdf (last visited June 10, 2010).
62. Police v. Razamjoo [2005] DCR 408 (District Court, Auckland).

CHAPTER 9

TERROR(IZING) THE "VEIL": AMERICAN MUSLIM WOMEN CAUGHT IN THE CROSSHAIRS OF INTERSECTIONALITY

SAHAR F. AZIZ

The September 11 terrorist attacks transformed the meaning of the Muslim headscarf.[1] No longer is the crux of the debate whether the "veil" is used to oppress women by controlling their sexuality and, by extension, their personal freedoms and life choices. Rather, a Muslim headscarf "marks" the wearer as a representative of the suspicious, inherently violent, and forever foreign "terrorist other" in our midst.[2]

In the post-9/11 era, many Muslim women donning a headscarf find themselves trapped at the intersection of bias against Islam, the racialized Muslim, and women. In contrast to their male counterparts, Muslim women face unique forms of discrimination not adequately addressed by Muslim civil rights advocacy organizations, women's rights organizations, or civil liberties advocates. Amid pervasive suspicion of Islam, continuing sexism, and bias against her particular race group, the Muslim woman is both a visible target and a silent victim.[3]

Whether guilty by association, through her marriage to a presumably terrorist husband, or an active accomplice in secret plots to terrorize Americans, the covered Muslim woman is rarely perceived as an individual capable of developing her own beliefs and protestations. Instead, she is viewed as a mere extension of her familial relationships with actual or prospective male terrorists. As national security prerogatives filter perceptions of Muslims through the prism of terrorism, the Muslim "veil" has become a symbol of terror.[4] This critical shift results in palpable adverse consequences to a Muslim woman's freedom of religion, freedom of individual expression, and safety interests.

The shift in meaning of the Muslim headscarf is due in large part to a recasting of Islam as a political ideology as opposed to a religion. Once this definitional shift occurs, acts that would otherwise qualify as actionable religious discrimination are accepted as legitimate, facially neutral national security law enforcement measures or protected political activity by private actors. The recasting serves as the basis for calls to deny Muslims of rights otherwise protected under the law.

The shift in symbolism of the headscarf results in two notable outcomes. First and foremost, Muslim women continue to be objectified within a larger conflict of ideas between predominantly male decision makers. Heated national security debates about the emergence of "homegrown terrorism," now code for domestic Muslim terrorists, focus primarily on persecuting or defending male suspects. Sparse attention is paid to the impact of the post-9/11 national security era on Muslim women, and specifically those that wear the headscarf. Irrespective of their place of origin or the color of their skin, the headscarf "marks" Muslim women as sympathetic to the enemy, presumptively disloyal to this country, and forever foreign.[5]

Second, any meaningful discourse surrounding a woman's right to wear a headscarf in America cannot be disconnected from the racial subtext of the "terrorist other" associated with the Muslim headscarf. Thus the label "Muslim" is both a religious and racial identifier. The shift in symbolism of the "veil" from subjugation to terrorism causes palpable discrimination against Muslim women. She now must worry about her and her families' physical safety, her ability to obtain employment, and the government's harsh prosecutorial tactics. That is in addition to the deprivation of her individual expressive and religious freedom rights.

Many Muslim women continue to suffer tangible economic harm as a result of choosing to wear the headscarf.[6] In a country where economic independence of women is promoted as a means of preserving their legal and political rights, the Muslim woman is forced to forfeit her right to practice her faith in her preferred manner in order to preserve her economic independence and the corresponding benefits. As the costs of wearing the headscarf become prohibitively high, the legal right to wear it rings hollow.

Accordingly, this chapter examines the implications of the shift in symbolic interpretation of the Muslim headscarf in America from gender subjugation to terror(ism). Specifically, this chapter argues that the Muslim woman is a casualty of the post-9/11 "war on terror" in different ways than Muslim men. She is trapped in the crosshairs of national security conflicts that profoundly affect her life but have yet to be adequately addressed by advocacy groups focused solely on defending either Muslims, or women's rights, or civil liberties post-9/11.

I. Recasting Islam from a Religion to a Hostile Political Ideology

As a result of the September 11, 2001, terrorist attacks, in a matter of days, Islam in America went from a relatively obscure religion to the focal point of public anxieties. Thirteen years later, the attention has far from waned. The odious acts of 19 Muslim hijackers placed the lives of 6 million[7] ordinary American citizens and residents under heightened scrutiny by the government and the public.

The September 11 terrorist attacks recast Islam as a hostile political ideology, as opposed to a bona fide religion.[8] As a result, what would otherwise qualify as "religiously driven racial discrimination" has become a legitimate safeguard to protect the homeland—a homeland that Muslims find increasingly antagonistic to their presence, despite their status as US citizens.

Otherwise invidious scrutiny has become acceptable because it is believed to be a neutral and rational national security measure that counters a virulent political ideology. Open and brazen Muslim-bashing invites little public shaming or political backlash.[9]

The "race-ed" Muslim lies at the unenviable intersection of preexisting American biases against racial, immigrant, and religious minority groups. Those suspicious of Muslims often contribute to a perceived grand civilization clash between the inherently violent, oppressive, and blood thirsty Islam of the "East," and the liberal, pluralistic, and free America of the "West."[10] The prejudice is rooted in an essentialist definition of a Muslim as prone to terrorism and disloyalty, coupled with an ingrained aversion to freedom.

Take for instance the furor in the fall of 2010 arising out of the approved plans to build a mosque two blocks from Ground Zero. What should have been a fringe right-wing effort to stop a lawful project exposed the entrenched animosity and distrust held against Muslims by a significant number of Americans.[11] Nine years after September 11, 2001, 25 percent of Americans believed that Muslim Americans were not patriotic.[12]

Similarly, 68 percent of Americans opposed the building of the mosque near Ground Zero primarily because they associated a mosque with the terrorists of September 11.[13] While some commentators and political leaders reminded the public of America's cherished principle of freedom of religion, many doubted its applicability to the Ground Zero Mosque. Islam's perceived status as a hostile political ideology thus exempts Muslims' otherwise religious practices from constitutional or statutory protections.

II. Politicizing "Muslim" as a Proxy for Racial Slurs

Shortly prior to the Ground Zero controversy, a Pew Poll found that, two years after his election, one in five Americans believed President Obama was a closeted Muslim.[14] These same allegations, intended as derogatory slurs, were hurled against him in the 2008 presidential elections. Since then, not much has changed, despite repeated efforts by Muslim communities to prove their fidelity to the nation. Such accusations say less about the veracity of Obama's religious beliefs and more about the affiliation with Islam as a political liability. Being called a Muslim has become a pejorative label aimed at a president whose drop in the polls is due more to an economic recession and controversial health care reform—both of which have nothing to do with Muslims per se.

Shortly after the September 11 attacks, when the nation was panic-stricken, commentators concluded that the severe backlash against Muslims, Arabs, and South Asians was merely a rational and temporary response to a traumatic national event.[15] But 13 years later, the resentment and deep distrust of over six million people has not abated. The manifestations of entrenched stereotypes are becoming institutionalized by government policies and practices and normalized as part of the public's discourse about Muslims.

In New York,[16] New Jersey,[17] Tennessee,[18] Wisconsin,[19] Connecticut,[20] Kentucky,[21] California,[22] and Oklahoma where concerted anti-Muslim and anti-mosque campaigns have formed,[23] mosques have been flooded with hate emails and threats including a video of a man destroying a mosque.[24] Mosques across the United States face threats of attack and vandalism. On April 10, 2011, the Islamic Center of Springfield in Missouri received a threatening letter stating that Muslims "stain the earth" and vowing that "Islam will not survive."[25] The letter ended with a drawing of a ram's head with "Death to Islam!" printed below it.[26] This was the second of such incidents at this center, where earlier in the year, the walls of the mosque were vandalized with graffiti stating, "You bash us in Pakistan, we bash you here."[27] The following week, on April 20, 2011, there was an attack on the Islamic Center of Cartersville in Georgia, shattering its doors and windows with rocks, one of which was reportedly painted with "Muslim murderers."[28]

These events illustrate how recasting Islam as hostile political ideology and Muslims as political actors reinforces public perceptions that otherwise discriminatory acts are morally sanctioned as defending the nation.

III. From Subjugation to Terrorism—The Muslim "Veil" Post-9/11

Prior to September 11, the Islamic faith garnered little attention from an American public generally indifferent about the religions of the Middle East, North Africa, and South Asia. The minimal attention paid to Islam was often limited to scholarly and activist debates about whether the Muslim headscarf undermined Western feminist ideals as a subjugating byproduct of patriarchy, coerced domestication, and gender oppression.[29] The discussions were often couched in a broader debate on whether the law should incorporate multiculturalism and more specifically whether multiculturalism was bad for women.

The September 11 attacks made moot the question of whether the Muslim "veil" oppressed women. Women were no longer viewed as victims of Muslim male patriarchs—but rather as conspirators with terrorists that victimized Americans. The oppressed Muslim woman suddenly became the aggressor against those who just a few years back had pledged to liberate these same women from the tyranny of certain religious practices.

A. The "Veil" as a Symbol of Subjugation

In the 1990s debates about multiculturalism's impact on the rights of women, some Western feminists categorically denounced any manifestations of patriarchy perpetuated by Islam—most visibly in the form of the headscarf. To some, it was unfathomable that a Muslim woman could "choose" to wear a headscarf.[30] Rather, they believed, she was coerced by male (or female) members of her family or indoctrinated from youth to accept the headscarf as mandatory for her spiritual salvation.[31] But if given a meaningful choice, according to many Western feminists, a Muslim woman seeking liberation would surely rebuke the "veil."[32]

What started out as an international issue quickly penetrated the domestic American legal discourse. Intellectuals began to question whether multiculturalism as a jurisprudential tool effectively legitimized patriarchy to the detriment of minority and immigrant women.[33] Feminists contested the deference that American society paid to culture, even when certain cultural practices seemingly oppressed women either physically or psychologically. To some, the Muslim veil, though not as egregious, was comparable to female genital mutilation in that its aim was to control women's sexuality.[34] Hence the "veil" was part of a larger debate on whether multiculturalism was bad for women.[35]

In one camp were multiculturalists, also known as cultural relativists, who supported granting protections and privileges to minority cultures to prevent them from extermination by majority cultures. In the other camp were a group of Western feminists[36] and progressives who questioned whether multiculturalism had any place within liberal Western society. Focusing specifically on gender equality, acclaimed feminists, such as Susan Moller Okin, argued against multiculturalism because protecting minority cultures perpetuates female oppression within those cultures.[37] If cultures endorse or facilitate control of women by men, then support of group rights is potentially antifeminist. Okin criticized Islam, among other religions, as being "rife with attempts to justify the control and subordination of women."[38] The Muslim "veil" was thus a tool for blaming and punishing women for men's failure to control their sexuality. Acknowledging group rights, therefore, strengthens male domination within Muslim cultural subgroups.[39] Ultimately, multiculturalism and feminism could not be reconciled.

In the other camp, Western multiculturalists, as well as some self-identified "Muslim feminists,"[40] responded that the Muslim headscarf was not necessarily antithetical to feminist ideals. Many Muslim women choose to wear it as a feminist statement, rejecting the hypersexualization of women's bodies by male dominated societies, both in the East and the West. Moreover, Okin and her followers were accused of objectifying Muslim women by imposing Western secular feminist ideologies upon Muslim women without allowing them to speak for themselves.[41]

But for the September 11 terrorist attacks, these debates could have continued to dominate American discourse on Islam well into the twenty-first century. However, concerns with individual rights of religious minority women now have been eclipsed by nationwide fears of terrorists in our midst who may hold American citizenship on paper but hold no loyalty to the nation in fact. Whether or not Muslim women are oppressed by patriarchy quickly became submerged by more important questions about their intentions to harm the nation.

B. The "Veil's" Transition to a Symbol of Terror

Against this political backdrop, the headscarved Muslim woman[42] in America finds herself in a precarious position. No longer does the headscarf reflect an individual decision (or lack thereof) about personal faith and dress. Rather, the headscarf marks her as a member of the enemy. The Muslim woman is merely an object in a purported civilizational conflict between the East and the West. Facing little control over the prohibitively costly consequences of wearing a religiously mandated headscarf, her legal right to wear it is of little value. She is faced with the false choice between, on the one hand, protecting her and her children's physical safety, obtaining employment, or actively engaging in the political process and, on the other hand, exercising her religious freedom and individual expressive rights.

Like Muslim males, the Muslim woman bears the brunt of entrenched stereotypes profiling Muslims as the primary threat to American national security.[43] But unlike her male counterpart, the headscarved Muslim woman is caught at the intersection of discrimination against Islam, women, and her particular racial group.

IV. Muslim Women Caught in the Crosshairs of Intersectionality

The deafening silence about the Muslim woman's perspective in the post-9/11 debates is analogous to the black woman's experiences in antiracist politics. Kimberle Crenshaw's seminal piece on the intersectionality of race and gender informs the analysis of Muslim women's experiences in the post-9/11 era.[44] Crenshaw argues that any analysis of antidiscrimination doctrine and antiracism politics "that does not take intersectionality into account cannot sufficiently address the particular manner in which Black women are subordinated."[45] For example, the centrality of white female experiences conceptualizes gender discrimination while the centrality of black male experiences conceptualizes race discrimination. Thus, black women are protected only to the extent that their experiences coincide with those of black men or white women.[46]

Like black women, Muslim women often experience discrimination as Muslim women—not the sum of race, religious, and sex discrimination.[47] Yet their rights are protected only to the extent that Muslim males or white women experience the same type of discrimination. While Muslim women experience some forms of discrimination in similar ways as Muslim males, the headscarf subordinates women in ways overlooked by generic strategies defending anti-Muslim (male) discrimination.

Meanwhile, although the stereotype of subjugation has been eclipsed by the "terrorist other" stereotype, it still lingers in the background, such that if a Muslim woman manages to evade one, she is likely to be subjected to the other. Hence Muslim women, unlike Muslim men, are ordained to subordination whether as terrorists, terrorist sympathizers, or victims of Muslim male patriarchy.

A. Facing Both Gender Stereotypes and the "Terrorist Other" Stereotype

The headscarved Muslim woman is trapped at the intersection of sexism and anti-Muslim bias that is not holistically addressed by civil rights advocates or the relevant government agencies. Take for instance the situation of a headscarved Muslim woman with an assertive personality. She is demonstrably smart, ambitious, and self-confident. She does not comport to a "good female employee" who is soft-spoken, deferential, and mild-mannered. Her male colleagues perceive her as the stereotypical "bitch" who exhibits an inappropriate sense of entitlement. As a consequence, she is denied a promotion and raise and given poor evaluations based on pretext, such as needing to "improve her attitude" and be a better team player. Not unlike a white woman in her same circumstances but for the headscarf, she is held to a different and more rigorous standard than a similarly situated white male.

Meanwhile, some of the Muslim woman's colleagues (both men and women) hold biases against Muslims due to a variety of factors, including personal experiences, national events, and negative stereotypes promoted in the media. These coworkers believe many Muslims are terrorists and/or disloyal to America. This is manifested through offensive comments about Muslims as terrorists and misogynists. The Muslim woman's loyalty to the nation and right to be in the workplace, especially in a leadership capacity, may be questioned either explicitly or implicitly. In general, she feels unwelcome in the workplace at least partially on account of her religion.

Muslim civil rights groups focus solely on the discrimination she faces as a Muslim who wears the headscarf. Indeed, it is questionable whether they would assist her if she did not wear the headscarf, as they may fail to see how such forms of discrimination (i.e., gender) fall within their mandate. If they do offer assistance to the headscarved woman, it is often provided by advocates who define their agenda based on a male-centric definition of anti-Muslim bias that does not see the issue beyond the right to practice one's faith. The Muslim civil rights groups may even decide that she is to blame for the discrimination because of her "bad attitude," as similar gender stereotypes of the "good Muslim woman" as obedient and deferential permeate the American Muslim communities.

An American women's rights group would likely overlook gender discrimination because they may mistakenly believe the bias is solely on account of her religion and thus not within their mandate.[48] Both Muslim civil rights and women's rights groups are likely to overlook one of the two dimensions of the bias, either gender or religion. As a consequence, the headscarved Muslim woman is caught in the crosshairs of intersectionality at her own peril.

This predicament is not merely an abstract concern. As demonstrated in recent events, a black Muslim woman's exclusion from the courthouse on account of her headscarf[49] would not happen to Muslim men, whatever their race, as they are not religiously mandated to cover their hair. Considered against America's history of discrimination against women and blacks, a black Muslim woman's denial of access to justice resurrects forms of discrimination believed to be a thing of the past. Likewise, when two South Asian Muslim women were evicted from a picture with presidential candidate Obama, the offense was against women, Muslims, and Middle-Eastern looking people.[50] Notably, Western feminists' silence on these incidents exposes their failure to recognize the significance of excluding women, whatever religion they may profess or their racial identity, from the political process. Instead, the cases are narrowly viewed as anti-Muslim (male) religious discrimination.[51]

These cases also highlight Western feminists' double standards as they criticize "Eastern" practices that subordinate Muslim women while failing to acknowledge their "Western" society's subordination of the same women.[52] Specifically, Western feminist groups, such as CODE Pink, EQUALITY NOW, and the Feminist Majority Foundation, have consistently called for the ban of the burka and spoken in defense of women's rights in Iraq, Afghanistan, and other Middle Eastern nations, all the while remaining silent on a Muslim woman's right to wear the hijab along with other gender rights in the United States. While Western feminists' focus on equal pay, abortion rights, and other gender specific issues certainly benefit Muslim women, the American women's rights agenda fails to address the unique forms of subordination experienced by Muslim women in the United States.

B. The Privileging of the Male Perspective in American Muslim Leadership

Further exacerbating the marginalization of Muslim women's rights is the privileging of male perspectives in the American Muslim leadership. As articulated by legal scholars Devon Carabado and Mitu Gulati, "political agendas of identity groups tend to focus on the interests of the privileged within the group."[53] Because Muslim women are generally politically subordinated within Muslim communities, especially where community activities center around a mosque, the articulation of political claims for equality by Muslims privileges the experiences of Muslim males over the experiences of Muslim females.[54] This intraracial hierarchy further constricts the agency of Muslim women in the post-9/11 era. They live in a community that is defined and subordinated by the racialized "Muslim" identity and culture while also subjected to patriarchy within their own communities.

The predominantly male perspective causes resources to be directed at forms of discrimination common to Muslim men, such that distinct discrimination experienced by Muslim women is obscured.[55] Muslim leaders and spokespersons claim to speak for "Muslims" but often fail to incorporate the perspectives of Muslim women.[56] Community-wide protests against unlawful government action often focus on cases involving profiling of Muslim men in airports, immigration enforcement, and law enforcement. With regard to private acts of discrimination, resources are expended toward protecting the right to build mosques, the right to religious accommodation in the workplace, and negative stereotyping in the media. The focus on women and discrimination is often limited to a case-by-case basis rather than a more effective systemic approach.

While these are legitimate concerns that warrant attention and affect both men and women, they constitute only part of the post-9/11 adverse impact on Muslim communities in America. For instance, in the context of religious accommodation in the workplace the Muslim woman faces discrimination against her faith and discrimination against her gender. The latter is often manifested in violence against her body. A strategy that considered this intersectionality would work with both women's rights and civil rights groups to defend the right of religious minorities *and* the rights of women to have equal opportunity in the workplace. Thus, if the religious freedom issue is resolved, then the gender equality issue need not fall by the wayside.

Less obvious is male leadership's preference that she wear the headscarf, as opposed to defending her right to choose whether she wants to wear it. Should she choose not to wear it, yet nonetheless face discrimination, it is unlikely that community resources are expended in her defense. Meanwhile, Western feminists have failed to identify with Muslim women beyond wanting to "liberate" them from oppressive patriarchies originating from their "Eastern" cultures. At the same time, they fail to recognize how their own "Western" patriarchy prevents some Muslim women from attaining the economic independence necessary for exercising individual rights.[57] In light of the near obsession with Muslim women's rights abroad by some American feminists, their silence over the past 13 years about the various forms of discrimination against Muslim women by non-Muslim Americans is deafening.

C. Sacrificing Muslim Women's Rights to Defend Muslim (Male) Civil Rights

Like many women of color in communities experiencing systemic discrimination, Muslim women are ambivalent about the degree of political and social capital that should be expended toward challenging gender barriers within their communities. Muslim women are understandably hesitant to compromise the broader Muslim civil rights agenda by challenging the patriarchy within their communities and institutions. As Muslim communities across the country experience mosque vandalizations, hate crimes, forced exile on no-fly lists, profiling in airports, and aggressive law enforcement tactics that border on entrapment,[58] intracommunity gender rights are marginalized. Further complicating women's predicament is the likelihood that internal power struggles based on allegations of male domination, even if true, only reinforce negative stereotypes of (male) Muslims as oppressive, pathologically authoritarian, and deserving of suspicion.[59]

Challenging male patriarchy within the Muslim communities subjects a woman to allegations of harming the collective interests of Muslims in America—additional harms they cannot afford in light of political and physical assaults by the public and the government. These practical concerns restrain Muslim women from the ability to contest interpretations of religious doctrine and cultural practices, thereby stifling a healthy evolution of Islam in America. As a consequence, the new generation of Muslim women leaders may be left with little choice but to support defensive strategies that collectively marginalize Muslim women as a group.[60]

Notably, and perhaps in response to the complications of intersectionality, a new generation of Muslim women post-9/11 have begun to break into the communities' leadership. Although Muslim women collectively remain at the periphery of community leadership, these new organizations are often founded and managed by women. Organizations such as Muslim Advocates,[61] South Asian Americans Leading Together,[62] and Karamah[63] are founded and operated by highly educated women who represent the few examples of female leadership at the national level.[64] Although there are certainly other talented Muslim female professionals in leading roles, many of them work for and report to predominantly male executives and male board members.

Another consequence of women's exclusion from Muslim leadership is the rise of female dissidents who converted out of Islam and now ally with far-right organizations holding anti-Muslim bias. Women such as Ayaan Hirsi Ali, Wafa Sultan, Bridgette Gabriel, and Nonie Darwish hold themselves out as experts on Islam but proffer views highly controversial, if not outright offensive, to a vast majority of Muslims in America. These women, with no identifiable Muslim constituency, are often touted by their benefactors as courageous voices against the oppressive ideology of Islam. While their views may be sincerely held, they appear to be exploited to do the bidding of right-wing political groups with clear anti-Muslim agendas, which further objectifies Muslim women within the larger national security debates. Indeed, many Muslims perceive such women as mere pawns in the grander assault on Muslim's civil rights in America.

In the end, Muslim women trapped at the intersection of race, religion, and gender tend to either suffer in silence to preserve community unity during a time of siege, take on the nearly insurmountable endeavor of starting their own organizations, or become surrogates of opponents of mainstream Muslim organizations as a channel for expressing their dissent and empowering their voices.

To avoid these distorted consequences, Muslim American women should have opportunities to play meaningful roles in existing institutions whose mandate is to defend the rights of women, Muslims, or civil liberties in a the post-9/11 era. And those roles should not be limited to those associated with traditional gender roles as mothers or teachers. Similarly, American feminist groups have an obligation to include American Muslim women in their constituency and gender rights advocacy campaigns. And civil liberties groups focused on adverse consequences of national security laws would be well served if they included American Muslim women in their discussions on identifying violations of individual rights of American Muslim communities. Such groups miss out on at least 50 percent of the experiences in these communities that may not be shared by Muslim men.

Until such changes occur, American Muslim women are likely to remain trapped at the intersection of bias against gender, race, and religion.

V. Moving beyond Symbols of Terror to Palpable Discrimination

The shift in the symbolism of the headscarf has transformed the Muslim woman's experience in America as she faces various forms of palpable discrimination. Indeed, an unprecedented number of Muslim women have felt compelled to remove the headscarf after September 11 in order to be free from physical harassment, to obtain gainful employment, and to participate meaningfully in American civic life.

The scarf is no longer merely religious headwear. It has been racialized to symbolically mark the woman and her familial affiliates as the suspect, "terrorist other" Muslim.[65] As the headscarf "outs" the woman, she and her family experience adverse consequences in various contexts. The woman's children become subjected to bullying and derogatory slurs based on the visibility of their mother's Muslim identity.[66] The headscarved woman also faces discrimination in employment, threats to her physical safety, and exclusion from courthouses on account of her "terrorist" marker. Cumulatively, these circumstances deny her the individual expressive right to choose to wear her headscarf as a reflection of her personal beliefs.[67]

A. Employment Discrimination

Nowhere is the effect of the symbolic shift from subjugation to terrorism more evident than in the employment context. Indeed, the US Equal Employment Opportunity Commission (EEOC) reported the number of complaints of unlawful discrimination against Muslim employees more than doubled from 697 in 2004 to 1490 in 2009.[68] Of those, 803 formal charges were filed on behalf of Muslim complainants, wherein 25 percent alleged religious discrimination.[69]

Thus, the Muslim woman finds herself increasingly unwelcome, particularly if she chooses to practice her faith by covering her hair.[70] And if outright termination is not the discriminatory act of choice, she finds herself subjected to ethnic and racial slurs conflating her religion with disloyalty and a basis to question her right to be employed there.[71]

In some cases, employers changed their policies after 9/11 to coerce Muslim women into taking off their headscarves. In *Mohamed-Sheik v. Golden Foods/Golden Brands, LLC*,[72] the Somali women plaintiffs began working for the employer before the 9/11 attacks, during which time they were permitted to wear their headscarves, to wear their shirts untucked to accommodate their desire for modesty, and to pray during their breaks. Despite these workable accommodations, the employer changed its policy after the 9/11 attacks to prohibit the headscarf and prayer at work. The temporal relationship between the denial of accommodation and the 9/11 attacks are unlikely a coincidence but rather a reflection of increased intolerance toward Muslim workers, especially women seeking to cover their hair.

In a case involving a convert to Islam who chose to wear her headscarf at work, a coworker told her to take her scarf off because she "was a disgrace and was a symbol of 9/11 to customers."[73] She was eventually fired for failing to file a timely personal injury accident report when luggage fell on her toe. This apparently pretext for terminating her employment, coupled with numerous incidents of religious harassment, was sufficient to defeat the employer's attempts to dismiss the case.

In 2008, a 17-year-old Muslim woman applied for a job at an Abercrombie Kids store and was recommended "as a very good candidate" by the store manager, who suggested that the applicant wear a different color headscarf that was consistent with the store's "Look Policy." After recommending her for the job, the store manager consulted with the district manager who told the manager not to hire the applicant because she wore the headscarf.[74] In late 2010, once again, an American-born Arab woman applied to work at another Abercrombie & Fitch store while wearing the headscarf. After being rejected for the position because she did not have the "Abercrombie look," the woman lamented, "The interview crushed me because I never imagined anyone in the Bay Area would reject me because of my head scarf."[75] Fearing future discrimination from prospective employers, the young woman decided to take off her headscarf out of her economic necessity to obtain a job.[76]

B. Racial Violence against Muslim Women

Discrimination in employment is but one avenue in which the terror(izing) of the Muslim woman's headscarf has taken place. A more lethal consequence is found in the significant increase in random acts of racial violence against cognizably Muslim women.

Shortly after the 9/11 attacks, several Muslim women had their headscarves ripped off and cigarette lighters thrust at their heads.[77] When a Muslim woman reporter for a Seattle newspaper put on the headscarf as an experiment to investigate how Muslim women were treated, she was pushed into the path of a truck.[78] More than three years later, in 2004, a Muslim woman was stopped in her car by three individuals who, after demanding a lighter, called her "Stupid Muslims, f-cking Muslims," kicked her car, punched her in the face, and tore off her headscarf.[79]

By late 2010, the frequency of violence committed against Muslim women on account of racial and religious animus was on the rise at a troubling rate. In the span of two months, at least six reported cases of hate crimes across the country were committed against Muslim women wearing the headscarf; in one case, a woman's four-year-old son was also physically attacked, causing him to bleed. On October 14, 2010, a Staten Island woman and her toddler were attacked by a pedestrian who punched her in the face, pulled on her scarf, asked her why she was in America, and called Muslims and Arabs terrorists.[80]

One week later, in Seattle, Washington, two American citizens of Somali descent were physically attacked at a gas station.[81] The female attacker called them suicide bombers and terrorists and told them to go back to their country. She then slammed the door on the leg of one of the women, kicked her, and pulled her headscarf. As the Muslim women were screaming for help, bystanders just watched the attack without taking action.

Just weeks later on December 20, 2010, a Muslim woman wearing the hijab in Columbus, Ohio, was allegedly stalked, verbally harassed, and then pepper-sprayed by a white man shouting religious and ethnic slurs, such as "Tell all of your Muslims that this is not your country," "Go back to wherever you came from," and threatening, "I will kill you."[82]

On July 6, 2011, a 56-year-old Muslim woman wearing a headscarf in Harlem was attacked by two women after she had asked one of them to stop taking her photo. One of her attackers called her "a f-ing terrorist," as she punched the victim in the eye and threatened to kill her. The two attackers pulled off the woman's headscarf and continued to verbally attack her.[83]

In a similar incident a week later, a 26-year-old Pakistani Muslim in a purple hijab was attacked on July 14, 2011, in Niagara Falls. Two women yelled ethnic slurs from a van while following the victim, who was on foot, before the two assailants pulled over and started slapping, punching, and kicking the victim, repeatedly.

As the scarf increasingly becomes a symbol of disloyalty and foreignness, the Muslim woman is no longer merely a private citizen free to choose how to practice her faith. Rather, she faces the false choice between freely expressing herself, based on religious, cultural, and personal values, or protecting herself and her family from the wrath of systemic societal bias.

VI. Rethinking Post-9/11 Civil and Women's Rights Strategies to Give Agency to Muslim Women

As the "post-9/11 era" enters its thirteenth year, the persistent discrimination against Arabs, Muslims, and South Asians can no longer be characterized as mere backlash. Public bias is on the rise and the government continues to ratchet up its aggressive preventative counterterrorism efforts directed at Muslims. Because women bear a significant brunt of the adverse consequences, most acutely in the public sphere, a rethinking of post-9/11 civil rights strategies is long overdue.

At the conceptual level, the debate can no longer be framed as merely about the legal right to wear the headscarf as a matter of religious freedom. Wearing the headscarf post-9/11 has become a psychological and physical hazard for Muslim women and their families. As a result, American feminists are faced with the reality that their society has contributed to denying Muslim women their fundamental individual "right to choose" how to express themselves, how to dress, and how to define modesty according to their personal beliefs.

Although some feminists may feel no loss at the end of the Islamic practice of "veiling" which they believe does not adhere to the values of liberalism, they cannot escape their own culpability in stripping Muslim women of agency and individuality—two fundamental principles undergirding American feminism. Muslim women in America, like their non-Muslim counter parts, deserve the social and political space to make their own decisions on how to live.

At the simplest level, one solution to problems highlighted in this paper is increased inclusion of Muslim women in leadership positions in Muslim, civil rights, and women's rights organizations. However, while promotion of Muslim women may mitigate the situation, a handful of women placed in key decision-making positions cannot single-handedly undo systemic problems. A focus on quotas rather than quality makes Muslim women susceptible to being tokenized as a substitute for meaningful inclusion. Thus, inclusion of Muslim women in decision-making capacities within mainstream institutions is merely a first step toward integrating diverse perspectives into efforts to combat post-9/11 discrimination.

The measure of women's meaningful empowerment within Muslim community life should be qualitative as well as quantitative. The number of women in leadership roles is certainly indicative of their influence. But equally important is ensuring that the women in leadership are high achievers in their public professional lives, with the requisite authority to apply their expertise toward the empowerment of the community. This would require Muslim males to share, and in some cases cede, their control of the leadership reins with women who are not only more skilled than them in certain areas but also interject a gendered perspective that addresses social, political, or legal challenges uniquely faced by Muslim women.

The more difficult task, however, is de-objectifying women in the psyche and practices of Western feminists and Muslim community life in America. As demonstrated in this article, the Muslim woman's headscarf has become the insignia of the nation's political enemies, thereby subjecting her to forms of discrimination uniquely different than discrimination experienced by women at large. Despite having more than 13 years to come to this realization, women's rights groups have yet to include "post-9/11 discrimination" in their scholarly and activist agendas, as they shortsightedly view it as a national security issue.

Within Muslim community space, women's meaningful participation is often constrained by the superimposed primacy of their roles as wives, daughters, and mothers over their roles as executives, lawyers, doctors, and other professional positions they play in mainstream American society. As a response to the persistent discrimination against women who wear the headscarf, a new generation of women is increasingly proactive in empowering themselves against such bias and repelling these stereotypes. For example, in a local political race in the Chicago area, five women ran for political office. "Where not all of them wear the headscarf, their presence on the ballot as well as their active campaigning inevitably dispelled stereotypes of women as either subjugated or terrorists."[84]

But even those women who reject this ordering of their multiple identities by interacting with (predominantly male) Muslim leadership as skilled professionals, they still find themselves marginalized either through subversive tactics by the new generation of Muslim males or explicit rejection by the older immigrant generation. Through this gendered filtering process, the women remaining who have not been either expelled or opted-out from frustration are often technocrats who use their skills to merely implement male-centric strategies.

Meanwhile, Western feminist organizations have failed to incorporate the perspectives of Muslim women, especially those who wear the headscarf, into their women's rights agendas.[85] Just as black women face circumstances defined by their race, Muslim women's experiences are heavily defined by their racialization as the "terrorist other." Western feminists' failure to challenge head-on the racism underlying discrimination against Muslim women ultimately reinforces the subordination of Muslims as a group and, by extension, Muslim women.[86]

If Western feminists want to be taken seriously in their call for universal women's rights abroad, they must face the skeletons in their own countries' closets. Women's rights organizations must confront the double standards whereby they adamantly defend the rights of women abroad in the "Muslim East" yet neglect their own society's oppression of Muslim women. Such oppression is not limited to garden variety discrimination but is also found in the national security context where it prohibitively costly to wear the headscarf. Adopting the banal and patronizing approaches common in international development programs where Muslim women are victims with no agency, to be "saved" by Western feminists, perpetuates their subordination.[87] Similarly, tokenizing a few Muslim women; talking about, rather than to, Muslim women; or throwing some money at the problem would do more harm than good, by creating a false impression of progress.

Western feminists should be looking to Muslim women to take the lead in developing strategies and projects tailored to experiences only they can articulate. Attempts to empower Muslim women in America should look to ordinary Muslim women to determine how to improve their lives based on their values and personal experiences.[88] It is crucial that Muslim women's rights go beyond the simple freedom from discrimination but also grants them the freedom to shape their religious and cultural communities, as well as broader public policy.[89]

What is ultimately at stake, and has been pre- and post-9/11, is that Muslim women should not be forced to make false choices between individual rights, freedom of religion, and physical safety—whether imposed by Muslim males, American feminists, or the American government.

VII. Conclusion

This chapter aims to provoke analysis of the post-9/11 era through the perspective of American Muslim women—a population largely ignored in the relevant policy and legal debates. Their visibility as a marked Muslim inevitably subjects them to the entrenched bias against Muslims in America. Meanwhile the disparities they have experienced in the past on account of their gender did not suddenly wane once their racialized Muslim identity took center stage. Quite the contrary, they now must overcome obstacles arising out of gender bias as well as religious and racial bias. Muslim women are caught at the crosshairs of intersectionality of these three characteristics.

Overt acts of violence and insidious forms of economic discrimination against headscarved women restrict a woman's freedom of choice in practicing her religion. The threat this poses to a woman's life and livelihood should not be taken lightly. The right to work directly impacts a woman's self-esteem, individual autonomy, and placement in the hierarchy of power within the family and her community. Similarly, her inability to feel safe as a result of the headscarf strips her of a fundamental right to safety.

The challenge now rests with Muslim rights, women's rights, and civil liberties advocacy groups to uphold the civil rights of all women and all Muslims, rather than subordinate these women's interests for the benefit of the (male) group's agenda. This urgency does not stem from a merely principled perspective but a civil rights perspective—veiled women have increasingly become targets of entrenched anti-Muslim attitudes and have suffered palpable harm. Combatting this is essential, not only to restore the rights of these women but also to realize American values of religious freedom and gender equality.

Notes

1. Adrien Katherine Wing and Monica Neigh Smith, "Critical Race Feminism Lifts the Veil? Muslim Women, France, and the Headscarf Ban," *U.C. Davis Law Review* 39 (March 2006): 750. This article discusses the origin and significance of the headscarf in Islamic history and in the French headscarf debate.

2. See Nadine Strossen, "Freedom and Fear Post-9/11: Are We Again Fearing Witches and Burning Women," *Nova Law Review* 31 (2007): 307. The author cites Neil MacFarquhar, "A Simple Scarf, but Meaning Much More Than Faith," *The New York Times*, September 8, 2006.
3. Ibid.
4. See Editorial, "Terrorists Hiding in Hijabs: Muslims Seek Special Treatment to Elude TSA Groping," *The Washington Times*, November 17, 2010.
5. See Robert A. Kahn, "The Headscarf as Threat: A Comparison of German and U.S. Legal Discourse," *Vanderbilt Journal of Transnational Law* 40 (2007): 417. See also Kathleen M. Moore, "Visible through the Veil: The Regulation of Islam in American Law," *Sociology of Religion* 68 (2007): 237–51. Although most Muslim women in the United States choose not to wear the hijab, the visibility of it as a focal point for controversy influences American perceptions about what constitutes Islam. Such cases as the Florida driver's license case of Sultaana Freeman putatively pit a benighted image of Islam against the necessities of national security, and they only serve to entrench already polarized opinions about the nature of Islam. Worse, such a binarism posits gender relations as an essential point of divergence between the Islamic world and secular democracies, and it promotes the simplistic view that cultures are set on an unavoidable collision course, a clash of civilizations. Not only is the hijab a volatile emblem that can be viewed as a symbol of male oppression or of modesty and religious or cultural identity, it is also intertwined with discussions about the assimilability of Muslims in Western societies.
6. See Jerry Markon, "Justice Department Sues on Behalf of Muslim Teacher, Triggering Debate," *The Washington Post*, March 22, 2011. See also Javier Lavagnino, "Muslim Police Officer Kimberlie Webb Loses Discrimination Claims Based on Headscarf Ban: Workplace Dress Codes and Discrimination," Findlaw, April 13, 2009, http://blogs.findlaw.com/law_and_life/2009/04/muslim-police-officer-kimberlie-webb-loses-discrimination-claims-based-on-headscarf-ban-workplace-dr.html; See also Debra Cassens Weiss, "Suit: Abercrombie & Fitch Told Muslim Job Seeker Scarf Not Part of Look," *ABA Journal*, September 2, 2010.
7. "About Islam and American Muslims," http://www.cair.com/AboutIslam/IslamBasics.aspx
8. The longevity of these suspicions is due in large part to our continued military engagement in Iraq and Afghanistan, where Muslim combatants physically oppose our presence.
9. See, for example, Mona Shadia and Paloma Esquivel, "Villa Park Councilwoman Deborah Pauly Ignites Controversy with Speech at Islamic Charity Event," *Los Angeles Times*, March 24, 2001. This article quoted councilwoman Pauly at a rally outside of a charitable fundraiser in Yorba Linda, California, where she said, "I know quite a few Marines who will be very happy to help these terrorists to an early meeting in paradise." See also David Folkenfilk, "NPR Ends Williams' Contract after Muslim Remarks," National Public Radio (NPR), October 21, 2010. This story discusses Juan

Williams's contract termination on the basis of his comment, "when I get on the plane, I got to tell you, if I see people who are in Muslim garb and I think, you know, they are identifying themselves first and foremost as Muslims, I get worried. I get nervous." A similar public acceptance of anti-Muslim bias tends to take place in Great Britain. See, for example, Alice Ritchie, "Baroness Warsi Attacks 'Acceptable' Islamophobia," Agence France-Presse (AFP), January 20, 2011.

10. Samuel P. Huntington, "The Clash of Civilizations?" *Foreign Affairs* 72 (1993): 22. Compare this with Marc Lynch, "Why the Clash of Civilizations Won't Go Away," *Foreign Policy*, July 22, 2010.
11. "Muslim Community Center in Lower Manhattan (Park 51)," *The New York Times*, August 3, 2011.
12. "Time Poll Results: Americans' Views on the Campaign, Religion and the Mosque Controversy," *Time*, August 18, 2010.
13. "CNN Opinion Research Poll," *CNN*, August 11, 2010, http://i2.cdn.turner.com/cnn/2010/images/08/11/rel11a.pdf.
14. See "This Just In . . . ," *The New York Times*, February 20, 2011. See also "Growing Number of Americans Say Obama Is a Muslim, "Pew Research Center, August 19, 2010, http://pewresearch.org/pubs/1701/poll-obama-muslim-christian-church-out-of-politics-political-leaders-religious. This article found that nearly one in five Americans (18 percent) say Obama is a Muslim.
15. See, for example, Michelle Malkin, "Racial Profiling: A Matter of Survival," USA *Today*, August 16, 2004.
16. Liz Goodwin, "New York Mosque Vandalized with Racial Slur," http://news.yahoo.com/blogs/upshot/york-mosque-vandalized-racial-slur.html. The article reports on the vandalization of a mosque in Hudson, New York, on Sept. 8, 2010 with "F-cking Sand Niggers" spray-painted on the side of the building.
17. See Sahar F. Aziz, "From the Oppressed to the Terrorist: Muslim American Women Caught in the Crosshairs of Intersectionality," *Hastings Race and Poverty Journal* 9 (2012), 191-264, referencing an article that details vandalism at a mosque site under construction in Toms River, New Jersey, defaced with Nazi graffiti, in addition to the throwing of beer and liquor bottles at a Union City mosque in New Jersey while congregants were inside mourning an Arab-American teenager who had been killed in a car crash.
18. "Arson Reported at Tennessee Mosque Construction Site," *USA Today*, August 28, 2010, at http://usatoday30.usatoday.com/news/religion/2010-08-29-arson28_ST_N.htm
19. Barabara Abel and Julia Lieblich, "Rural Controversy: A Mosque in Sheboygan," *Time*, August 19, 2010.
20. Daryl Johnson, "Hamden Mosque Vandalized," February 28, 2011, http://www.wfsb.com/story/14807873/hamden-mosque-vandalized-2-25-2011. This article reports on the defacing of a Hamden mosque spray-painted with profanity and graffiti, one of four instances of vandalism in the past two years.

21. "Democracy Now: Islamic Center Vandalized in California; Kentucky Board Rejects Mosque," Democracy Now, August 26, 2010, http://www.democracynow.org/2010/8/26/headlines/islamic_center_vandalized_in_california_kentucky_board_rejects_mosque. The article reports on the rejection of a building permit for a new mosque in the town of Mayfield, Kentucky, with cheers after the decision was announced to a packed hearing.
22. Ibid. The article documents a report of vandalism at Masjid Madera center in Madera, California, with signs reading, "No Temple for the God of terrorism at Ground Zero" and "Wake up America, the Enemy is here."
23. See Kara L. Richardson, "Bridgewater Looking for Bigger Venue to Fit Crowd to Hear Mosque Application," January 25, 2011, http://www.mycentraljersey.com/article/20110125/NEWS/101250355/Bridgewater-looking-bigger-venue-fit-crowd-hear-mosque-application. The article reports that 400 people arrived at the Planning Board meeting regarding the application to convert a closed Redwood Inn into a mosque; residents find that the mosque represents "a coming in and taking over an entire community by the Islamic World." See also Donna Leinwand, "More States Enter Debate on Sharia Law," *USA Today*, December 9, 2010. The author cites seven states other than Oklahoma as states having proposed legislation that, as stated by Newt Gingrich, "clearly and unequivocally states that we're not going to tolerate any imported law."
24. See James C. McKinley, Jr., "Oklahoma Surprise: Islam as an Election Issue," *The New York Times*, November 15, 2010.
25. "CAIR: Mo. Mosque Targeted with 'Terrorist Threat,' Desecrated Quran," http://www.prnewswire.com/news-releases/cair-mo-mosque-targeted-with-terrorist-threat-desecrated-qurans-119850384.html.
26. Jess Rollins, "Islamic Center Reports Threat, Finds Charred Qur'an," *USA Today*, April 19, 2011.
27. Associated Press, "Missouri Mosque Officials Say Vandalism Was Hate Crime," *Missourian*, January 13, 2011.
28. PR Newswire, "CAIR: Georgia Mosque Targeted by Hate Vandalism," Reuters, April 19, 2011.
29. See, for example, Cyra Akila Choudhury, "Empowerment or Estrangement? Liberal Feminism's Visions of the 'Progress' of Muslim Women," *University of Baltimore Law Forum* 39 (2008): 164. The article describes the Feminist Majority Foundation's strategy of showing the powerlessness and oppression of women caused by the burka to garner public support for Muslim women's rights in Afghanistan; see also Sheryll Cashin, "To Be Muslim or 'Muslim-Looking' In America: A Comparative Exploration of Racial and Religious Prejudice in the 21st Century," *Duke Forum for Law and Sociological Change* 2 (2010): 131–33. The article notes that when participants in implicit bias surveys are asked open-ended questions about what they knew or heard about Muslims through the media, common responses included discrimination against women.
30. See Choudhury, "Empowerment or Estrangement?"

31. See Katha Pollitt, "Whose Culture?" in *Is Multiculturalism Bad for Women?* (Princeton: Princeton Univ. Press, 1999), 30.
32. See Choudhury, "Empowerment or Estrangement?"
33. See, for example, Madhavi Sunder, "Piercing the Veil," *Yale Law Journal* 112 (2003): 1427.
34. See, for example, Maryam Namazie, "Unveiling the Debate on Secularism and Rights," January 19, 2004, http://www.maryamnamazie.com/articles/on_ban_relgious_symbols_veil.html.
35. See Susan Moller Okin, *Is Multiculturalism Bad for Women?* (Princeton University Press, 1999), 18.
36. See Okin, *Is Multiculturalism Bad?*, 10. The author defines feminism as "the belief that women should not be disadvantaged by their sex, that they should be recognized as having human dignity equal to that of men, and that they should have the opportunity to live as fulfilling and as freely chosen lives as men can."
37. Ibid.
38. See Okin, *Is Multiculturalism Bad?*, 16.
39. See Yael Tamir, "Revisiting the Civic Sphere" in *Freedom of Association*, ed. Amy Gutmann (Princeton: Princeton University Press, 1998), 47.
40. See Azizah al-Hibri, "Deconstructing Patriarchal Jurisprudence in Islamic Law: A Faithful Approach," in *Global Critical Race Feminism: An International Reader*, ed. Adrien Katherine Wing (New York: New York University Press, 2000), 221–33.
41. See Al-Hibri, "Deconstructing Patriarchal Jurisprudence," 44.
42. Admittedly, one cannot speak of the "Muslim woman" or "Muslim women" as a singular, monolithic category. Women that are Muslim originate from various racial, ethnic, and immigrant backgrounds. Moreover, they hold diverse political, social, and religious views that cannot be summed up in one term. When I use the term "Muslim woman," I assume and accept such diversity.
43. See Tara Bahrampour, "TSA Procedures Offend Followers of Many Faiths," *The Washington Post*, December 23, 2010.
44. Kimberle Crenshaw, "Mapping the Margins: Intersectionality Identity, Politics, and Violence against Women of Color," *Stanford Law Review* 43 (1990): 1241. See also her article, "Intersectionality: The Double Bind of Race and Gender," 2004, American Bar Association, http://www.americanbar.org/content/dam/aba/publishing/perspectives_magazine/women_perspectives_Spring2004CrenshawPSP.authcheckdam.pdf.
45. Kimberle W. Crenshaw, "Demarginalizing the Intersection of Race and Sex: A Black Feminist Critique of Antidiscrimination Doctrine, Feminist Theory and Antiracist Politics," *University of Chicago Legal Forum* 1989 (1989): 139.
46. Ibid., 143.
47. Muslim males can "pass" by shaving their beard and wearing Western clothing without compromising their religious beliefs, because to many practicing Muslims, the beard and traditional Islamic dress are optional unlike

the headscarf. Moreover, because Muslim men have not been historically patronized and objectified in the same way as Muslim women vis-à-vis the "West," it is one less burden they carry within the hostile post-9/11 environment.

48. See Leti Volpp, "Feminism Versus Multiculturalism," *Columbia Law Review* 101 (2001): 1185. "The discourse of feminism versus multiculturalism presumes that minority cultures are more patriarchal than Western liberal cultures."
49. See, for example, David Beasley, "Muslim Woman Sues Georgia City over Headscarf Arrest," Reuters, December 14, 2010, http://www.reuters.com/article/2010/12/14/us-headscarf-lawsuit-idUSTRE6BD6LL20101214?feedName=OutloudFeed&feedType=RSS&rpc=1120. The article reports on a Georgia Muslim woman who was arrested and jailed after she refused to remove her hijab before entering a Georgia court.
50. See Ben Smith, "Muslims Barred from Picture at Obama Event," Politico, June 18, 2008, http://www.politico.com/news/stories/0608/11168.html.
51. See, for example, David Beasley, "Muslim Woman Sues." See also Clark-Flory, "Abercrombie Hates Your Hijab."
52. See Volpp, "Feminism Versus Multiculturalism."
53. See Devon W. Carbado and Mitu Gulati, "The Fifth Black Woman," *Journal of Contemporary Legal Issues* 11 (2000–2001): 709.
54. Ibid.
55. In nearly every joint national press conference by Muslim organizations, the individuals speaking in a representational role are consistently males despite their 50 percent female constituency.
56. See Crenshaw, "Demarginalizing the Intersection of Race and Sex," 160.
57. Western feminists have consistently called for the ban of the burka and spoken in defense of women's rights in Iraq, Afghanistan, and other Middle Eastern nations, but they have largely remained silent on a Muslim woman's right to wear the hijab along with other gender rights in the United States. See, for example, "MADRE: Demanding Rights, Resources & Results for Women Worldwide," http://www.madre.org/index/meet-madre-1/our-projects-20.html. This is an international organization that calls for greater women's rights in Iraq and Afghanistan, but it remains completely silent on women's issues post-9/11 in the "Western" world. See also "Association for Women's Rights in Development," http://www.awid.org/Our-Initiatives. This focuses primarily on combating mandatory requirements for women to wear the hijab in foreign countries; see also "Feminist Majority Foundation," http://feminist.org/welcome/index.html. This article focuses on women's rights issues primarily in Afghanistan and Iran, more specifically, on banning the burka in Afghanistan and changes in discriminatory laws in Iran. Organizations such as Vital Voices, CODE Pink, and EQUALITY NOW all focus primarily on international women's rights efforts in Iraq, Iran, Afghanistan, and other countries of the global south and are largely silent on the issue of domestic women's rights issues, particularly the issues of Arab/South-Asian/Muslim women.

58. See "Democracy Now!: Entrapment or Foiling Terror? FBI's Reliance on Paid Informants Raises Questions about Validity of Terrorism Cases," radio broadcast, October 6, 2010.
59. The same occurs within communities of color when women complain about domestic violence; rather than focusing on the needs of the women of color, society interprets the complaints as evidence that black men are uncontrollably violent consistent with stereotypes. See Crenshaw, "Demarginalizing the Intersection of Race and Sex," 361.
60. See Crenshaw, "Demarginalizing the Intersection of Race and Sex," 162; however, note the increase in women who claim to be experts on Muslims or Islam but proffer views highly controversial, if not outright offensive, to a broad group of Muslims in America. See, for example, Samer Araabi, "Apostate Politics: How Some Recanted Muslims Have Bolstered Militarist U.S. Policies," Institute on Policy Studies, December 18, 2010, http://www.rightweb.irc-online.org/articles/display/apostate_politics_how_some_recanted_muslims_have_bolstered_militarist_us_po. I posit that this phenomenon is partially attributable to the exclusion of women from leadership positions, especially those who hold controversial views or are exceptionally talented. Hence, Muslim women stuck at the intersectionality of race, religion, and gender tend to either suffer in silence to preserve community unity, start their own organizations with varying success, or become adamant opponents of mainstream Muslim organizations exploited by groups holding anti-Muslim biases.
61. Having emerged in 2005 as a nonprofit sister entity to the National Association of Muslim Lawyers (NAML), Muslim Advocates is a professional association of approximately 500 Muslim lawyers, law students, and other legal professionals.
62. While this civil rights and civic engagement organization was founded and is lead by a non-Muslim South Asian woman, SAALT has a large Muslim South Asian constituency.
63. This organization works to build this global network of informed, empowered advocates in two ways—first, by creating and sharing knowledge about the rights Islamic law grants to women and, second, by educating Muslim women in Islamic jurisprudence, leadership, and conflict resolution, so that they may become the leading agents of change within their communities.
64. Similar examples exist at the local level where Muslim women have founded female-focused and led organizations to address social, economic, and political issues faced by women and ignored by male-dominated mosques or other community organizations. See, for example, Texas Muslim Women's Foundation.
65. See Volpp, "The Citizen And The Terrorist." See also Cashin, "To Be Muslim."
66. See "Legal Advocacy and Policy Review: Significant Increase in Legal Complaints," American-Arab Anti-Discrimination Committee, March 3, 2010, http://www.adc.org/media/press-releases/2011/march-2011/2010-adc-legal-report-significant-increase-in-legal-complaints.

67. See, for example, Karen Gardner, "Headscarf Causes Controversy at Basketball Game," *Frederick News Post*, January 18, 2011.
68. "Religious Freedom Has a Place in the Workplace," FindLaw, November 9, 2010, http://knowledgebase.findlaw.com/kb/2010/Nov/208334.html.
69. Brian Murphy, "Stop the Hate—Anti Muslim Discrimination Complaints at Record Levels," Submityourarticle.com, November 12, 2010, http://www.submityourarticle.com/articles/Brian-Mahany-8446/employment-discrimination-lawyer-123783.php.
70. See also Debra J. Groom, "Former Pulaski Health Center Worker Files Federal Complaint Stating He Was Fired Because He Is Muslim," *The Post-Standard*, February 7, 2011. See also *Abercrombie & Fitch* (SFDO) filed 9/1/10—Charging Party is Muslim. She was denied a reasonable accommodation (hijab) and denied hire into a stockroom position because of her religion; *Abercrombie & Fitch* (SLDO) filed 9/29/09—Charging Party is Muslim. She was not hired by defendant because she wore a headscarf to her interview; *Kaze Japanese Steakhouse* (CTDO) filed 9/7/10—Charging Party converted to Islam. She was denied the reasonable accommodation of wearing a hijab and discharged from her servicer position because of her religion; *Imperial Security* (PHDO) filed 9/16/10—Charging Party is Muslim. She was denied the reasonable accommodation of wearing a Khimar and discharged from her security guard position because of her religion; *White Lodging Services Corp.* (INDO) filed 7/4/06, resolved 7/21/10 ($40,000)—A Marriott hotel did not hire four Muslim women for housekeeping jobs because the women wore religious head coverings; *Ivy Hall Assisted Living* (ATDO) filed 9/30/08, resolved 1/28/10 ($43,000)—Charging Party, a housekeeper, was denied a religious accommodation to wear a traditional religious head covering, a hijab, and was discharged for violating defendant's dress code.
71. *Project Group of Illinois* (CHDO) filed 3/29/07, resolved 10/9/08 ($25,000)—a Palestinian Muslim was subjected to derogatory remarks about her head covering and was referred to as a terrorist.
72. Mohamed-Sheik v. Golden Foods/Golden Brands, LLC, No. Civ.A 303CV737H, 2006 WL 709573 (W.D. Ky. Mar. 16, 2006).
73. Campbell v. Avis Rent A Car System, Inc., No. 05-74472, 2006 WL 2865169 at *2 (E.D. Mich. Oct. 5, 2006).
74. EEOC v. Abercrombie and Fitch Co., No. 09-CV-602-GKF-FHM, 2011 WL 2748406 (N.D. Okla. July 13, 2011).
75. EEOC v. Abercrombie and Fitch, Co., No. 5:10-CV03911 (N.D. Cal. 2010).
76. First Amended Complaint and Demand for Jury Trial, EEOC v. Abercrombie & Fitch, Co., No. CV10-3911-HRL, 2010 WL 4638269 (N.D. Cal. Oct. 7, 2010).
77. See Mackenzie Carpenter, "Muslim Women Say Veil Is More about Expression than Oppression," *Pittsburgh Post-Gazette*, October 28, 2001.
78. Ibid.
79. Ibid.

80. See Doyle, "New 'Bias' Attack."
81. Janet I. Tu, "Woman Charged with Hate Crime against Two Muslim Women," *The Seattle Times*, October 22, 2010.
82. Gina Potthoff, "FBI Investigates Reported Assault on Local Muslim," *The Columbus Dispatch*, Dec. 20, 2010.
83. Jamie Schram and Maura O'Connor, "Muslim Gal Assaulted in Harlem," *New York Post,* July 8, 2011.
84. Kane Farabaugh, "Seven Muslim Americans on Ballot in Chicago, Voice of America, April 4, 2011, http://www.voanews.com/english/news/usa/Seven-Muslim-Americans-on-Ballot-in-Suburban-Chicago-119217129.html.
85. Crenshaw, "Demarginalizing the Intersection of Race and Sex," 360.
86. Ibid.
87. See Choudhury, "Empowerment or Estrangement?," 168–70.
88. Ibid.
89. Sunder, "Piercing the Veil," 1413.

Part 4

Concluding Thoughts

CHAPTER 10

RULES OF LAW AND GOD: LIBERAL DEMOCRATIC REFLECTIONS ON FREEDOM, EQUALITY, AND RELIGION

RICHARD B. MILLER

1. PRELIMINARIES

Our topic is the rule of law and the rule of God and, more specifically, the proper role of religious citizens who seek to enshrine their religious convictions in public policy and practice. Such adherents of "political religions," as Mark Lilla uses that term, are infrequently apathetic about public affairs. Quite the contrary: religious believers often aim to shape others' behavior and opportunities by having their religious values embodied in law and policy and enforced through the coercive powers of the state. That aspect of religion should remind us of a more general fact about how religions—and not only political religions—often behave: among the many things that religions do, they argue. They make claims over and against other positions, points of view, settled convictions, and pictures of the good life. Religions are not necessarily tolerant. Even when they are tolerant, religions often find it difficult to accede to other forms of authority. When they do accede, religions typically do so on terms that they themselves set—on terms established by their own authoritative teachings and traditions. In that way, as Andrew March's discussion of

Islamic jurisprudence makes plain, religions seek to offer legitimation to norms or principles established by other nonreligious authorities.

More generally, religions are—again, among other things—normative discourses. They do not merely describe wider processes and patterns of history and the world, along with our place in them. They do not simply organize human activity for ritualistic and other similar purposes. They do not only discipline adherents by means of spiritual and bodily practices, ascetic or otherwise. They *avow* visions about what is right and good for their adherents and, at times, the world at large. In that way religions sort out acceptable from unacceptable modes of character and conduct. The fact that they do so with such visibility and vigor today should come as no surprise to any student of religious history, theories of secularization notwithstanding. How they ought to do so through the medium of regulation, especially political regulation and legal enforcement, is an important matter to consider.

As John Kelsay reminds us in his contribution to this volume, inquiry into the rules of law and the rules of God should not presume that religious rules and political rules seamlessly cohere. This is true even when political regulations are understood to issue forth from more general religious rules and convictions. But I want to focus on theoretical and practical questions that arise when political rules secure their justification on terms independent of religious traditions or belief systems—when they don't issue forth from more general religious rules and convictions. Like rival lovers, rules of God and rules of law may compete with each other for an individual's embrace. In such instances, political regulations sometimes prohibit or make difficult the fulfillment of duties that are guided by religious rules and beliefs. Likewise, religious rules and beliefs can sometimes prohibit or make difficult the fulfillment of duties guided by political obligations. How to adjudicate such conflicts in practical affairs finds no obvious solution.

Theoretical and practical tensions between rules of God and rules of law are especially exigent in liberal, democratic societies. In such contexts, one question is whether, or to what extent, religious practices and laws might be accommodated within existing legal frameworks and institutions of liberal democracies. In American public life, this question is of constitutional importance: disputes about religious accommodation implicate the First Amendment's disestablishment and freedom of religion clauses. US citizens are sometimes asked whether the state should make allowances for religious practices or allow policies that might appear to involve the state in the business of endorsing particular religious institutions or religious laws.

I use the modifier "liberal" when referencing the liberal democratic state to highlight questions that our previous chapters take up directly or indirectly. On one account of liberalism, the liberal state is and should remain neutral to broad comprehensive doctrines of the good. That understanding of liberal doctrine, defended by John Rawls and Ronald Dworkin, among others, claims that liberalism as a political philosophy is not itself a worldview but offers terms for the ethical design of social and political institutions within the context of cultural pluralism. On this account, liberalism defines a broad political framework according to which adherents of different religious doctrines and other worldviews can coexist and find fair and stable terms of social cooperation. The ideal picture of the liberal state is thus neutral in a specific sense: the liberal state takes no stand, affirmatively or negatively, regarding the truth of any religious or other comprehensive doctrine. That is not to say that the liberal state's decisions cannot or should not affect religious communities positively or negatively. It only means that whatever effects a social policy might have on a religious organization are not a function of the putative truth or falsity of that organization's particular beliefs. Moreover, and equally important, the ethical design of liberal democracy often seeks to set terms for social cooperation that are rooted in principles of fairness rather than in a balance of power—a *modus vivendi*. Two of the most basic of such principles are respect for conscience and equal liberty; these principles allow us to justify policies that protect the freedom of religious expression and that require religious toleration.

Liberalism on this account is religiously agnostic. It is not a secular doctrine that imposes a nonreligious or antireligious vision on its adherents. Liberalism does not seek to neutralize the public square of religious conviction or marginalize religious views from public life. But neither does liberalism want the state to encourage religious beliefs or endorse one or another religious worldview. Liberalism's agnosticism walks the line between secularism and endorsement.

The fact that liberal doctrine is agnostic about religious claims should not suggest that liberalism views religion as a trivial matter for democratic citizens. Quite the contrary: liberalism takes religion seriously by relegating the authority for making religious commitments to individual citizens instead of public officials. Political institutions constrained by liberal norms seek not to interfere in the faith of citizens by purposefully encouraging or discouraging one or another comprehensive doctrine. The proper liberal stance to religion is one of noninterference within the limits assigned by the norm of equal liberty. On this description, liberalism assigns to the individual the authority to develop, change, dispute, or reject any particular comprehensive belief. Liberalism is premised in part on our interest in freely developing and critically revising our desires against a background of meaningful options. "Freedom of conscience," as

William Schweiker envisions that idea, is close to, if not identical with, liberal notions of moral subjectivity. In the words of Rawls, individuals "do not view themselves as inevitably tied to the pursuit of the particular conception of the good and its final ends which they espouse at any given time." Instead, they "are capable of revising and changing this conception."[1] Liberals thus assign value to autonomy or "human subjectivity," understood as our capacity to critically evaluate our immediate first-order desires to determine whether they are indeed desirable and worthy of our commitment.[2] The enforcement of religious orthodoxy or the criminalization of apostasy is not the appropriate business of law and policy. We do well to remember that liberalism is, among other things, a doctrine about the limited authority of the state. Limits to state authority are set by the authority assigned to citizens to determine how they may freely organize their lives and convictions. In this way, liberalism embodies the idea of respect for political autonomy, understood as the right of citizens to set their ends absent state interference within the constraints implied by equal liberty for all.

Insofar as liberals assign decisional authority regarding religious matters to individual citizens, liberalism is frequently charged with "privatizing" religion. Moreover, and more controversially, privatizing religion is often understood—perhaps under the influence of legal scholar Stephen Carter—as "trivializing" religion.[3] Indeed, the public mandate of the symposium that partly gave rise to this book describes religion as "once . . . sidelined in the past in the West as a private matter [moving] . . . on a slow path to social insignificance."[4] That statement makes plain the putative link between privatization and trivialization. But here, as elsewhere, distinctions are important: privatizing religion and trivializing religion are quite different matters. Indeed, as I noted above, privatizing religion is a function of considering it a serious matter, not a trivial one. Its significance is indicated by setting it beyond the proper limits of state regulation.[5] The privatization of religion is one aspect of the state's limited authority. In that way liberals mark—indeed protect—religion as a matter crucially important for the individual and his or her conscience. I thus believe that privatizing religion as I have described it—assigning final authority to the individual citizen in matters of religious belief and practice—is both right and proper.

I state this point about liberalism's neutrality (or agnosticism) in very basic terms knowing—as the political philosopher Will Kymlicka has forcefully argued—that the liberal state is scarcely neutral in establishing the language of signage, public holidays, civic heroes, and the terms of political franchise and representation.[6] The state makes its own claims on our practices and commitments, often with an eye to practical matters regarding cultural legacy and cohesion rather than to ideal-theoretical accounts regarding justice, citizenship, and the state. But the neutrality of which I am speaking concerns not these cultural practices. It rather concerns, more narrowly, the state's relationship to matters of religious belief and practice.

To be sure, distinguishing between religious beliefs and practices, on the one hand, and cultural legacies, on the other, is often difficult. I am proceeding on the hypothesis that we can do so. Regarding religious matters, liberalism is often misunderstood and misrepresented by its critics. I want to focus most of my comments on liberalism's stance toward religion as a way of framing my thoughts about many of the contributions to this volume. Liberalism shadows several of our authors' arguments in important and provocative ways, providing a conceptual backdrop for their theoretical concerns and concrete examples. I will turn to those concerns and examples soon, and I will assess a few of them in light of the liberal notion of human dignity as that idea attaches to the notion of moral subjectivity as I have defined it above. I'll describe those ideas in the process of developing my commentary below. But by way of stage setting, it will help to be clear about how core ideas in liberal thinking illumine several of our authors' chapters.

1. The Liberal Imaginary

Consider first the contribution by legal scholar Frank Ravitch. Ravitch (and other contributors to this volume, as I will make plain) addresses legal questions in ways that presuppose the liberal imaginary, by which I mean the imaginative framework according to which liberal citizens conceive the relationship between the state and religious practices, among other things. That imaginary forms the background of his analysis insofar as he addresses questions of legal neutrality regarding church-state controversies. Ravitch is skeptical about the idea of neutrality in general. He argues that the concept is itself a fiction and that the Supreme Court's use of the concept works to legitimize its decisions given the esteem we place on neutrality. By that Ravtich means that appeals to neutrality offer the patina of legal objectivity and impartiality, but only that. In his mind, the concept of neutrality cannot coherently *justify* the court's decisions given that the effects of those decisions on religious institutions are scarcely neutral. There are winners and losers in church-state decisions, and that fact embarrasses claims of legal neutrality.

Such disputes repose against the backdrop of liberal ideas and practices. Indebted to liberalism as we are, neutrality is a norm to which we often aspire and according to which we claim to view the proper role of the state in relation to religion and religious citizens. Without that backdrop, church-state disputes would seem idle if not incoherent. The appeal to neutrality is a liberal's way of expressing agnosticism in public and political life regarding matters of religious truth; as a norm, neutrality aims to ensure that policy decisions about any religion prescind from judging the truth of that religion.

But perhaps neutrality is being deployed to do more than put limits on the powers of the state. Perhaps the work it is being asked to perform goes beyond the special duties of expressing agnosticism. Ravitch thus invites us to step back and ponder a broader question of the sort that Nietzsche would have us ask, namely, what is the *value* of neutrality?[7] What is it about the concept that inclines us to use it as our default way of authorizing legal decisions? I will return to such questions below. For now, I want us to note that the disputes, to which Ravitch calls our attention, reveal that we share some common understandings as a condition for inquiring into what neutrality is all about. However vague or contested, liberal aspirations to neutrality are part and parcel of our lifeworld.

Consider as well the contributions by Anita Allen and Andrew March. In their chapters, background agreements regarding liberal doctrine seem more obvious. For Allen and March, the core question is how, or on what terms, can liberal doctrine accommodate Islamic law as espoused by minority Muslim groups in democratic societies? Allen gets at this question by thinking about how case law and precedent can resolve a dispute in Michigan surrounding a Muslim woman, Ginnah Muhammad, who wished to wear the niqab in court. Allen calls attention to legal decisions in which veiling to ensure modesty and privacy is protected by law, along with other court decisions that protect religious free exercise regarding the citizens who, for religious reasons, refuse to have their photographs taken for legal purposes. Case precedent shows that, generally speaking, state interest is not sufficiently compelling to encumber religious adherents in disputes surrounding religious free exercise regarding rules of dress and female modesty. Case precedent also shows how other forms of (non-Muslim) religious practice have been accommodated by the state, even at some inconvenience to the state. This latter set of legal examples illustrates the pressure exhibited by the norm of neutrality in cases surrounding free exercise. Encumbering the Muslim practice of wearing the niqab in court appears to discriminate against Muslim women, given that religious adherents of other traditions are being accommodated in analogous cases.

March gets at the question of religious accommodation, not by starting from precedent in US law as a way of addressing more recent legal controversies, but by starting from Islamic law and tradition to determine whether, and on what terms, it can find common ground with "an exogenously determined liberal framework." Such questions are especially vexing when liberal laws permit what Islamic law prohibits, or when liberal laws prohibit what Islamic law requires. Here again questions about religion in public affairs arise against a background according to which we understand the liberal state's agnosticism regarding religious belief. In March's chapter, those questions congeal around the problem of whether, or to what extent, Islamic law can assign legitimacy to liberal political frameworks and institutions.

As with Ravitch, the problems to which March and Allen direct our attention repose against some common understandings about state neutrality regarding religious practices and beliefs and substantive visions of the good more generally.[8] Once again I want to say that such understandings are a part of our lifeworld, a habit of mind for liberal democrats. Controversies of the proper place of Islam for Muslims as political minorities arise in light of some shared understandings about the state, its limits, and the authority that liberalism assigns to individual citizens regarding matters of religious belief and practice. Ravitch, Allen, and March thereby address questions that presuppose the liberal imaginary. Even when that imaginary is seen as problematical, as it seems to be among some of the authors to whom March refers, that imaginary would have us view individuals as possessing the final authority to determine the nature and shape of religious belief and practice within the limits assigned (to everyone) by the norm of equal liberty.

How the norm of equal liberty ought to constrain appeals to religious belief, or accommodation of religion, is brought into sharp relief by Michael Curtis. Curtis trenchantly identifies how efforts at religious accommodation can infringe upon other legal and moral norms. He focuses on the infringement of equal liberty, as it bears on a right to be free, in the commercial sphere, from discrimination based on gay marriage or more generally based on sexual orientation. Curtis targets how the idea of religious freedom is used to invoke religious norms to justify exemptions from state laws that ban discrimination in the commercial sphere based on sexual orientation. In his account, such arguments fail to abide by antidiscrimination norms. Proposals for exemptions in the case of gay marriage—or sexual orientation generally—would put same-sex citizens in a uniquely disadvantaged class. In a number of state laws, discrimination in the commercial sphere is typically prohibited when based on race, religion, gender, national origin, or sexual orientation—and it is currently prohibited without an exception for those with religious or moral objections to the mandate of equal treatment. Some proposals suggest at least a limited exemption from such laws, when the act is discrimination against people in same-sex relationships and the discrimination is religiously or morally motivated. Married or unmarried, same-sex persons would be denied the full and equal protection of such laws enjoyed by other groups.

Curtis's chapter shows not only how disputes regarding freedom of religion take shape within the liberal imaginary, but also how liberal ideas can function as tools for social criticism. The core point, as I have mentioned above, is that the norm of equal liberty limits what can be granted under protections of religious expression. Curtis insists that in the case of sexual orientation, as in the cases of discrimination based on race, gender, national origin or religion, discrimination enforces a caste system.

Religious claims can work, not merely to express and protect individual piety, but also to enforce a series of power relations. Liberalism that affirms not only religious liberty but also constraints on such liberty, in light of equality, has powers (and reasons) to resist conservative religious rhetoric, especially but not only when such rhetoric conspires to turn a segment of the population into second-class citizens.

When religion works ideologically as a tool of subordination, then liberal norms can and should put religion to scrutiny as a form of ideology. Viewing religion as ideology is not to say, as it is commonly said, that religion offers a false world that enables one to escape the real world. Rather, as Denys Turner writes, when a belief is ideological, "the believer relates not a false world by means of an alternative to the real world but to the real world in and through the prism of belief in a false world. Religion [as ideology] misconstrues this particular world."[9]

Ideology-critique targets religious and other comprehensive doctrines that seek to legitimize parochial interests and antiegalitarian visions of social relations. This legitimation proceeds by rendering such interests and relationships as normal and good. In these contexts, liberal norms work not so much to constrain religious practices as to *expose* how religion can lend an aura of sanctity to a specific policy position.

That work of exposé is different from more straightforward attempts to restrict the privileging of religion when it finds itself endorsed by state policy. Liberals are mindful not only about the extensive powers of the state but how those in political power can find legitimation from religion and other cultural sources to disempower various groups or classes.

Simeon Ilesanmi's chapter illustrates how liberal norms might straightforwardly constrain appeals to religion and certainly endorsements of religious practice in Nigeria, especially that state's support of pilgrimage to the Holy Lands of Jerusalem and Mecca. Such support, Ilesanmi observes, goes beyond the removal of travel restrictions to an all-inclusive package of government generosity at both the federal and state levels, and it targets Muslim and Christian citizens alike. This case differs notably from disputes about religion in public life, as they are carried out in North American contexts, given that the Nigerian policy is underwritten by an understanding of religious liberty not as a negative right against noninterference but as a positive right that entails an entitlement to government support. Given that Muslims and Christians are only a part of the Nigerian population, however, it is necessary to ask whether extensive state involvement can be justified in light of relevant religious provisions in the Nigerian Constitution. On Ilesanmi's account, such support is challenged by norms of religious non-adoption and nondiscrimination. On his reckoning, state involvement makes a "preferential option" for members of Nigeria's two dominant religions, thereby treating others as second-class citizens. For Ilesanmi, as for Allen and Curtis, policy assessment should be informed by considerations of equal liberty. Once again we see how the norm of equality qualifies religious liberty, even when (perhaps especially when) such liberty is conceived as a positive rather than a negative right.

2. Rules: External or Immanent?

Thought reposes against a lifeworld in yet another way that is relevant to our volume. Here we turn from political philosophy to philosophy of mind. My point here, and the broader challenge that it presents, concerns an underlying assumption about rules and/or laws—assumptions about how rules arise and how they behave. I have in mind both "constructed rules" as well as rules in "revealed moralities." On one description of rules—a description I want to challenge—rules are external mental constructs that exist "out there" as terms that we deploy to evaluate past conduct or direct the course of present and future conduct. Rules on that description are extrinsic to our imaginative and behavioral practices, experienced from without, insofar as they find their existence in some external source. That source may be revelation, a freestanding legal body, or a philosopher's mind. Rules on this description are like Platonic ideas, residing above and outside of our lifeworld. In that respect, I will call this view of rules "idealistic."

I believe that this idealistic view of rules is misguided. I propose that we view rules in relation to behavior immanently rather than idealistically, on analogy of grammar's relationship to speech. Thus understood, rules are to behavior as *parole* is to *langue.* The former is only possible because of the preexistence of the latter. Grammatical rules inhere in the practice of interlocution, enabling the very act of communication. We understand each other when we speak, insofar as we all rely on a set of rules that structure our patterns of discussion and dialogue. Such rules exist to the degree that we have embodied and internalized them as a condition for discourse. On this non-platonic description, rules are not "out there" as mental constructs. They are rather embodied—shaping and guiding our practices in infrastructural ways. Thus understood, rules are internal to a role or institution and guide it as such.[10] They are cultural artifacts, identifying paradigmatic practices and examples that are commendable or reprehensible.[11] Stated another way, rules provide shorthand for what we deem exemplary by way of good or bad behavior.

This is not to say that rules do not or cannot have conceptual backing or that articulating rules is merely to appeal to "how we customarily do things here." It is rather to say that the reasons we invoke when challenging a rule, or revising a rule, aim to articulate what it is about the rule that fails to track irregularities, innovations, or new intuitions that seek to nest themselves into social practices and a way of life. Challenges to a rule, or attempts to revise a rule, thus require us to proceed from an immanent understanding of a rule to an understanding that reflexively opens itself up to reasoned articulation and refinement in light of competing values that themselves gesture toward prescriptive, proscriptive, or permissive articulations.

The implications of this more immanentist account of rules are as follows: Challenges to rules of God that arise from efforts to follow the rules of law cut deep. That is to say, challenges posed to rules of God from other rules of law are typically conflicts that include differences between ways of life. When rules of law pose problems for rules of God, those problems typically implicate how God and world are to be interpreted or reinterpreted. Likewise, when rules of God pose problems for rules of law, those problems typically implicate how social and political ends are to be conceived or reconceived. Rules don't simply regulate behavior. They implicate identities and, with that, ways of experiencing each other and the world.

3. Questions

With these preliminaries about (1) liberalism and (2) rules behind us, let me now turn to a few particulars of our collective project regarding the rule of God and the rule of law. I'll begin with questions for Professor Ravitch's chapter.

Ravitch argues against the idea of neutrality as a norm for resolving church-state disputes. His complaint moves along two tracks that, taken alone and taken together, require more argument. One complaint claims that neutrality does not exist because no neutral baseline exists to which the norm of neutrality can be traced and grounded. It is incoherent, he claims, to ground neutrality on a non-neutral norm, one that is itself located in a context, relative to time and place. Neutrality aspires to achieve a vantage point that is a view from nowhere, and such epistemic aspirations, he alleges, have shown to be illusory.

I find this complaint to be unpersuasive for disputing neutrality for several reasons. The first concerns the putative incoherence of grounding neutrality by attaching it to a non-neutral baseline. More needs to be said here. Consider an analogy: we secure the principle of religious liberty on secular terms and hardly find that form of argument to be incoherent. That is to say, we value religious liberty for nonreligious reasons—because religious liberty expresses respect for persons, for example, or because respecting religious liberty is good for democracy, or because it is part of a larger endorsement of expressive freedom. None of these is a religious reason for valuing religious liberty. We needn't trace the value to its mirror image in order to proceed coherently. Likewise with neutrality, we value it for substantive reasons. Neutrality expresses attitudes toward others that we think they deserve as citizens with political autonomy. That is to say, there are the non-neutral values that are served by adherence to the norm of neutrality.

Ravitch might reply that neutrality is a fiction because a court's decision has winners and losers, and that fact embarrasses claims to neutrality. Any decision by a court leaves some religious communities or individuals at a disadvantage relative to others, and that fact means that a decision cannot claim neutrality in its effects. But surely that conclusion is misleading. Consider the analogy of instructional grading. When professors return exams to their students, some students are advantaged more than others in the pursuit of a high grade, but such effects hardly impugn the neutrality of the examiner in grading her students' work. The key question is whether neutrality is sought in the relevant way and for the right reasons. If neutrality is a *normative* concept and not merely a descriptive one, its application in identifying differences in student performance, or in adjudicating a legal dispute, will leave some at a disadvantage to others vis-à-vis relevant social goods.

The largest difficulty with Ravitch's argument arises when we put these two claims together. If neutrality does not exist because it cannot be traced to a neutral baseline, then it is not clear how he can claim that some decisions are non-neutral in their effects. That is to say, if no criteria exist for identifying a neutral decision, then we have no criteria for marking the absence of neutrality. If criteria for identifying X do not exist and cannot exist, then all we can be left with is agnosticism regarding X. Ravitch can't have it both ways, arguing first that no criteria exist to establish neutrality and then claiming that neutrality has not been satisfied by one or another court decision.

A more general response to Ravitch would be to ask him why we should want to jettison neutrality in the first place. Here it is important to ask what work the concept can perform. Stated in the Nietzschean terms to which I alluded above, it would have us ask what *value* we attach, or should attach, to the value of neutrality. I have only general intuitions along these lines, but all of them suggest that neutrality offers more than a patina of legitimacy to a legal decision. It expresses liberalism's commitment to the state's limited authority regarding matters that are properly left to individual citizens. That is to say, neutrality signals to citizens that the state recognizes the boundaries within which it should operate when addressing matters that implicate religious belief and practice. Neutrality is the state's idiom for expressing *respect* for citizens' political autonomy to establish and revise their ends within the constraints imposed by equal liberty for all. Such respect is not an endorsement *of* any particular exercise of political autonomy; it is rather respect *for* the authority exercised by individual citizens.[12] That is to say, courts respect citizens' authority to make their own decisions within the constraints imposed by equal liberty, even when judges may not esteem the decisions that citizens make. Neutrality aims to ensure that members of a democracy do not find themselves subjected to inferior legal status, the status of second-class citizenship. To be sure, the *Zelman* decision may show the incoherence of certain renderings of neutrality or expose where the idea seems stretched beyond its means. But we should not judge the work that neutrality can perform based on court decisions that may get it wrong.

Likewise, I have a question for Professor March's essay. It concerns his effort to find some common ground between Islamic law and "complex purposivism," on the one hand, and the framework of political liberalism, on the other. On his account, complex purposivism provides a set of terms and distinctions according to which Islamic jurists might find in liberal regimes some common ground, thereby allowing jurists to assign legitimacy to such regimes. Muslim jurists might, for example, be able to distinguish between the ends of law and the means of punishment, and thereby see that liberal laws forbid the same wrongs as do Muslims, but enforce their sanctions differently. Complex purposivism might also enable Muslims to distinguish between dispensible and indispensible practices for living a good Islamic life, enabling Muslims to evaluate the relative merits of liberal permissions and prohibitions. On these terms, March suggests, constructive dialogue between Islamic law and political liberalism is possible.

But there is a serious stumbling block standing in the way of such dialogue. That stumbling block concerns the basis for assigning toleration of and respect for religious differences from within the legal reasoning of complex purposivism. If, as March argues, "advancing religion" is one of the five aims of the law, according to complex purposivism, then I wonder wherein lies his optimism regarding prospects for common ground between liberal democratic politics and Islamic law. I say this not only for the obvious reason that "advancing religion" implicates establishment concerns in democratic societies, such as ours in the United States. Ilesanmi's chapter reveals reasons for concern regarding establishment issues in other political contexts. More generally, it is not clear that Muslim theocrats have solid bases for respecting others and their religious beliefs. At the root of my concern, here is whether there are grounds for securing equal respect between or among citizens according to the tenets of complex purposivism.

I can sharpen my comments to Ravitch and March into focus by offering an admittedly brief and truncated genealogy of the idea of the liberal political subject and the idea of equal respect, as it developed in modern Western thought. My story has less to do with the "Great Separation" regarding matters of belief, politics, and law, as Mark Lilla describes these ideas, than with two distinct ways of envisioning authority and our relationship to it in early modern European thought. Clarifying those two ways is central to understanding the liberal imaginary, especially with regard to norms of respect for political autonomy, nondiscrimination, and ideology-critique, as these shaped the lifeworld of liberal democratic citizens.

I have spoken of liberalism's commitment to ideas of political autonomy and equal liberty. Let us bring these ideas under the rubric of equal respect, understood as a normative principle in democratic public life. Central to liberalism's understanding of equal respect is the distinction between two forms of subjection, each of which presumes a different relationship between an individual and authority.[13] One relationship is that of *submission* to authority, the other is *respect* for authority.[14] Submission is the acknowledgment of de facto authority, the status of being ruled. It expresses no view about that authority; one can submit to a rule or regime that one considers unjust. Respect, in contrast, expresses a normative attitude toward authority; it involves the subject's internal acceptance of a sovereign's rule. Therein lies the basic difference between submission and respect. As Stephen Darwall rightly observes, with respect, "although the subject is governed by the sovereign de facto, there is a sense in which she also governs herself, since she is not submitting to something she does not herself accept."[15] One can respect an authority out of awe because it has superior dignity, as in hierarchical relationships, or one can respect an authority because it has equal dignity, thereby entailing mutual or equal respect. In either forms of respect—hierarchical or mutual—the core idea is that there is something about authority that satisfies an independent norm. Respect for authority, unlike submission, is contingent upon that authority's ability to satisfy criteria that stand apart from its social status or control of power. Those who respect authority on such terms are ruling and being ruled at the same time.

In early modern Europe, ideas about authority and religious belief were complicated by the fact that individual and institutional authority were seen as divinely willed and dependent upon obedience to God. Central to this picture of authority was the idea of theological voluntarism and divine command morality, defended by Duns Scotus and William of Ockham in the late medieval period, and subsequently developed in the political theologies of the mainline Reformers. Luther and Calvin both believed that moral and political authority derives from God's will, as expressed in divine commands. For the sake of brevity, let me focus on Luther's argument. Luther held that "God is He for Whose will no cause or ground may be laid down as its rule and standard; for nothing is on a level with it or above it, but it is itself the rule for all things. . . . What God wills is not right because He ought, or was bound, so to will; on the contrary, what takes place must be right, because He so wills it."[16] Luther continued this line of reasoning in "Secular Authority," in which he sought to "establish secular law and the sword, that no one may doubt that it is in the world by God's will and ordinance."[17] Drawing exclusively on biblical passages (especially Romans 13), Luther claimed that it is "sufficiently clear and certain that it is God's will that the sword and secular law be used for the punishment of the wicked and the protection of the upright."[18] Luther developed these ideas in part to restrict the reach of secular authority to the realm of external behavior, arguing that faith was the Christian's individual responsibility and thus not subject to coercion. "Where temporal power presumes to prescribe laws for the soul," Luther wrote, "it encroaches upon God's government and only misleads and destroys the souls."[19] Yet Luther had no compunction about enjoining public authorities to punish those who practice the Catholic Mass. "If cursing and swearing are forbidden in a country," Luther reasoned, "it is still more right here that the lay lords should prohibit and punish, because such blasphemy and such insults to God are as evident and public in the Mass as when a rascal blasphemes in the street."[20]

When political authority is grounded in theological terms in this way, Darwall notes, "there will be an obvious sense in which religious difference will seem to contest political authority, at least potentially."[21] Those who worship God differently, or who worship a different deity, will have reason to question the de jure authority of a sovereign. At a minimum, they will see a potential conflict between obedience to divine and political authorities. Central to the problem of religious toleration in early Europe, "was the idea that the authority of human beings and human political institutions derives from God's superior right of command, that to be a human moral subject is to be subject to God's authority."[22] The opportunities for violations and umbrage are clear. As Darwall observes: "In a world in which dignity and moral identity are gauged by subjection, by the relation human individuals and institutions have to superior divine authority, an attack on God must be understood as an attack on the source of one's own dignity and, hence, as a personal insult which, if not avenged, risks dishonor and devaluation to oneself, as it does to anything whose dignity derives from God's."[23] That is to say, when dignity is contingent upon belief in God or in a certain community's interpretation of a certain God, then dignity and respect can be denied. This seems to be the danger to which Schweiker alerts us in his comments about "hypertheism": if you don't worship my god, then you, along with your beliefs and practices, do not deserve my respect. Equal respect is thereby contingent upon possessing the right beliefs; equality is exclusive rather than inclusive.

In contrast to a regime of toleration premised on submission, there is the liberal idea of mutual respect. I can only sketch the idea here. Central to this idea is a feature of human beings, namely, moral subjectivity, "the capacity to lead and take responsibility for one's own life."[24] On the liberal view that I would defend, we need freedom to choose and critically to revise our commitments against a background of meaningful options. On my view, then, autonomy is valuable as a necessary ingredient in our personal pursuit of the good. We thus assign to each person the authority to lead his or her own life as an expression of respect for her intrinsic dignity as a free and equal person, respect that is constrained by fairness and mutual respect. Religious toleration on this view expresses respect for this intrinsic dignity.[25] What is salient about religious toleration, understood along these liberal lines, is "its centrality to political institutions that express respect for the dignity any individual has in herself, independently of her religious belief and practice—respect for citizens as equals."[26]

I sketch these differences between a theocratic understanding of submission and a liberal political account of respect to sharpen what I believe to be an obstacle facing March's argument to find bases for rapprochement between Islamic theocratic law and political liberalism. Recall his core claim: complex purposivism provides a basis for thinking that Muslims and non-Muslims might assign legitimacy to secular or non-Muslim rule. But March's argument stays at the level of jurisprudential reasoning while missing what I believe to be a basic philosophical difference between a theocratic and a political liberal's view of citizen-state and citizen-citizen relationships. Hence these questions: Do theocratic Muslims have Muslim grounds in complex purposivism to respect laws that protect everyone's religious liberty? More generally, are there grounds in complex purposivism to respect the beliefs of non-Muslims or, more specifically, to respect others as free and equal citizens, regardless of the content of their belief (or disbelief), in a non-Muslim state? It would seem not. That is because complex purposivism has as one of its intrinsic goods the "advancement of religion," understood as Muslim faith. For political liberals, however, what other citizens deserve is equal respect owing to an understanding of all of us as bearers of intrinsic dignity to choose and, if necessary, revise our beliefs against a background of meaningful options.[27]

Notes

1. John Rawls, "Kantian Constructivism in Moral Theory," *Journal of Philosophy* 77.9 (September 1980): 544.
2. This account of first- and second-order desires draws from Charles Taylor, "What Is Human Agency?" in *Philosophical Papers I* (Cambridge: Cambridge University Press, 1985), 15–44.
3. Stephen Carter, *The Culture of Disbelief: How American Law and Politics Trivialize Religious Devotion* (New York: Basic Books, 1993).
4. http://provost.wfu.edu/news-and-events/conferences/the-rule-of-law-and-the-rule-of-god/
5. Again, within constraints set by the norm of equal liberty, as I will make plain below.
6. Will Kymlicka, *Multicultural Citizenship: A Liberal Defense of Minority Rights* (Oxford: Clarendon Press, 1995).
7. Friedrich Nietzsche, *On the Genealogy of Morals*, trans. Walter Kaufmann and R. J. Hollingdale (New York: Vintage Books, 1989).
8. This is not to say that religious freedom is absolute, only that any legal effort to restrict it shoulders a considerable burden of proof.
9. Denys Turner, describing Marx's view of ideology in Turner, "Religion: Illusions and Liberation," in *The Cambridge Companion to Marx*, ed. Terrell Carver (Cambridge: Cambridge University Press, 1991), 324. For a discussion of how liberal thought can perform social criticism of religious convictions and practices, see Richard B. Miller, *Terror, Religion, and Liberal Thought* (New York: Columbia University Press, 2010), chap. 7.
10. John Rawls, "Two Concepts of Rules," in *Theories of Ethics*, ed. Philippa Foot (Oxford: Oxford University Press, 1967), 144–70.
11. Richard B. Miller, "Rules," in *Oxford Handbook of Theological Ethics,* ed. Gilbert Meilaender and William Werpehowski (New York: Oxford University Press, 2005), 220–36.
12. Miller, *Terror, Religion, and Liberal Thought*, chaps. 4–5.
13. The following brief genealogy borrows from my *Terror, Religion, and Liberal Thought*, 75–79.

14. Stephen Darwall, "Peace as Politics," in *Religion, Politics, and Peace,* ed. Leroy S. Rouner (Notre Dame, IN: University of Notre Dame Press, 1999), 89. The following discussion of submission and respect borrows from Miller, *Terror, Religion, and Liberal Thought*, chap. 4. Although I focus on Muslim radicals in that book, my ideas apply to matters of theocratic politics and authority more generally.
15. Ibid., 90.
16. Martin Luther, "The Bondage of the Will," in *Martin Luther: Selections from His Writings*, ed., with an Introduction by, John Dillenberger (New York: Doubleday, 1961), 196.
17. Martin Luther, "Secular Authority," in *Martin Luther: Selections from His Writings*, 366.
18. Ibid., 367.
19. Ibid., 383.
20. Luther, quoted in Joseph Lecler, *Toleration and the Reformation* (New York: Association Press, 1960), 147–64, cited in Darwall, "Peace as Politics," 96.
21. Darwall, "Peace as Politics," 95.
22. Ibid., 101.
23. Ibid., 96.
24. Ibid., 98.
25. Ibid.
26. Ibid.
27. For one effort to secure Muslim grounds for universal respect, see Abdulaziz Sachedina, *The Islamic Roots of Democratic Pluralism* (New York: Oxford University Press, 2001). I discuss Sachedina's views in *Terror, Religion, and Liberal Thought*, chap. 6.

POSTSCRIPT:

The "Arab Spring" of 2011 and *Case of Lautsi and Others v. Italy*

J. Wilson Parker

As part of our project for this book, *The Rule of Law and the Rule of God*, the editors organized a symposium of the same title in Spring 2010. Two events have occurred since the symposium that vividly illustrate the significance of the issues at the heart of this book and merit further discussion. The first was the series of events known as the "Arab Spring" of 2011 (and its aftermath). The second was the European Court of Human Rights approving the mandatory Italian practice of displaying crucifixes in public school classrooms in *Case of Lautsi and Others v. Italy* (2011).[1]

In early December 2011, Egypt held parliamentary elections for the first time in decades. Long lines of eager voters waited patiently to cast their ballots—to assert a voice in political life that had too long been muted. Weeks later, the demand for a voice grew louder, as thousands of Egyptian women marched through downtown Cairo, protesting for the end of military rule.[2] In a traditionally patriarchal society, their call for a role in Egyptian politics was loudly progressive. But, the victories of conservative Islamists during the first round of parliamentary elections, preceding the women's protest (as well as a number of other developments in the succeeding three year period), disappointingly were not always positive.

A particularly poignant illustration of the repressive behavior of the Mubarak government was the beating of a young woman protestor by a half-dozen soldiers during the December 2011 Cairo demonstration. She was left lying on the ground, black abaya ripped off to reveal a blue bra and a baton-bruised body.[3] The video and photographs of her humiliating assault were circulated globally on the Internet and television.

Another widely viewed image of freedom unrealized is that of Mohamed Bouazizi. A 26-year-old fruit and vegetable vendor, Bouazizi was routinely harassed by corrupt police and governmental officials for years as he struggled to eke out a living in the small Tunisian town of Sidi Bouzid.[4] On December 17, 2010, after a policewoman confiscated his goods and slapped him, Bouazizi sought relief at both the police station and provincial-capital building. When his complaints fell on deaf ears, he walked to the gate of the provincial-capital building, doused himself in petrol, and lit a match.[5] Bouazizi's self-immolation expressed in blazing terms the "collective sense of hopelessness and despair"[6] felt by many Arabs. His image became seared into the consciousness of the Arab world, sparking not only a mass uprising in Tunisia but also the "Arab Spring"—a series of revolutionary protests in Egypt, Yemen, Libya, Syria, and throughout the Middle East. Political turmoil continues in the Arab world in 2014 and shows no sign of abating.

Fueled by a common desire to break free from the shackles of governmental authoritarianism, both secularists and Islamists have participated in civil uprisings in Algeria, Bahrain, Egypt, Iraq, Kuwait, Libya, Morocco, Syria, Tunisia, and Yemen. As of the time of writing this chapter in the summer of 2014, longtime autocratic rulers had been overthrown in Egypt, Libya, Tunisia, and Yemen. In August 2011, after months of violent fighting in Libya, protestors brought an end to the longtime rule of Muammar al-Qadhafi. Egypt's comparatively peaceful revolution overthrew the government of authoritarian President Hosni Mubarak in February 2011. Revolutionary efforts in Yemen forced the resignation of President Ali Abdullah Saleh, who was replaced by Abd Rabbuh Mansur Al-Hadi, in February 2012.

Yet, the transition remains uncertain. In other Arab states—like Syria, for example, where President Bashar Assad's military is literally crushing protestors—upheavals are progressing at a painfully slower pace.[7] Moreover, the lingering influence of Qadhafi supporters in Libya and the reassertion of military control in Egypt in 2013 cast doubt over the type of leadership that will emerge from the Arab Spring revolutions. The incursion of the extremist theocratic ISIS forces into portions of Iraq in the summer of 2014 represents a devastating blow to the possibility of widespread democratic government arising from the recent chaos gripping Syria and Iraq.

A constitutional referendum in Egypt, elections in Morocco, and four million citizens voting to form a constitutional assembly in Tunisia, suggested that the fall of despots might trigger the beginnings of constitutional democracy. Indeed, many hoped that the revolts—driven by deep-rooted economic, demographic, and political factors—would produce democratic governments in which secular, not religious, law was predominant and human rights were more fully protected. However, it seems that it is not secularist revolutionaries that are blooming from the Arab Spring, but sectarian Islamists. And the Islamists are "winning fairly" (ISIS notwithstanding), as religious parties have swept open elections held in Tunisia, Morocco, and Egypt. By "tapping into ideological roots that were laid down long before the revolts began,"[8] political Islam is filling the chaotic void left by the corrupt regimes it has long condemned.

In particular, the Muslim Brotherhood gained temporary control of the political scene in both Egypt[9] and Tunisia,[10] reaping the biggest initial harvest of the Arab Spring. With ties in Jordan, Iraq, Algeria, Bahrain, Kuwait, Yemen, and Egypt (as Egypt's oldest Islamist organization), the Brotherhood is a seasoned veteran in Middle East politics. In November 2011, King Muhammad VI of Morocco appointed the head of the Brotherhood's Justice and Development party as the country's new prime minister.[11] And in January 2012, its Freedom and Justice Party emerged from Egypt's parliamentary elections with just under half of the 508 seats in the lower house and nearly 60 percent of the 180 seats in the upper house. Their power in the Egyptian parliament was further extended in February 2012, when the Freedom and Justice Party's Ahmed Fahmy was elected speaker of the house,[12] although as noted the Egyptian military ended their rule in July of 2013.

The Brotherhood's platform officially promoted "evolutionary, rather than revolutionary change" and attempted to focus more upon "questions of Islamic identity than with imposing rigid God-given rules."[13] Instead of imposing moral law, the party proposed to "nudge Egyptian society by the power of example" by establishing a government that would ask artists and writers to sign a voluntary "code of ethics" and support cultural arts that commend religious and family values.[14] Yet, their political message was far from consistent. For example, at a campaign rally in Giza, one Brotherhood speaker advocated for "the rule of God, not the rule of the people" and stated that "the enemy media" were "already saying that 'those who love Jews, the United States, and Europe should make every effort to keep the Islamic spirit dormant. Look at the conspiracy.'"[15] Another Brotherhood speaker then expressed the Brotherhood's commitment to nonsectarian citizenship and equal rights for both Christians and Muslims.

Such statements avowing moderation and a freedom not based on Islamic law were repeatedly criticized by the Salafists, a puritanical Islamist group, who claimed the Brotherhood was diluting the Islamist agenda to alleviate Western apprehension.[16] The Salafists advocate the exclusion of women from politics, severe religious penalties for fornication, and traditional Islamic corporal punishment, like stoning, for adultery. Their election platform, for "citizenship restricted by Islamic Shariah, freedom restricted by Islamic Shariah, [and] equality restricted by Islamic Shariah,"[17] sounded disturbingly similar to the political agendas followed in Islamic theocracies. Yet, the Salafists still won the second-largest number of seats in both houses during the parliamentary elections in Egypt, leaving secular and liberal candidates a powerless minority.[18] Given the clout of the ultraconservative Salafists, the suspiciously fickle moderation of the Brotherhood, and the fact that every major party in Egypt—whether liberal or Islamist—supported retaining the constitutional clause stating that Islam is the source of Egyptian law, many feared that "one political dictatorship [had been] exchanged through democratic vote for a stifling new set of rules based on religion."[19]

And this fear was not unfounded, as Coptic Christians continued to be killed, Islamist legislators qualified their oaths of office with religious incantations during the assembly's opening session, and secularists protesting Egypt's "parliament with a beard" hurled trash at Brotherhood speakers during the one year anniversary celebration in Tahir Square. A similar sentiment was expressed February 25, 2012, in Tunisia, when over four thousand members of the General Union of Tunisian Workers' marched through the capital denouncing the Islamist led government. Although Ennahda, Tunisia's moderate Islamist governing party following the revolution, claimed to lead the country's government in a "spirit of religious pluralism and toleration," its left-wing and secular opponents remained skeptical.[20] Echoing these suspicions, protesters demanded another revolution, claiming that the new government had just stepped into the old one's "repressive shoes."[21] The accusation they made is a powerful one—Islamism may not merely be the "common inherited language of dissent"[22] shared by Arab revolutionaries with widely varying cultures and histories, but also a nation-making tool that can be wielded to disguise government deficiencies, corruption, and accountability.

No matter how carefully the Islamists who were swept into power attempted to craft their new governments, structural tensions within those governments could not stay hidden for long. New conflicts and calls for change soon arose in countries that Western media outlets and authorities had previously hailed as potential beacons of a democratic future. Richard Spencer was among the first journalists to call this new period the "Arab Winter," marking the shift from hopeful regional revolutionary movements toward deepening political divisions and increasing levels of violence.[23]

Egypt experienced by far the most public and obvious shift: a second revolution in 2013, marked by both sharp contrasts and fighting between supporters of the Islamist regime and disenfranchised moderates, that ended when the military pushed Mohamed Morsi and the Muslim Brotherhood out of power on July 3, 2013. Morsi called the regime changes "a complete military coup,"[24] while Gen. Abdul-Fattah el-Sisi argued that the only interest the military had in ousting the Brotherhood was Morsi's failure to govern effectively. While the change certainly satisfied pro-democracy moderates, Morsi's accusation of a military coup was itself prescient: by June 8, 2014, el-Sisi had stepped down from his position as Commander-in-Chief of the Egyptian military and was sworn in as the sixth President of Egypt.[25]

The vast majority of post-Arab Winter governments in the region have also faced tumultuous years, with conflicts ranging from public protests and political assassinations in Tunisia to outright infiltration and occupation by Islamic terror groups in Libya (one of which was responsible for the attack on the American diplomatic institution in Benghazi on September 11, 2012). Among these other conflicted governments is that of Yemen, which is plagued by the presence of Al-Qaeda groups who occupy significant territory within the nation's borders. The Yemeni government declared war on Al-Qaeda in late 2010,[26] but heavy fighting has continued into the present, despite U.S. intervention.

While some terror groups merely attempted to carve out their own territories in the wake of the Arab Winter, one group was far more ambitious and has sought to carve out a new nation: the Islamic State of Iraq and Syria, or ISIS (also known as the Islamic State of Iraq and the Levant, or ISIL). Abu Bakr al-Baghdadi, a longtime al-Qaeda in Iraq (AQI) operative, founded the group in 2010 after the U.S. assassinated key AQI leaders and he was left in charge.[27] Slowly amassing resources and taking over territories in Syria during the civil war, the group exploded onto the scene in 2014 as it expanded rapidly in the wake of the American withdrawal from Iraq. On June 9, 2014, shortly after ISIS forces captured Mosul (the second largest city in Iraq), the group declared the territory it controlled throughout Iraq and Syria to be the "restoration of the caliphate" as foretold by the Prophet Mohammed.[28] The group's decision to declare itself the return of the Caliphate, and to name its leader al-Baghdadi as the new Caliph, clearly defines its regime as theocratic rather than secular.

ISIS's actions in establishing a ruling regime followed suit: the group moved to impose Sharia law in their territory within days of gaining control.[29] In addition to requiring women to wear the *burqa* and punishing theft by cutting off one of the thieves' hands, ISIS struck a blow against religious plurality by enforcing the *jizyah*.[30] Non-Muslims in the region were faced with three options: paying a tax to ISIS in order to continue living in ISIS-occupied territories, leaving their homes and abandoning their possessions, or being executed.

Though these latest developments in the Middle East pose the greatest concerns for the future of religious pluralism and secular democracy in the region, they also strike closest to the issues that lie at the heart of this book. It is fair to say that the title of this book, *The Rule of Law and the Rule of God,* implicitly suggests that the "Rule of Law" at issue is the accepted *secular,* empirically justified law of the post-Enlightenment West, and it further suggests that the book will explore the tensions societies face when "modern" secular institutions confront demands from religious communities that are based upon the religious believers' commitment to revelatory or transcendent truths.

Mark Lilla's opening chapter, "The Return of Political Theology," challenges a common binary assumption: sophisticated secular law versus primitive religion. Lilla defines "political theology" as "a doctrine that legitimates public authority, and the institutions that exercise it, on the basis of a divine revelation." (*Supra,* 16) Lilla then suggests that the institutional rule of law in a country need not be secular at all, and that the Western approach to government and religion after the "Great Separation" of Thomas Hobbes was neither inevitable nor necessary. Lilla argues that theocracies are not always generated by the social dysfunction of poverty and lack of education. However, it is only speculation on his part that increased literacy and financial well-being will not in fact render empirical secular government more appealing in emerging countries. (Of course, it is equally speculative to contend that secular government is inevitable in a "modern" society.) Religious fundamentalists appear to be winning in the aftermath of the Arab Spring, but it is premature to predict what the cultural results of improved living conditions might be in these very same countries.

However, Lilla's fundamental point—that humans long for the coherence that a unifying religious vision provides—should not be dismissed lightly. Lilla elaborates:

> Theology is an intellectual discipline; it is a way of thinking. It begins by assuming a divinely revealed nexus between God, man, and world, which it investigates rationally. Political theology, as I wish to define it, derives principles of political legitimacy from that nexus. . . . (*Supra*, 17)

If there is going to be a battle for the "hearts and minds" of the citizens in emerging third world countries, secularists underestimate the power of sincere religious experience and its political ramifications—Lilla's "political theology"—at their own peril.

Ironically, ostensibly pious proponents of *public* religion in the West are often proclaiming a sanitized vision of religion that religious leaders in emerging third world countries may find problematic. (By "public religion," I mean the inclusion of overtly religious symbols or practices in governmental activities.) If this vision of public religion forecasts what inevitably happens to religion in secular democracies, an outsider might conclude that theocracies are in fact the best option for true believers.

This "sanitized vision of religion" can be seen in two cases: one from the European Court of Human Rights and the other from the US Supreme Court. In both cases, religious groups made demands upon secular governments to incorporate religious displays on public property. In both, the courts approved the inclusion of the objects. Though seemingly victories for the proponents of public religion, ironically these decisions were reached only by the courts' trivializing the religious authenticity of the objects.

In *Case of Lautsi and Others v. Italy*,[31] a parent challenged the requirement that all public classrooms in Italy display a crucifix—a central symbol of Christianity. (A crucifix is a cross with the body of Christ attached, as opposed to a simple bare cross.) Lautsi contended that the policy violated religious freedom provisions in the Italian Constitution and the European Convention of Human Rights. After losing before administrative courts in Italy, Lautsi appealed to the European Court of Human Rights and in 2009 won 7–0 before a Chamber panel. The result set off a firestorm of controversy throughout Europe, as public opinion rallied to support Italy. (It should be recalled that there had been an unsuccessful attempt to include a reference to Europe's "Christian" heritage during 2003–2007, as Europe engaged in a failed attempt to draft a constitution.) Italy appealed to the Grand Chamber and prevailed. In a 15–2 decision, the Grand Chamber ruled that Italy was entitled to a margin of appreciation on the crucifix policy and that the Convention was not violated. The Court said in part:

> [I]t is true that by prescribing the presence of crucifixes in State-school classrooms—a sign which, whether or not it is accorded in addition a secular symbolic value, undoubtedly refers to Christianity—the regulations confer on the country's majority religion preponderant visibility in the school environment.
>
> That is not in itself sufficient, however, to denote a process of indoctrination on the respondent State's part and establish a breach of the requirements of Article 2 of Protocol No. 1. . . .

> [A] crucifix on a wall is an essentially passive symbol and this point is of importance in the Court's view, particularly having regard to the principle of neutrality. . . . It cannot be deemed to have an influence on pupils comparable to that of didactic speech or participation in religious activities. . . .[32]

The crucifix rule was first established in 1860 and renewed in various eras. The current rule derives from a 1928 royal decree demanding that every classroom display a portrait of the King and a crucifix. This decree followed a governmental order in 1922, which stated in part:

> . . . in the last few years in many of the Kingdom's primary schools the image of Christ [the crucifix] and the portrait of the King have been removed. That is a manifest and intolerable breach of the regulations and especially an attack on the *dominant religion of the State* and the unity of the Nation. We therefore order all municipal administrative authorities in the Kingdom to restore, to those schools which lack them, the two *sacred* symbols of the faith and the consciousness of nationhood.[33] (Emphasis added.)

Lautsi alleged that such displays violated the religious freedom provisions of both the Italian Constitution and the parallel sections of the European Convention on Human Rights.[34] Reading the entire case offers the opportunity for an extended meditation on the social conflict between religious and secular belief, because in tracking the evolution of Europe's commitment to secular government, it identifies religious values as the origin of the modern Italian commitment to secularism.

There are written decisions from an Italian Administrative Court, the Italian Consiglio di Stato (Supreme Administrative Court), a Chamber panel (7 judges) of the European Court of Human Rights, and a Grand Chamber panel (17 judges) of the European Court of Human Rights. The central reasoning underlying all of the decisions rejecting the claim is that the crucifix can be seen as a *cultural* symbol of Italy. The Grand Chamber opinion cites portions of the various opinions below:

> [The Administrative Court] took the view, in particular, that although the crucifix was undeniably a religious symbol, it was a symbol of Christianity in general rather than of Catholicism alone, so that it served as a point of reference for other creeds. It went on to say that the crucifix was a historical and cultural symbol, possessing on that account an "identity-linked value" for the Italian people, in that it "represent[ed] in a way the historical and cultural development characteristic of [Italy] and in general of the whole of Europe, and [was] a good synthesis of that development." The Administrative Court further held that the crucifix

should also be considered a symbol of a value system underpinning the Italian Constitution.[35]

The Grand Chamber opinion continues to cite the Administrative Court opinion:

> Looking beyond appearances makes it possible to discern a thread linking the Christian revolution of two thousand years ago to the affirmation in Europe of the right to liberty of the person and to the key elements in the Enlightenment (even though that movement, historically speaking, strongly opposed religion), namely the liberty and freedom of every person, the declaration of the rights of man, and ultimately the modern secular State. All the historic phenomena mentioned are based to a significant extent—though certainly not exclusively—on the Christian conception of the world. It has been observed—judiciously—that the rallying call "liberty, equality, fraternity" can easily be endorsed by a Christian, albeit with a clear emphasis on the third word.
>
> In conclusion, it does not seem to be going too far to assert that, through the various twists and turns of European history, the secular nature of the modern State has been achieved at a high price, and was prompted in part, though of course not exclusively so, by a more or less conscious reference to the founding values of Christianity. That explains why in Europe and in Italy many jurists belonging to the Christian faith have featured among the strongest supporters of the secular State. . . .[36]

The Grand Chamber opinion continues to cite the Administrative Court opinion, as the Administrative Court argues that in spite of the record of European Christians persecuting members of other religions, there is a causal connection between Christianity and modern secular values:

> Moreover, with the benefit of hindsight, it is easy to identify in the constant central core of Christian faith, despite the inquisition, despite anti-Semitism and despite the crusades, the principles of human dignity, tolerance and freedom, including religious freedom, and therefore, in the last analysis, the foundations of the secular State.
>
> This court is admittedly not unaware of the fact that, in the past, other values have been attributed to the symbol of the crucifix, such as, at the time of the Albertine Statute, the sign of Catholicism understood as the State religion, and therefore used to Christianise and consolidate power and authority.
>
> The court is well aware, moreover, that it is still possible today to give various interpretations of the sign of the cross, and above all a strictly religious meaning referring to Christianity in general and Catholicism in particular. It is also aware that some pupils attending State schools might

> freely and legitimately attribute to the cross values which are different again, such as the sign of an unacceptable preference for one religion in relation to others, or an infringement of individual freedom and accordingly of the secular nature of the State, or at the extreme limit a reference to temporal political control over a State religion, or the inquisition, or even a free catechism voucher tacitly distributed even to non-believers in an inappropriate place, or subliminal propaganda in favour of Christian creeds. Although all those points of view are respectable, they are ultimately irrelevant in the present case. . . .[37]

The Consiglio di Stato affirmed. The Grand Chamber opinion cited part of its opinion:

> The Constitutional Court has accepted on a number of occasions that secularism is a supreme principle of our constitutional order, capable of resolving certain questions of constitutional legitimacy (among numerous judgments, see those which concern the provisions relating to the compulsory nature of religious teaching in school or the jurisdiction of the courts over cases concerning the validity of marriages contracted according to canon law and recorded in the registers of marriages).
>
> This is a principle which is not proclaimed in express terms in our Constitution, a principle which is rich with ideological resonances and has a history full of controversy, but one nevertheless which has a legal importance that can be deduced from the fundamental norms of our system. In reality the Court derives this principle specifically from Articles 2, 3, 7, 8, 19 and 20 of the Constitution.[38]

The initial panel of the European Court of Human Rights reversed the Italian Courts and found a violation (7–0), only to be reversed by the Grand Chamber (15–2). It is naive to believe that the current influx of Muslims into Europe was not a significant subtext to the resolution of this case. Twenty European countries supported Italy's appeal.

The "crucifix as primarily culture" argument denigrates the sacramental significance of the crucifix. The Italian administrative court went so far as to opine on Christian theology in an effort to justify the crucifix rule: the cross is a symbol of charity and its display cannot be intimidating because Christians *must* be charitable to others.

> [W]e can clearly perceive an affinity between . . . the "hard core" of Christianity, which, placing charity above everything else, including faith, emphasises the acceptance of difference, and the "hard core" of the republican Constitution, which, in a spirit of solidarity, attaches value to the freedom of all, and therefore constitutes the legal guarantee of respect for others. . . .

> In Christianity even the faith in an omniscient god is secondary in relation to charity, meaning respect for one's fellow human beings. It follows that the rejection of a non-Christian by a Christian implies a radical negation of Christianity itself, a substantive abjuration; but that is not true of other religious faiths, for which such an attitude amounts at most to the infringement of an important precept.[39]

A review of the *Nicene Creed* from 325 AD, a statement of the required beliefs of Christianity used throughout Christendom to this day, shows what actually lays at the "hard core" of Christianity:

> **The Nicene Creed**
>
> I believe in one God, the Father almighty, maker of heaven and earth, of all things visible and invisible. I believe in one Lord Jesus Christ, the Only-begotten Son of God, born of the Father before all ages. God from God, Light from Light, true God from true God, begotten, not made, consubstantial with the Father, through him all things were made. For us men and for our salvation he came down from heaven, and became man, and by the Holy Spirit was incarnate of the Virgin Mary, and became man. For our sake he was crucified under Pontius Pilate, He suffered death, and was buried, and rose again on the third day in accordance with the Scriptures. He ascended into heaven and is seated at the right hand of the Father. He will come again in glory to judge the living and the dead and his kingdom will have no end. I believe in the Holy Spirit, the Lord, the giver of life, who proceeds from the Father and the Son, who with the Father and the Son is adored and glorified, who has spoken through the prophets. I believe in one, holy, catholic and apostolic Church. I confess one Baptism for the forgiveness of sins and I look forward to the resurrection of the dead and the life of the world to come. Amen.

Christianity is indeed a *revealed* religion. Decisions like *Lautsi* mistakenly accept cultural familiarity as empirical evidence of transcendent authenticity.

A 1987 case decided by the German Constitutional Court correctly rejected the "crucifix as culture" argument. In the "Classroom Crucifix Case,"[40] the Court made clear that universal displays of sacred religious that are justified by generalities about good citizenship in fact diminish, not advance, religion. The Court held:

> b) The cross is a symbol of a particular religious conviction and not merely an expression of the Western culture marked partly by Christianity.
>
> Undoubtedly, through the centuries numerous Christian traditions have been incorporated in the general cultural foundations of society, and

> even opponents of Christianity and critics of its historical heritage cannot elude them. These must however be distinguished from the specific content of beliefs of the Christian religion, and still more from a particular confession including its ritual presentation and symbolic portrayal. The State's professing of these contents of belief, to which third parties too are exposed in contacts with the State, affects religious freedom. . . .
>
> The cross continues to be one of the specific faith symbols of Christianity. It is, indeed, its symbol of faith as such. It symbolizes the salvation of man from original sin brought about through Christ's sacrificial death, but at the same time also Christ's victory over Satan and death and his lordship over the world: suffering and triumph simultaneously. . . . For the believing Christian it is accordingly in many ways an object of reverence and of piety. The equipping of a building or a room with a cross is still today understood as an enhanced profession of the Christian faith by the owner. For the non-Christian or the atheist, just because of the importance that Christianity attaches to it and that it has had in history, the cross becomes a symbolic expression of particular religious convictions and a symbol of their missionary dissemination. It would be a profanation of the cross running counter to the self-perception of Christianity and the Christian churches to regard it, as the decisions challenged do, as a mere expression of Western tradition or cult token without a specific reference to faith.[41]

In US constitutional law, Justice William Brennan made a similar point in his dissent in *Lynch v. Donnelly*.[42] In *Lynch*, the City of Pawtucket, Rhode Island had a crèche in its seasonal Christmas display because many in the city wanted "to keep Christ in Christmas." Although the District Court had ordered the removal of the crèche, finding that it had no secular purpose within the meaning of the three-part Establishment Clause analyses set out in *Lemon v. Kurtzman*,[43] the US Supreme Court reversed and allowed the crèche to remain. Central to its analysis that the creche's inclusion had a secular purpose was the fact that the symbol constituted part of a seasonal display encouraging shoppers to come to the central business district. The majority opinion held:

> The District Court inferred from the religious nature of the creche that the city has no secular purpose for the display. In so doing, it rejected the city's claim that its reasons for including the creche are essentially the same as its reasons for sponsoring the display as a whole. The District Court plainly erred by focusing almost exclusively on the creche. When viewed in the proper context of the Christmas Holiday season, it is apparent that, on this record, there is insufficient evidence to establish that the inclusion of the creche is a purposeful or surreptitious effort to express some kind of subtle governmental advocacy of a particular religious message. In a

> pluralistic society a variety of motives and purposes are implicated. The city, like the Congresses and Presidents, however, has principally taken note of a significant historical religious event long celebrated in the Western World. The creche in the display depicts the historical origins of this traditional event long recognized as a National Holiday. . . .
>
> The narrow question is whether there is a secular purpose for Pawtucket's display of the creche. The display is sponsored by the city to celebrate the Holiday and to depict the origins of that Holiday. These are legitimate secular purposes. The District Court's inference, drawn from the religious nature of the creche, that the city has no secular purpose was, on this record, clearly erroneous.[44]

Justice Brennan vehemently disagreed that placing a crèche in a seasonal display had a secular purpose. However, he also disagreed that it was a good way to "keep Christ in Christmas."

> The inclusion of a creche in Pawtucket's otherwise secular celebration of Christmas clearly violates [Establishment Clause] principles. Unlike such secular figures as Santa Claus, reindeer, and carolers, a nativity scene represents far more than a mere "traditional" symbol of Christmas. The essence of the creche's symbolic purpose and effect is to prompt the observer to experience a sense of simple awe and wonder appropriate to the contemplation of one of the central elements of Christian dogma—that God sent His Son into the world to be a Messiah. Contrary to the Court's suggestion, the creche is far from a mere representation of a "particular historic religious event." It is, instead, best understood as a mystical re-creation of an event that lies at the heart of Christian faith. To suggest, as the Court does, that such a symbol is merely "traditional" and therefore no different from Santa's house or reindeer is not only offensive to those for whom the creche has profound significance, but insulting to those who insist for religious or personal reasons that the story of Christ is in no sense a part of "history" nor an unavoidable element of our national "heritage."[45]

It is clear that proponents of public religion in Italy, Germany, and the United States mask their religious goals with claims of generalized historic or cultural motivation. However, as both the German Constitutional Court and Justice Brennan point out, such justifications come at a cost. As the West advocates a separation of religion and politics to those countries currently in the embrace of "political theology," it must have a model of vibrant religion to offer those who wish to be believers. Ironically, obscuring religious goals under the guise of secular justification may reduce religion to merely another potential source of ethical positions—an approach many sincere believers may reject.

It is easy to forget that the historic purpose of a wall of separation between church and state in America was to protect religion from the government, just as much as it was to protect government from religion.[46] Is it possible that widespread dissemination of religious symbols by the government can actually reduce religious piety among that country's citizens (or at least does not prevent erosion)? The evidence in Italy suggests the answer is yes.[47]

As the Arab Spring continues and many predominantly Muslim countries emerge from medieval cultures, the West must offer the citizens in those countries a viable alternative to "political theology." These people must be able to see that secular government is the best way to allow a flourishing private religious sphere, as sketched out in Richard Miller's concluding essay. Enshrining Christian symbols in governmental activities is certainly not the way to show Muslims that government can be evenhanded. And it is not the way to foster Christian piety among the Western populations. It would be well to consider Learned Hand's warning about the need for the individuals who constitute society to harbor a commitment to constitutional principles, rather than leaving the burden of their maintenance to fall on public institutions:

> [A] society so riven that the spirit of moderation is gone, no court *can* save; . . . a society where that spirit flourishes, no court *need* save; . . . in a society which evades its responsibility by thrusting upon the courts the nurture of that spirit, that spirit in the end will perish.[48]

Consider Hand's warning in the context of a similar commitment to religious values: "In a society which evades its responsibility by thrusting upon [*government*] [rather than churches] the nurture of [the *religious*] spirit, that spirit in the end will perish."

Notes

1. *Case of Lautsi and Others v. Italy*, Application no. 30814/06, March 18, 2011, http://cmiskp.echr.coe.int/tkp197/view.asp?action=html&documentId=883169&portal=hbkm&source=externalbydocnumber&table=F69A27FD8FB86142BF01C1166DEA398649.
2. Matthew Kaminski, "Arab Democracy Is the Best Bet for Muslim Reformation," *Wall Street Journal*, 3 January 2012, A15.
3. Amro Hassan and Julian Borger, "Young woman beaten and dragged by Egyptian soldiers wants anonymity," *The Guardian*, 18 December 2011. http://www.theguardian.com/world/2011/dec/18/egpyt-military-tahrir-square-woman
4. Roula Khalaf, "After the Arab Spring," *Financial Times*, 7 May 2011, *FT Weekend Supplement*, 1.

5. Ibid.; see also Kurt Andersen, "The Protester," *Time Magazine*, December 14, 2011, vol. 178 no. 25 page 1. The annual "person of the year" article describes the prelude to the Arab Springs and the trajectory of the wave of protests it inspired on a global level.
6. Alwaleed Bin Talal, "The Lesson of the Arab Spring," *Wall Street Journal*, 6 February 2012, A.13.
7. Patricia Smith, "Arab Spring: What's Next?," *The New York Times Upfront*, 19 September 2011, 6.
8. John Owen, "Why Islamism Is Winning," *The New York Times*, 7 January 2012, 21.
9. In July 2013, President Morsi was overthrown by the Egyptian military. David D. Kirkpatrick, "Army Ousts Egypt's President; Morsi is Taken into Military Custody," *The New York Times*, July 3, 2013. http://www.nytimes.com/2013/07/04/world/middleeast/egypt.html?pagewanted=all&_r=0. At the end of 2013, the Muslim Brotherhood was declared a terrorist organization in Egypt. See http://www.bbc.com/news/world-middle-east-25515932.
10. Emily Crane, "Prime Minister Laarayedh Announces Resignation," *Tunisia Live*, 9 January 2014. http://www.tunisia-live.net/2014/01/09/prime-minister-laarayedh-to-announce-resignation-today/.
11. "The Arab Spring, A Long March," *The Economist,* 18 February 2012, http://www.economist.com/node/21547853/print.
12. "Brotherhood's Fahmy named Egypt Shura Council speaker," *Ahram Online, MENA, 28 Feb 2012,* http://english.ahram.org.eg/NewsContent/1/64/35602/Egypt/Politics-/Brotherhoods-Fahmy-named-Egypt-Shura-Council-speak.aspx.
13. "The Arab Spring, A Long March."
14. David Kirkpatrick, "Egypt's Vote Puts Emphasis on Split over Religious Rule," *Times*, December 3, 2011, www.nytimes.com/2011/12/4/world/middleeast/egypt-vote-propels-islamic-law-into-spotlight.html.
15. Ibid.
16. "The Arab Spring, A Long March."
17. Kirkpatrick, "Egypt's Vote."
18. "Brotherhood's Fahmy named Egypt Shura Council speaker."
19. Susan Jacoby, "Egypt's Elections and the Risky Rule of God," http://www.faithstreet.com/onfaith/2011/12/07/egypts-elections-and-the-risky-rule-of-god/10899.
20. Bouzza Ben Bouzza, "Thousands of Trade Unionists Protest in Tunis," *Associated Press*, February 25, 2012.
21. Ibid.
22. John Owen, "Why Islamism Is Winning."
23. Richard Spencer, "Middle East review of 2012: the Arab Winter," December 31, 2012. http://www.telegraph.co.uk/news/worldnews/middleeast/9753123/Middle-East-review-of-2012-the-Arab-Winter.html.
24. David D. Kirkpatrick, "Army Ousts Egypt's President."

25. "El-Sisi Sworn In as Egypt President," *Ahram Online*, June 8, 2014. http://english.ahram.org.eg/News/103147.aspx.
26. "Yemeni al-Qaeda suspects 'killed'," *Al Jazeera*, January 16, 2010. http://www.aljazeera.com/news/middleeast/2010/01/2010115141954305381.html.
27. Patrick Cockburn. "Mosul: Who is the Isis jihadi leader Abu Bakr al-Baghdadi?," *The Independent,* 10 June 2014. http://www.independent.co.uk/news/world/middle-east/mosul-emergency-who-is-abu-bakr-albaghdadi-9523070.html.
28. Adam Withnall, "Iraq crisis: Isis declares its territories a new Islamic state with 'restoration of caliphate' in Middle East," *The Independent*, June 30, 2014. http://www.independent.co.uk/news/world/middle-east/isis-declares-new-islamic-state-in-middle-east-with-abu-bakr-albaghdadi-as-emir-removing-iraq-and-syria-from-its-name-9571374.html.
29. Jack Moore, "Iraq Isis Crisis: Medieval Sharia Law Imposed on Millions in Nineveh Province," *The International Business Times*, June 12, 2014. http://www.ibtimes.co.uk/iraq-isis-crisis-medieval-sharia-law-imposed-millions-nineveh-province-1452401.
30. Imran Khan, "Iraqi Christians get Islamic State's warning," *Al Jazeera*, July 19, 2014. http://www.aljazeera.com/news/middleeast/2014/07/iraq-christians-told-convert-face-death-201471811040982432.html.
31. *Lautsi*.
32. Ibid., 29.
33. All citations to opinions in the lower courts in the *Lautsi* litigation are taken from the Grand Chamber opinion (see note 1 above at 10).
34. The parent alleged "an infringement of the principle of secularism, relying in that connection on Articles 3 (principle of equality) and 19 (religious freedom) of the Italian Constitution, Article 9 of the Convention, and on the principle of the impartiality of public administrative authorities (Article 97 of the Constitution)," see note 1 above at 4.
35. Ibid., 5.
36. Ibid.
37. Ibid., 6.
38. Ibid., 8.
39. Ibid., 6.
40. BVerfGE 93, 1 1 BvR 1087/91 Kruzifix-decision "Crucifix Case (Classroom Crucifix Case)," May12, 1987. Translation available at http://www.utexas.edu/law/academics/centers/transnational/work_new/german/case.php?id=615.
41. Ibid. at part II, 2 (b).
42. *Lynch v. Donnelly,* 465 U.S. 668 (1984).
43. *Lemon v. Kurtzman*, 403 U.S. 602 (1971). The so-called "*Lemon* test" asked whether: (1) the challenged law or conduct has a secular purpose, (2) its principal or primary effect is to advance or inhibit religion, and (3) it creates an excessive entanglement of government with religion.

44. 465 U.S. 668, 680–681.
45. 465 U.S. 668, 711–712 (Brennan, J., dissenting.)
46. See Elizabeth Katz, "Founders Designed Establishment Clause to Protect Religion, McConnell Says," October 31, 2005, http://www.law.virginia.edu/html/news/2005_fall/mcconnell.htm.
47. A 2007 study by the Patriarchate of Venice, which actually asked worshippers inside 619 churches how often they had been in the past month, found only 15 percent of worshippers attend Mass every Sunday, and 8 percent said they had been at some point in the last month. In total, only 23 percent reported attending church regularly. Malcolm Moore, "Italian Church Attendance Lower than Thought," February 23, 2007, http://www.telegraph.co.uk/news/worldnews/1543643/Italian-church-attendance-lower-than-thought.html.
48. Learned Hand, "The Contribution of an Independent Judiciary to Civilization," in *The Spirit of Liberty* (3rd ed., I. Dilliard, ed., 1960): 164. Cited quote is from a speech Learned Hand delivered in 1942.

List of Contributors

Anita L. Allen is an expert on privacy law, bioethics, and contemporary values; she is recognized for her scholarship about legal philosophy, women's rights, and race relations. In 2013, Allen was appointed vice provost for faculty at the University of Pennsylvania. In 2010 she was appointed by President Obama to the Presidential Commission for the Study of Bioethical Issues. Her books include *Unpopular Privacy: What Must We Hide* (Oxford, 2011); *The New Ethics: A Guided Tour of the 21st Century Moral Landscape* (Miramax/Hyperion, 2004); *Why Privacy Isn't Everything: Feminist Reflections on Personal Accountability* (Rowman and Littlefield, 2003); and *Uneasy Access: Privacy for Women in a Free Society* (Rowman and Littlefield, 1988). She coedited (with Milton Regan) *Debating Democracy's Discontent* (Oxford, 1998). Allen, who has written more than a 100 scholarly articles, has also contributed to popular magazines and blogs and has frequently appeared on nationally broadcast television and radio programs. Allen has served on numerous editorial and advisory boards and on the boards of a number of local and national nonprofits and professional associations, including the Hastings Center, EPIC, and the Bazelon Center.

Sahar F. Aziz is an associate professor at Texas A&M University School of Law. Professor Aziz's scholarship focuses on the intersection of national security and civil rights law with a focus on the post-9/11 era. Professor Aziz incorporates critical race theory, feminist theory, and constitutional law into her examination of the disparate impact of post-9/11 laws and public policy on ethnic, racial, and religious minority groups in the United States. Professor Aziz analyzes these issues in various contexts, including employment, counterterrorism, criminal justice, and civil rights litigation. Professor Aziz also writes on the rule of law and democracy in Egypt, including gender rights, transparency laws, and election laws.

Michael Kent Curtis is the Judge Donald Smith Professor of Constitutional Law at Wake Forest University School of Law where he teaches constitutional law, legal and constitutional history, freedom of speech and press, and classical rhetoric for lawyers (with Harold Lloyd). He is the author of *No State Shall Abridge: The Fourteenth Amendment and the Bill of Rights* (1986) and *Free Speech: "The People's Darling Privilege"* (2000); the coauthor of *Constitutional Law in Context* (third edition, 2010; supplement, 2013); and author of numerous articles dealing with civil liberties and constitutional history.

Simeon O. Ilesanmi is the Washington M. Wingate Professor of Religion at Wake Forest University. A former Laurance S. Rockefeller Visiting Fellow at Princeton University, he is the author of *Religious Pluralism and the Nigerian State* (Ohio University Press, 1997), and he has published extensively on human rights, the ethics of war, and religion and law.

John Kelsay is a distinguished research professor (religion) at the Florida State University in Tallahassee, Florida (USA). A Guggenheim Fellow in 2002–2003, Professor Kelsay's publications include *Arguing the Just War in Islam* (Harvard University Press, 2007).

Win-chiat Lee is a professor of philosophy and Chair of the Philosophy Department at Wake Forest University. His published work is mostly on legal and political philosophy, including global justice and the philosophy of international criminal law. His most recent article, "The Judgeship of All Citizens: Dworkin's Protestantism about Law," appears in *Law and Philosophy*.

Mark Lilla is a professor of humanities at Columbia University. A frequent contributor to *The New York Review of Books* and other publications, he has taught at New York University and the Committee on Social Thought at the University of Chicago. His books include *G. B. Vico: The Making of an Anti-Modern*, *The Reckless Mind*, and most recently, *The Stillborn God: Religion, Politics, and the Modern West,* which was based on his Carlyle Lectures at Oxford University in 2003.

Andrew F. March (andrew.march@yale.edu) is an associate professor in the Department of Political Science at Yale University. He is the author of *Islam and Liberal Citizenship: The Search for an Overlapping Consensus* (Oxford, 2009).

Richard Miller is professor of religious ethics at the University of Chicago Divinity School. He is the author of *Interpretations of Conflict: Ethics, Pacifism, and the Just-War Tradition*; *Casuistry and Modern Ethics: A Poetics of Practical Reasoning*; *Children, Ethics, and Modern Medicine*; and *Terror, Religion, and Liberal Thought*. He is currently at work on two projects on method and history in religious ethics and religious studies.

J. Wilson Parker (parkerjw@wfu.edu) is a professor of law at the Wake Forest University School of Law. His scholarship and teaching focus on constitutional law, comparative constitutional law, and the history of the United States Supreme Court. He is primary author, with Michael Kent Curtis, of *Constitutional Law in Context*, third edition, (Carolina Academic Press).

Frank S. Ravitch is the Walter H. Stowers Chair in Law and Religion and Director of the Kyoto, Japan Summer Abroad Program at the Michigan State University College of Law. He is the author of the books, *Marketing Creation: The Law and Intelligent Design* (Cambridge University Press, 2011); *Masters of Illusion: The Supreme Court and the Religion Clauses* (NYU Press 2007); *Law and Religion, a Reader: Cases, Concepts, and Theory*, second edition (West, 2008) (first edition, 2004; third edition, expected 2014); *Employment Discrimination Law* (Prentice Hall, 2005) (with Pamela Sumners and Janis McDonald); and *School Prayer and Discrimination: The Civil Rights of Religious Minorities and Dissenters* (Northeastern University Press, 1999; paperback edition, 2001). Professor Ravitch is currently working on a treatise with the late Boris Bittker and Scott Idelman called *Religion and the State in American Law*, which is supported by a grant from the Lilly Endowment and will be published by Cambridge University Press. He has also published a number of law review articles dealing with law and religion, Japanese law, civil rights law, and disability discrimination in journals such as the *Georgia Law Review*, *Wake Forest Law Review*, *BYU Law Review*, *Boston College Law Review*, and *Cardozo Law Review*. In 2001, Professor Ravitch was named a Fulbright Scholar and served on the faculty of law at Doshisha University in Kyoto, Japan, where he taught US constitutional law and law and religion and engaged in research.

William Schweiker (w-schweiker@uchicago.edu) is the Edward L. Ryerson Distinguished Service Professor of Theological Ethics at the University of Chicago. His scholarship and teaching engage theological and ethical questions attentive to global dynamics, comparative religious ethics, the history of ethics, and hermeneutical philosophy. Professor Schweiker's books include *Mimetic Reflections: A Study in Hermeneutics, Theology and Ethics* (1990); *Responsibility and Christian Ethics* (1995); *Power, Value and Conviction: Theological Ethics in the Postmodern Age* (1998); *Theological Ethics and Global Dynamics: In the Time of Many Worlds* (2004); *Religion and the Human Future: An Essay in Theological Humanism* (2008, with David E. Klemm); and most recently, *Dust that Breathes: Christian Faith and the New Humanisms* (2010). He is also chief editor and contributor to *A Companion to Religious Ethics* (2004), a comprehensive and innovative work in the field of comparative religious ethics. Professor Schweiker is an ordained minister in the United Methodist Church.

Bibliography

al-Alwani, Taha Jabir. *Towards a Fiqh for Minorities: Some Basic Reflections*. Herndon, VA: International Institute of Islamic Thought, 2003.

al-Hibri, Azizah. "Deconstructing Patriarchal Jurisprudence in Islamic Law: A Faithful Approach." In *Global Critical Race Feminism: An International Reader*. Edited by Adrien Katherine Wing, 221–233. New York: New York University Press, 2000.

An-Na'im, Abdullahi. *Islam and the Secular State: Negotiating the Future of Shari'a*. Cambridge, MA: Harvard University Press, 2008.

Assman, Jan. *Moses the Egyptian: The Memory of Egypt in Western Monotheism*. Cambridge, MA: Harvard, 1998.

Attia, Gamal Eldin. *Towards Realization of the Higher Intents of Islamic Law*. Translated by Nancy Roberts. London: International Institute of Islamic Thought, 2007.

Auda, Jasser. *Maqasid al-shari'ah as Philosophy of Islamic Law: A Systems Approach*. London: International Institute of Islamic Thought, 2008.

Audi, Robert, and Nicholas Wolterstorff, *Religion in the Public Square: The Place of Religious Convictions in Political Debate*. Lanham, MD: Rowman & Littlefield, 1997.

Baier, Kurt. "Justice and the Aims of Political Philosophy." *Ethics* 99 (1989): 771–90.

Balagangadhara S. N., and Jakob De Roover. "The Secular State and Religious Conflict: Liberal Neutrality and the Indian Case of Pluralism." *Journal of Political Philosophy* 15 (2007): 67–92.

Bianchi, Robert R. *Guests of God: Pilgrimage and Politics in the Islamic World*. Oxford: Oxford University Press, 2004.

Bitton-Ashkelony, Brouria. *Encountering the Sacred: The Debate on Christian Pilgrimage in Late Antiquity*. Berkeley: University of California Press, 2005.

Brownstein, Alan E. "Interpreting the Religion Clauses in Terms of Liberty, Equality, and Free Speech Values—A Critical Analysis of 'Neutrality Theory' and Charitable Choice." *Notre Dame Journal of Legal Ethics and Public Policy* 13 (1999): 243–84.

Carbado, Devon W., and Mitu Gulati. "The Fifth Black Woman." *Journal of Contemporary Legal Issues* 11 (2000–2001): 701–30.

Carter, Stephen. *The Culture of Disbelief: How American Law and Politics Trivialize Religious Devotion*. New York: Basic Books, 1993.

Cashin, Sheryll. "To Be Muslim or 'Muslim-Looking' in America: A Comparative Exploration of Racial and Religious Prejudice in the 21st Century." *Duke Forum for Law and Sociological Change* 2 (2010): 125–39.

Choudhury, Cyra Akila. "Empowerment or Estrangement? Liberal Feminism's Visions of the 'Progress' of Muslim Women." *University of Baltimore Law Forum* 39 (2008): 153–72.

Cohen, Joshua. "Minimalism about Human Rights: The Most We Can Hope For?" *Journal of Political Philosophy* 12 (2004): 190–213.

Crenshaw, Kimberle W. "Demarginalizing the Intersection of Race and Sex: A Black Feminist Critique of Antidiscrimination Doctrine, Feminist Theory and Antiracist Politics." *University of Chicago Legal Forum* 1989 (1989): 139–68.

Crenshaw, Kimberle W. "Mapping the Margins: Intersectionality Identity, Politics, and Violence against Women of Color." *Stanford Law Review* 43 (1990): 1241–300.

Curtis, Michael Kent. "Be Careful What You Wish For: Gays, Dueling High School T-Shirts, and the Perils of Suppression." *Wake Forest Law Review* 44 (2009): 431–96.

Curtis, Michael Kent. *Free Speech, "The People's Darling Privilege": Struggles for Freedom of Expression in American History*. Durham, NC: Duke University Press, 2000.

Curtis, Michael K., and Shannon Gilreath. "Transforming Teenagers into Oral Sex Felons: The Persistence of the Crime against Nature after *Lawrence v. Texas*." *Wake Forest Law Review* 43 (2008): 155–222.

Dennett, Daniel. *Breaking the Spell: Religion as a Natural Phenomenon*. New York, NY: Penguin, 2007.

Eagleton, Terry. *On Evil*. New Haven: Yale University Press, 2010.

Dailey, Jane. "Sex, Segregation, and the Sacred after Brown." *The Journal of American History* 91, no. 1 (2004): 119–44.

Darwall, Stephen. "Peace as Politics." In *Religion, Politics, and Peace*. Edited by Leroy S. Rouner, 85–103. Notre Dame, IN: University of Notre Dame Press, 1999.

Ediozie, Rita Kiki. "Democratization in Multi-Religious Contexts: Amina vs. the (Disunited) States of Nigeria." In *Local Institutions, Global Controversies: Islam in Sub-Saharan African Contexts*. Edited by Kamari Clarke, 145–76. New Haven: Yale University Press, 2007.

Eisgruber, Christopher L., and Lawrence Sager. *Religious Freedom and the Constitution*. Cambridge, MA: Harvard University Press, 2007.

Elaigwu, J. Isawa. "The Shadow of Sharia over Nigerian Federalism." *Publius: Journal of Federalism* 33 (2003): 123–44.

El Fadl, Abou. *The Place of Tolerance in Islam*. Boston: Beacon, 2002.

El Fadl, Khaled Abou. "Islamic law and Muslim Minorities: The Juristic Discourse on Muslim Minorities from the Second/Eighth to the Eleventh/Seventeenth Centuries." *Islamic Law and Society* 1 (1994): 141–87.

Epps, Garrett. "What We Talk about When We Talk about Free Exercise." *Arizona State Law Journal* 30 (1998): 563–602.

Feldman, Noah. "The Intellectual Origins of the Establishment Clause." *New York University Law Review* 77 (2002): 346–428.

Fischer-Fabian, S. *Die Macht des Gewissen: Von Sokrates bis Sophie Scholl.* München: Th. Knaur, 1987.
Gehrke-White, Donna. *The Face behind the Veil: The Extraordinary Lives of Muslim Women in America.* New York: Kensington Publication, 2006.
Gelvin, James L. "Al-Qaeda and Anarchism." *Terrorism and Political Violence* 20 (2008): 563–81.
Giddens, Anthony. *Modernity and Self-Identity: Self and Society in the Late Modern Age.* Stanford, CA: Stanford University Press, 1991.
Gillespie, G.T. *A Christian View on Segregation.* Greenwood, MS: Educational Fund of the Citizens' Councils, 1954.
Go, Julian. "Modeling the State: Postcolonial Constitutions in Asia and Africa." *Southeast Asian Studies* 39, no. 4 (2002): 558–83.
Green, Steven K. "Of (Un)equal Jurisprudential Pedigree, Rectifying the Imbalance between Neutrality and Separationism." *Boston College Law Review* 43 (2001–2002): 1111–38.
Greenawalt, Kent. *Religion and the Constitution: Establishment and Fairness* (Princeton, NJ: Princeton University Press 2008).
Hadda, Yvonne Yazbeck, Jane I. Smith, and Kathleen M. Moore, *Muslim Women in America.* New York: Oxford, 2006.
Hamburger, Philip. *Separation of Church and State.* Cambridge, MA: Harvard University Press, 2004.
Hathout, Maher. *In Pursuit of Justice: The Jurisprudence of Human Rights in Islam.* Los Angeles: Muslim Public Affairs Council, 2006.
Hourani, George F. *Reason and Tradition in Islamic Ethics.* Cambridge: Cambridge University Press, 1985.
Hume, David. *The Natural History of Religion.* Edited by J. Fieser. New York, NY: Macmillan/Library of Liberal Arts, 1992.
Huntington, Samuel. *The Clash of Civilizations and the Remaking of the World Order.* New York, NY: Simon & Schuster, 1998.
Ikenga-Metuh, Edmund Emefie. "Pilgrimage in African Religion: A Quest for the Ultimate." *Dialogue & Alliance* 6, no. 4 (1992–93): 3–13.
Jackson, Sherman A. "Literalism, Empiricism, and Induction: Apprehending and Concretizing Islamic Law's *Maqasid Al-Shari'ah* in the Modern World." *Michigan State Law Review* 5 (2006): 1469–86.
Johnston, David L. "*Maqasid Al-Shari'a*: Epistemology and Hermeneutics of Muslim Theologies of Human Rights." *Die Welt des Islams* 47 (2007): 149–87.
Kahn, Robert A. "The Headscarf as Threat: A Comparison of German and U.S. Legal Discourse." *Vanderbilt Journal of Transnational Law* 40 (2007): 417–44.
Kelsay, John. *Arguing the Just War in Islam.* Cambridge, MA: Harvard University Press, 2007.
Khadduri, Majid. *The Islamic Law of Nations: Shaybani's Siyar.* Baltimore, MD: Johns Hopkins University Press, 1966.
Klarman, Michael J. *From Jim Crow to Civil Rights: The Supreme Court and the Struggle for Racial Equality.* New York: Oxford University Press, 2004.
Klemm, David E., and William Schweiker. *Religion and the Human Future: An Essay in Theological Humanism.* Oxford: Wiley-Blackwell, 2008.

Koppelman, Andrew. "Secular Purpose." *Virginia Law Review* 88 (2002): 87–166.

Kymlicka, Will. *Multicultural Citizenship: A Liberal Defense of Minority Rights.* Oxford: Clarendon Press, 1995.

Laycock, Douglas. "Formal, Substantive, and Disaggregated Neutrality toward Religion." *Depaul Law Review* 39 (1990): 993–1018.

Laycock, Douglas. "The Underlying Unity of Separation and Neutrality." *Emory Law Journal* 46 (1997), 43–74.

Lecler, Joseph. *Toleration and the Reformation.* New York, NY: Association Press, 1960.

Leonard, Bill J. "A Theology for Racism: Southern Fundamentalists and the Civil Rights Movement." *Baptist History and Heritage* 34 (1999): 49–68.

Lilla, Mark. *The Stillborn God: Religion, Politics, and the Modern West.* New York, NY: Vintage, 2007.

Lloyd, Harold Anthony. "'Original' Means Old, 'Original' Means New: An 'Original' Look at What 'Originalists' Do." *National Lawyers Guild Review* 67 (2010): 135–55.

Ludwig, Frieder. "Christian-Muslim Relations in Northern Nigeria since the Introduction of Shari'ah in 1999." *Journal of the American Academy of Religion* 76 (2008): 602–37.

Lund, Christopher C. "Religious Liberty after Gonzalez: A Look at State RFRAs." *South Dakota Law Review* 55 (2010): 466–97.

Lupu, Ira C. and Robert W. Tuttle. "Same-Sex Family Equality and Religious Freedom." *Northwestern Journal of Law and Social Policy* 5 (2010): 274–306.

Luther, Martin. *Martin Luther: Selections from His Writings.* Edited with an Introduction by John Dillenberger. New York: Doubleday, 1961.

Marty, Martin E. *When Faiths Collide.* Oxford: Blackwell, 2005.

March, Andrew F. *Islam and Liberal Citizenship: The Search for an Overlapping Consensus.* Oxford: Oxford University Press, 2009.

Mary, Andre. "Pilgrimage to Imeko (Nigeria): An African Church in the Time of the 'Global Village.'" *International Journal of Urban and Regional Research* 26, no. 1 (2002): 106–20.

McConnell, Michael W. "Religious Freedom at a Crossroads." *University of Chicago Law Review* 59 (1992): 115–94.

Miller, Richard B. "Rules." In *Oxford Handbook of Theological Ethics.* Edited by Gilbert Meilaender and William Werpehowski, 220–36. New York: Oxford University Press, 2005.

Miller, Richard B. *Terror, Religion, and Liberal Thought* New York: Columbia University Press, 2010.

Moore, Kathleen M. "Visible through the Veil: The Regulation of Islam in American Law." *Sociology of Religion* 68, no. 3 (2007): 237–51.

Niebuhr, H. Richard. *Radical Monotheism and Western Culture.* Louisville, KY: Westminster/John Knox Press, 1993.

Nietzsche, Friedrich. *On the Genealogy of Morals.* Translated by Walter Kaufmann and R. J. Hollingdale. New York: Vintage Books, 1989.

O'Brien, Donal B. Cruise. *Symbolic Confrontations: Muslims Imagining the State in Africa.* New York: Palgrave 2003.

Obadare, Ebenezer. "In Search of a Public Sphere: The Fundamentalist Challenge to Civil Society in Nigeria." 38 *Patterns of Prejudice* 38 (2004): 177–97.

Okin, Susan Moller Okin. *Is Multiculturalism Bad for Women?* Princeton, NJ: Princeton University Press, 1999.

Paden, John N. *Ahmadu Bello Sardauna of Sokoto: Values and Leadership in Nigeria*. Zaria, Nigeria: Hudahuda Publishing Co., 1986.

Ramadan, Tariq. *Radical Reform: Islamic Ethics and Liberation*. New York: Oxford University Press, 2009.

Ramadan, Tariq. *Western Muslims and the Future of Islam*. Oxford: Oxford University Press, 2004.

Ravitch, Frank S. *Masters of Illusion: The Supreme Court and the Religion Clauses*. New York: NYU Press, 2007.

Rawls, John. "Kantian Constructivism in Moral Theory." *Journal of Philosophy* (1980): 515–72.

Rawls, John. "Two Concepts of Rules." In *Theories of Ethics*. Edited by Philippa Foot, 144–70. Oxford: Oxford University Press, 1967.

Rosenblum, Nancy. *Obligations of Citizenship and Demands of Faith*. Princeton, NJ: Princeton University Press, 2000.

Sachedina, Abdulaziz. *Islam and the Challenge of Human Rights*. New York: Oxford University Press, 2009.

Sachedina, Abdulaziz. *The Islamic Roots of Democratic Pluralism*. New York: Oxford University Press, 2001.

Sacks, Jonathan. *The Dignity of Difference: How to Avoid the Clash of Civilizations*. London: Continuum, 2003.

Schweiker, William, ed., *The Blackwell Companion to Religious Ethics*. Oxford: Blackwell, 2005.

Schweiker, William. *Theological Ethics and Global Dynamics: In the Time of Many Worlds*. Oxford: Blackwell, 2004.

Schweiker, W., M. Johnson, and K. Jung, ed., *Humanity before God: Contemporary Faces of Jewish, Christian and Islamic Ethics*. Minneapolis, MN: Fortress Press, 2006.

Sklar, Richard L. "On the Study of Constitutional Government in Africa." In *Constitutionalism and Society in Africa*. Edited by Okon Akiba, 43–54. Aldershot: Ashgate, 2004.

Smith, Steven D. *Foreordained Failure: The Quest for a Constitutional Principle of Religious Freedom*. New York: Oxford University Press, 1995.

Smith, Steven D. "Symbols, Perceptions, and Doctrinal Illusions: Establishment Neutrality and the 'No Endorsement' Test." *Michigan Law Review* 86 (1987): 266–332.

Spinner-Halev, Jeff. "Cultural Pluralism and Partial Citizenship." *Multicultural Questions*. Edited by Christian Joppke and Steven Lukes, 65–86. Oxford: Oxford University Press, 1999.

Stone, Suzanne Last. "Cultural Pluralism, Nationalism, and Universal Rights." *Cardozo Law Review* 21 (2000): 1211–24.

Strossen, Nadine. "Freedom and Fear Post-9/11: Are We Again Fearing Witches and Burning Women." *Nova Law Review* 31 (2007): 279–314.

Sulaiman, Ibraheem. *The Islamic State and the Challenge of History: Ideas, Policies, and Operation of the Sokoto Caliphate.* London: Mansell Publishing Limited, 1987.

Sunder, Madhavi. "Piercing the Veil." *Yale Law Journal* 112 (2003): 1399–472.

Swaine, Lucas. *The Liberal Conscience: Politics and Principle in a World of Religious Pluralism.* New York: Columbia University Press, 2006.

Taiwo, Olufemi. *How Colonialism Preempted Modernity in Africa.* Bloomington: Indiana University Press, 2010.

Tamir, Yael. "Revisiting the Civic Sphere." In *Freedom of Association.* Edited by Amy Gutmann, 214–38. Princeton, NJ: Princeton University Press, 1998.

Tangban, O. E. "The Hajj and the Nigerian Economy." *Journal of Religion in Africa* 21, no. 3 (1991): 241–55.

Taylor, Charles. *Philosophical Papers I.* Cambridge: Cambridge University Press, 1985.

Taylor, Charles. *A Secular Age.* Cambridge, MA: Harvard, 2007.

Thigpen, Robert B., and Lyle A. Downing. "Rawls and the Challenge of Theocracy to Freedom." *Journal of Church and State* 40 (1998): 757–73.

Tibi, Bassam. *Islamism and Islam.* New Haven and London: Yale University Press, 2012.

Tibi, Bassam. "Political Islam as a Forum of Religious Fundamentalism and the Religionisation of Politics." In *Totalitarian Movements and Political Ideologies* 10/2 (June 2009): 97–120.

Tomlison, John. *Globalization and Culture.* Chicago, IL: The University of Chicago Press, 1999.

Turner, Denys. "Religion: Illusions and Liberation." In *The Cambridge Companion to Marx.* Edited by Terrell Carver, 320–38. Cambridge: Cambridge University Press, 1991.

Volpp, Leti. "Feminism versus Multiculturalism." *Columbia Law Review* 101 (2001): 1181–218.

Wahba, Wafaa H., trans., *The Ordinances of Government.* Reading, UK: Garnet Publishing, 1996.

Warner, Michael, Jonathan VanAntwerpen, and Craig Calhoun, *Varieties of Secularism.* Cambridge, MA: Harvard University Press, 2010.

Williams, Aaron J. "The Veiled Truth: Can the Credibility of Testimony Given by a Niqab-Wearing Witness Be Judged without the Assistance of Facial Expressions?" *University of Detroit Mercy Law Review* 85 (2008): 273–92.

Wing, Adrien Katherine, and Monica Neigh Smith. "Critical Race Feminism Lifts the Veil? Muslim Women, France, and the Headscarf Ban." *U.C. Davis Law Review* 39 (March 2006): 743–86.

Yates, Joshua J. "Mapping the Good World: The New Cosmopolitans and Our Changing World Picture." In *The Hedgehog Review* 11, no. 3 (2010): 7–29.

INDEX

Printed and bound in the United States of America